WOMEN WARRIORS

AN UNEXPECTED HISTORY

PAMELA D. TOLER

BEACON PRESS
BOSTON

BEACON PRESS
Boston, Massachusetts
www.beacon.org

Beacon Press books
are published under the auspices of
the Unitarian Universalist Association of Congregations.

22 21 20 19   8 7 6 5 4 3 2 1

This book is printed on acid-free paper that meets the uncoated paper
ANSI/NISO specifications for permanence as revised in 1992.

Text design and composition by Kim Arney

An excerpt from the "Poem of Mulan," trans. Wilt L. Idema, from *Mulan: Five Versions
of a Classic Chinese Legend*, ed. Shiamin Kwa and Wilt L. Idema (Indianapolis:
Hackett Publishing, 2010), is reprinted by permission of Hackett Publishing Company, Inc.

Library of Congress Cataloging-in-Publication Data

Names: Toler, Pamela D., author.
Title: Women warriors : an unexpected history / Pamela D. Toler.
Description: Boston : Beacon Press, 2019. | Includes bibliographical references and index.
Identifiers: LCCN 2018028811 (print) | LCCN 2018034228 (ebook) |
ISBN 9780807064641 (ebook) | ISBN 9780807064320 (hardback)
Subjects: LCSH: Women and war. | Women soldiers—Biography. | BISAC: HISTORY
/ Military / General. | SOCIAL SCIENCE / Women's Studies.
Classification: LCC UB416 (ebook) | LCC UB416 .T65 2019 (print) |
DDC 355.0092/52—dc23
LC record available at https://lccn.loc.gov/2018028811

*"I did not come to the front to give it
the once over with a cleaning rag in my hand."*

—MANOLITA, a *partisana* in the Spanish Civil War

CONTENTS

"WOMEN DO NOT FIGHT"

W hen Antonia Fraser's *Warrior Queens* came out in 1988, I greeted it with delight.

The idea that some women in the past had taken up arms and fought beside their brothers, fathers, cousins, and neighbors was not a new one to me. As a nerdy little girl growing up outside Wilson's Creek National Battlefield in southwest Missouri, I learned that women disguised themselves as men to fight in the American Civil War. As a nerdy tweenager I read everything I could find on Joan of Arc, from biographies designed to give young girls role models to George Bernard Shaw's *Saint Joan.** As a less obviously nerdy graduate student, I was fascinated by Lakshmi Bai, the Rani of Jhansi, who led her soldiers onto the battlefield to fight the British in the Indian Mutiny of 1857. Fraser's book introduced me not only to women I'd never heard of before but to the idea that women "fought, literally

---

* I wasn't alone in my fascination with Joan. When I first began to think about this book, I asked a group of family and friends to tell me what they knew about Joan of Arc off the top of their heads. The accuracy and detail of the answers varied, but one thing stood out: the people who remembered the most were all women who had been fascinated by Joan's story at that age—sometime between nine and death—when smart girls look for historical role models to tell them that it's okay to be tough/mouthy/opinionated/different. I'd love to think modern preteens don't need these role models the same way we did in the dark ages before the women's movement of the late 1960s and early 1970s, but I'm afraid it's not true. Hence the popularity of the website A Mighty Girl.

A late-nineteenth-century image of Lakshmi Bai, the Rani of Jhansi—already honored as a national heroine.

fought, as a normal part of the army in far more epochs and far more civilizations than is generally appreciated."*

Once I was aware that women warriors had existed in many times and places, I ran across references to them everywhere. I began to collect their stories in a casual way, adding notes on the Trung sisters of Vietnam, or Queen Njinga of Angola, or Jeanne Hachette of France to the file when I ran across them. I didn't do much with those stories beyond an occasional article or blog post. I had other things to write and the world at large didn't seem to share my fascination with women warriors.†

That's changed. Women warriors have entered the cultural mainstream. Fantasy heroines and historical female soldiers engage the public imagination in serious historical fiction, television series, comic books, and war-gaming forums. Not to mention the popular excitement over Patty Jenkins's *Wonder Woman* and the women warriors of Wakanda in Ryan Coogler's *Black Panther*—both of which not only enjoyed box-office success but also served as catalysts for cultural discussion.

Real-life women warriors evoke a more complicated public response. For more than twenty years, beginning with the Persian Gulf War, American servicewomen have fought officially in air and naval units and unofficially in raids and security patrols on the ground. Public perception is divided on the subject. Female combat veterans run political campaigns that center on their military service, as their male counterparts have done since the first days of the United States.‡ They are honored as heroes at major league baseball games and showcased on the covers of publications as diverse as the *New York Times* and *StreetWise*, the newspaper peddled by homeless people on the streets of Chicago. They even appear as central characters in romance novels—where their unlikely presence is testimony that women in the military have become a fact of American life. At

---

* Antonia Fraser, *The Warrior Queens: The Legends and the Lives of the Women Who Have Led Their Nations in War* (New York: Vintage Books, 1994), 8. Working on this book for the last eighteen months (or three years, or thirty years, depending on where you start the count), I've learned the accuracy of Dame Fraser's statement depends on how you define normal and army. Or for that matter how you define war. Not easy questions in a work that begins with a woman warrior buried in the second millennium BCE and ends the day before yesterday.

† Though I had my hopes when Xena fought her way across the television screen in 1995.

‡ In all fairness, *General* Washington did not actually campaign for the presidency.

the same time, despite this apparent public acceptance, the repeal of the ground combat exclusion policy in 2013 and the military's grindingly slow efforts to implement that change have generated outraged howls from those who argue that women cannot and should not fight—howls that did not diminish when two women successfully completed Ranger School, the US Army's elite infantry training program, in October 2015. In an effort to avoid the media frenzy, positive and negative, that followed the news that women had received their Ranger tabs, the military announced more recent gains by America's servicewomen—such as the first woman to complete Marine Corps infantry officer training in September 2017 and the six women of the Eighty-Second Airborne Division who earned the Expert Infantryman Badge in January 2018—with less fanfare. They succeeded in avoiding angry headlines, but not ugliness in the comments sections of online news articles.

INSIGNIFICANT EXCEPTIONS?

Both the current appeal of pop cultural heroines and ongoing battles over the role of female soldiers in the modern military assume women who go to war are historical anomalies: Joan of Arc, not G.I. Joan. This position is summed up in military historian John Keegan's magnificently inaccurate claim that "warfare is . . . the one human activity from which women, *with the most insignificant exceptions* [emphasis mine], have always and everywhere stood apart. . . . Women have followed the drum, nursed the wounded, tended the field and herded the flocks when the man of the family has followed his leader, have even dug the trenches for men to defend and laboured in the workshops to send them their weapons. Women, however, do not fight . . . and they never, in any military sense, fight men."*

In fact, women have always gone to war: fighting to avenge their families, defend their homes (or cities or nations), win independence from a foreign power, expand their kingdom's boundaries, or satisfy their ambition.

---

* John Keegan, *A History of Warfare* (New York: Vintage Books, 1993), 76. Lest anyone make the mistake of thinking that Keegan was an extremist with a small audience of like-minded friends, *Time* named *A History of Warfare* one of the best books of the year and described Keegan as "one of the century's most distinguished military historians." See "The Best Books of 1993," *Time*, January 3, 1994, 77, and Lance Morrow, "Chronicling a Filthy 4000-Year-Old Habit," *Time*, November 29, 1993, 74.

A handful of women warriors have elbowed their way into historical accounts. Sometimes they are remembered in their home countries
as national heroines, even if they have been forgotten by the larger
world. But for the most part, women warriors—in uniform or not,
eager to fight or driven by desperation to defend themselves—have
been pushed into the historical shadows, hidden in the footnotes, or
half-erased. Some disappeared because they disguised themselves as
men in order to fight, appearing in the records as women only when
their disguises failed. Some have been defined out of the picture: my
favorite version of this is the historian who claimed that a woman who
fought during the French siege of Zaragoza in 1808 did not count as
a combatant because her life was in danger and she was defending
herself.* Others who fought in the distant past are dismissed as legends, myths, folklore, exaggerations, or just plain lies on the grounds
that records of their actions/existence are slight—an indignity to
which their male counterparts are less prone. Some women warriors
are deliberately written out of history. After World War II, for instance, the Soviet government explicitly instructed Russia's squadrons
of highly decorated female fighter pilots not to speak of their wartime
experiences. Even the history of modern female soldiers has begun to
blur. When I told people I was writing about women warriors, most
were startled to realize that American women have officially served in
air and naval combat units for the past twenty years.

At some level, the disappearance of women warriors is part of
our larger tendency to write history as "his story." The tendency is
explicit in the world of military history. As military historian David
Hay points out, "The assumption that war is something essentially
male—be it the apotheosis of masculinity or the incarnation of patriarchy—has banned the study of the female combatant to academic
purgatory."[1] But women's contributions in science, literature, politics,
and economics are also routinely minimized, dismissed, or forgotten. Look at almost any subject and you'll discover another example,
whether it's classicist Alice Kober's critical role in the decipherment
of Linear B or the existence of all-female volunteer fire brigades in the
early twentieth century. Rachel Swaby describes writing about these
forgotten contributions as "revealing a hidden history of the world."[2]

In the case of women warriors, the tendency to erase women's
roles in history is complicated by the contested question of whether

---

* She also defended a number of artillerymen whose battery was under attack.

women should fight. Many people who cheer for the highly sexual-
ized women warriors of popular culture are less comfortable when
confronted with real-life images of camouflage-wearing women with
shaved heads at boot camp or Ranger School.* In fact, that contrast
gets at the heart of much of the long-standing, cross-cultural social
discomfort with women warriors—the fear that women who chose to
fight will lose their femininity or, conversely, that their presence will
"feminize" the army, thereby rendering it less effective, less aggressive,
less serious, or just less. It is an old discussion: when Plato argued
that women should be given the same training as men and used in all
the same tasks, including training in war, he warned "we must not be
afraid of all the jokes of the kind that the wits will make about such a
change in physical and artistic culture, and not least about the women
carrying arms and riding horses."[3]

If we look closely at debates over whether women should be allowed to participate in direct combat in the American military, it becomes clear that those who stand on opposite sides of the argument
are not even asking the same questions—and that they haven't for a
long time.† After World War II, when Congress considered whether
or not to allow women to serve as permanent regular members of
the armed services, supporters of the Women's Armed Services Integration Act, including General Dwight D. Eisenhower and Admiral
Chester W. Nimitz, argued in terms of the value of using women in
"traditionally female" jobs and the potential need for rapid mobiliza-
tion as a result of Cold War tensions. Critics of the legislation raised

---

* Wonder Woman, the female warriors of Wakanda, Black Widow, and other female
warriors in comics, fantasy novels, video games, television, and movies are dressed in (the
passive voice is purposeful here) outfits designed with sexuality rather than fighting in
mind. Many wear some version of what the geek community calls "boob armor": form-
fitting breastplates, complete with bra cups. Some versions of boob armor are more overt
than others—Xena's armor not only has bra cups but swirls designed to call attention
to the same. At first glance, boob armor is one step better than the pervasive "armor bi-
kini"—which is made of some material generally associated with armor but which does
not cover any of the body parts you would want armor to protect in case of a fight. But
the illusion of greater protection is just that: an illusion. As many impassioned blog posts
and videos make clear, body-fitting armor could get a woman warrior killed. (One of the
best discussions of this can be found in the YouTube video "The Physics of Boob Armor,"
https://youtu.be/jZJGvLF8tEU.) It is intended to suggest that the character is a badass
of the bad-est variety while still leaving her *ahem* assets uncovered.

† A discussion that did not end with the lifting of the combat exclusion policy
in 2013.

questions about the impact of female biological "impairments"* on the army's effectiveness, the masculinization of female soldiers, and the return to a peacetime culture of female domesticity.

Today, proponents of allowing women to take direct combat roles argue in terms of equal rights and the nature of combat in modern warfare, and about what constitutes a combatant, a noncombatant, and the front.† In contrast, arguments as to why women should not go to war are deeply rooted in ideas about what it means to be female—and what it means to be a man. Such arguments range from cultural ideas and taboos surrounding family, motherhood, pregnancy, and menstruation to mundane questions about providing physical facilities for female soldiers. Opponents of women in combat express fears that a female soldier will become pregnant in order to avoid deployment, pointing out that pregnancy is the only temporary disability a service member can inflict on herself without penalty.‡ They ask how female soldiers will use the latrine in a combat zone.§ They argue that women are not emotionally fit for combat because they are innately more nurturing than men—and alternatively that because men are programmed to protect women, the presence of women on the battlefield will distract male comrades from doing their jobs.¶ They assert that women do not have the physical strength or stamina for the job, whether that means wearing a medieval suit of plate armor or modern body armor, keeping up on a forced march, carrying a fifty-pound machine gun into battle, or rescuing a fallen comrade.

---

* By which they meant menstruation, pregnancy, and menopause. The idea that the routine functioning of the female body constitutes an anomaly or, worse, a disability, is problematic well beyond discussions of women in the military.

† Congresswoman Patricia Schroeder, then chair of the House Military Installations and Facilities Subcommittee, summed up issues regarding the nature of combat. Citing the example of an Army recruiting commercial that featured a female soldier operating a communications van—a position classified as noncombatant—Schroeder argued, "I think all of us know that if you were in real battle, the first person you usually try to hit is the person running the communications van. So it appears that women can be the first killed, but they are not allowed at the front line and supposedly in battle." Quoted in Rosemarie Skaine, *Women at War: Gender Issues of Americans in Combat* (Jefferson, NC: McFarland, 1999), 31.

‡ So many things are wrong with this thought process. Where to start?

§ Rosemarie Skaine reports the answer of one young female officer as "What's the big deal? Pull a tarp over your head and squat." Not a solution for everyone, but clear proof that some problems aren't that complex (Skaine, *Women at War*, 167).

¶ There is often a lose-lose quality to these arguments.

Many of these arguments look familiar to students of women's history. At various times, defenders of the status quo used similar concerns to argue against educating women, hiring women, or promoting women. In the 1860s, doctors in the US Army's medical department used the same general ideas to fight the use of female nurses in the Civil War. Police and fire departments in the 1980s offered similar justifications for not assigning female police officers to patrol duty and not hiring female firefighters and EMTs.

The strength and continuity of such arguments points to a sense of social discomfort that goes beyond the specific arguments offered by opponents to women in combat—what Elaine Donnelly, founder of the Center for Military Readiness, describes as "cultural dissonance" related to the idea of women in the military.* For much of human history, the dominant images of war, and consequently of peace, have been gender-based. War is considered men's business, a position summed up by activist and poet Grace Paley:

> I have to say that war is man-made. It's made by men. It's their thing, it's their world, and they're terribly injured by it. They suffer terribly in it, but it's made by men. How do they come to live this way? It took me years to understand this. Because when I was a little girl, I was a boy—like a lot of little girls who like to get into things and want to be where the action is, which is up at the corner someplace, where the boys are. And I understood this very well, because that was what really interested me. I could hardly wait to continue being a boy so that I could go to war and do all the other exciting boys' things.[4]

If men are seen as warriors, women are not-warriors.

In its most positive form, the "not-warrior" role is framed in terms of motherhood, potential and actual. Women are considered too precious a resource to endanger, as American war correspondent William G. Shepherd expounded in an article about Russia's battalions of women soldiers in the March 1918 issue of the *Delineator*. "Women have got something the men haven't," he explained through his interpreter to the young female soldier he was interviewing. "They have

---

* If you spend any amount of time reading the literature produced on both sides of the argument, you will find that there are no unbiased observers. Advocates on both sides are guilty of special pleading, cherry-picking the evidence, and presenting opinion as irrefutable fact.

potential motherhood, and if you kill that, you kill the whole race."* At the same time, women are seen as being natural pacifists precisely because they are mothers (a position that is historically dubious).† In modern debate, the idea of mother as not-warrior is often cloaked in seemingly practical terms: What happens to children when a mother deploys? Worse, what happens to children if both parents deploy? Would the service of large numbers of young women in the military adversely affect a nation's birthrate?‡ Ideas of this type lead to the conclusion that even if women are capable of performing in combat, allowing them to do so might not be in the larger interest of society.

The image of women as not-warriors does not imply that women are not involved in war. Keegan's claim that women do not fight is wrapped around a list of ways in which women have been involved in war: "Women have followed the drum, nursed the wounded, tended the field and herded the flocks when the man of the family has followed his leader, have even dug the trenches for men to defend and laboured in the workshops to send them their weapons." Military historian and theorist Martin van Creveld made the same point in darker terms when he outlined the not-warrior roles that "women have played in war, namely as its causes, its objects and its victims."§

---

* William G. Shepherd, "The Soul That Stirs in 'Battalions of Death': Their Motives and Methods, as Revealed in Interviews with Them Obtained for the Delineator in Petrograd," *Delineator* 92, no. 3 (March 1918): 7. Obviously "mansplaining" is not a new phenomenon.

† Social conservatives and proponents of some versions of radical feminism share common ground in the idea that motherhood is antithetical to war. Where many feminists argue for women to be allowed to take part in combat on grounds of equal rights, some reject female involvement in the military in favor of a social critique that renounces hierarchy and the use of force. We will explore the ideas surrounding the opposition of warriors and mothers, and the resulting concept of mothers as natural pacifists, in more detail in chapter 1.

‡ The related questions of growing populations in developing countries and falling birthrates in developed countries are almost as divisive as the question of women in the military.

§ Martin van Creveld, *Men, Women & War: Do Women Belong in the Front Line?* (London: Cassell, 2001), 27. It will come as no surprise to the reader that van Creveld answers his own question with a bellowed "No!" In fact, he is the author of the single most astonishing statement I have read by a contemporary author as to why women should not be in combat: "Except under very special circumstances, such as last-minute defense or insurgencies, women's participation in war will take away one of the cardinal reasons why men fight, which is to assert their own glory" (Van Creveld, *Men, Women & War*, 167). The academic equivalent of "No gurlz allowed"?

Van Creveld makes explicit the idea that underlies what I think of as the "body bag argument": opponents of allowing women in combat often invoke the image of a mother or daughter coming home in a body bag as if it were an argument against the use of women in combat in its own right, and as if the death of a mother in combat is inherently more horrifying than the death of a father. Writing from the other side of the divide, historian Linda Grant De Pauw suggests the problem is not that it is a woman in the body bag: "The horror of women in body bags is not a horror of a dead woman. It's that the woman was a warrior, that she is not a victim. American culture does not want to accept that women can be both warriors and mothers. . . . To accept women as warriors means a challenge to patriarchy at its most fundamental level."[5]

LET'S START AT THE VERY BEGINNING

The arguments against women in combat are as old as war itself—and yet women have gone to war.

The horse-riding nomadic tribes of the Eurasian steppes may win the prize for being the earliest (and most consistent) cultures to allow women to openly fight alongside their male counterparts.

Most of what we know about ancient steppe cultures comes from their burial mounds, known as *kurgans*, which can be found from the Balkans to Siberia.* These rich physical finds are supplemented by the often sensational accounts written by outsiders, beginning with Herodotus,† and occasionally with reference to the oral traditions and customs of the existing peoples of the Eurasian steppes.‡

---

* The cultures of the Eurasian steppes had no written language until the early thirteenth century, when Genghis Khan commissioned a Uyghur clerk to create a written language for the Mongols based on the Uyghur script.

† For example, Herodotus, known as both the Father of History and the Father of Lies, gives this description of the role of women among the Sauromatians, whom he believed were the offspring of the Amazons and their Scythian husbands: "Riding to the hunt on horseback, sometimes with, sometimes without, their menfolk, taking part in war, and wearing the same sort of clothes as men. . . . They have a marriage law which forbids a girl to marry until she has killed an enemy in battle; some of their women, unable to fulfill this condition, grow old and die in spinsterhood" From Herodotus, *The Histories* 4, trans. Aubrey de Selincourt (Baltimore: Penguin, 1965), 279. (All quotations from Herodotus are from this edition.)

‡ The practice of drawing conclusions about the lives of ancient peoples based on the customs of their twenty-first-century counterparts makes this historian queasy.

The earliest evidence for a female warrior comes from a burial mound in the Caucasus. In 1927, archaeologists discovered the grave, which has been dated to the second millennium BCE, of three armed women in Semo-Awtchala, Georgia. They were buried with grave goods that included a bronze sword, iron spearheads, and a horse's head. One died with an arrowhead embedded in her skull. Another had a pointed axe wound in the left side of her skull that had begun to heal before she died—preempting arguments that the grave goods buried with her were purely ceremonial.*

Moving ahead a thousand years or so, we find multiple burials of possible women warriors in sites associated with the Scythian, Sauromatian, and Sarmatian cultures, which date from the late seventh through the second centuries BCE. Notable among these are remains from forty-four *kurgans* located near the town of Pokrovka, in Kazakhstan near the Russian border. A joint Russian and American archaeological team, led by Leonid Yablonsky and Jeannine Davis-Kimball, excavated the Pokrovka *kurgans* in the 1990s.† The burials yielded 192 adult skeletons that were intact enough to allow their ages and sexes to be identified. Ninety-four percent of the men were buried with the types of goods that lead archaeologists to identify them as warriors: bronze and iron arrowheads, swords, daggers, and, in some cases, horse gear—not surprising in a culture of warrior nomads. Fifteen percent of the women were also buried with weapons, armor, and horse gear—as well as "feminine" items, such as earrings, beads, and spindle whorls.‡ For the most part, they were buried with light weapons—spears, bows, and arrows, and the distinctive double-edged short-swords called *akinakes*, which were designed to be worn in a belt scabbard and were used throughout the

---

* No one would question that a man buried with such goods in ancient times was a warrior, or at least a powerful figure. But the remains of women are held to a higher standard of proof, as was demonstrated by the controversies that arose in 2017 when DNA testing of the remains of an iconic Viking warrior known as the "Birka man" proved that "he" was actually a woman—a subject we will discuss at greater length at the end of the book.

† Russian archaeologists first discovered women's graves containing weapons, armor, and riding gear in sixth-century BCE *kurgans* in the 1950s but focused on male burials when they interpreted their excavations. Because that's what's important, right?

‡ In my opinion, if we aren't willing to assume that remains buried with a sword are automatically those of a male, we should not assume the presence of earrings means a female. Gender profiling can cut two ways.

eastern Mediterranean in the first century BCE. Some bear battle wounds that mark them as warriors rather than hunters. The body cavity of one woman held a bronze arrowhead, the tip damaged as if it had hit a bone as it lodged itself in her abdomen. Other women suffered injuries to their left arms that suggest they shielded themselves with that arm while attacking with the right. Most were in their teens when they died, lending some credence to Herodotus's report on the marriage customs of the Sauromatians. The evidence for women warriors is even stronger in burial mounds from Scythia dating from the fifth and fourth centuries BCE. Some 130 graves of women from this period included weapons as grave goods, roughly 25 percent of the female graves excavated in Scythia. The remains of many of the Scythian women show signs of battle injuries similar to those found on the remains of males buried with similar weapons— serious blows or stabs to the skull or arrowheads stuck in their bones suggest these women died in battle. Moreover, these burials often included heavier weapons, such as spears, lances, and axes, in addition to arrowheads and *akinakes*. In one extraordinary Scythian burial, a young woman warrior was buried with the complete equipment of a member of the heavy cavalry, including a helmet, scale armor, and an iron shield.

The horse-riding, bow-wielding women of the ancient steppes may have been the earliest women warriors. They were by no means the last.

LOOKING ACROSS BOUNDARIES OF TIME AND SPACE

My intention in writing this book is to bring women warriors out of the historical shadows, even if it means kicking some historical shins along the way. In the following chapters, we will consider the reasons women historically have taken up arms, how those reasons relate to women's roles as daughters, wives, mothers and widows, peacemakers, peasant girls, prostitutes, poets, and queens—and what happened when women stepped outside those roles to take other identities. Looking at specific examples of historical women warriors and why they fought, we will consider queens and commoners, those who commanded from the rear and those who fought in the front lines, those who fought because they wanted to, because they had to, or because they could. We will look at ordinary women who did extraordinary things as well as the truly exceptional.

I came to the project well aware of the challenges associated with adding women back in to the history of the world. It is a common topic of conversation among the historians, literary scholars, and journalists who are interested in this subject. What I didn't expect to find was that writing a global history of women warriors posed challenges beyond those shared by all of us who write about women as actors in history.

1. The challenge of filling in the background

The primary challenge of writing a global history of women warriors is that it is in fact global. (Why this took me by surprise is not clear.)

There is a reason scholars tend to sink their roots into a specific time and space. It is both terrifying and thrilling to drop the safety net of an academic field and explore scholarly foreign territory.

For my sake, as well as the reader's, I needed to root every story I told in its historical context. (I'm not good at faking it.) If I wrote, "The Roman Empire was in crisis in the third century BCE," I needed to know what that meant, even if I had to stop and build a timeline of the reign of the Roman emperors.* I wrote thousands of words explaining the social movements and political contexts behind wars, the extended biographies of individual warriors, and troop movements in individual battles that didn't make it into this book. I trimmed sections on the border squabbles between the Roman and Persian empires, on the Danish occupation of Britain, and on the political issues surrounding Joan of Arc's rise to fame down to the sentence or two needed to tell the story of a particular woman warrior. I dropped one-sentence explanations of, say, the Thirty Years' War or the Battle of Leucate in 1637 because they were not critical to the point at hand. It was painful.†

---

* With twenty-six emperors and at least forty wannabes over a period of fifty years, you can't tell the players without a program.

† I've tried to provide the necessary context for every story I tell, but that doesn't mean I've managed to provide all the context any given reader might want. Maps, in particular, were an impossibility given the scope of time and territory. I've included a few sources, digital and otherwise, in the suggested reading section at the end of the book to help those of you who want to look at maps, who need a term explained, or who just want to explore further.

Worse, from my perspective at least, I wrote hundreds of pages on women who didn't make it into the book at all.

Which brings me to:

2. The question of definitions

I went into this book with a simple definition of women warriors as women for whom battle wasn't a metaphor. It was a nice starting point, but I quickly realized I needed precise standards as I sifted through the thousands of possible stories to tell.

Women warriors, like any other category of human beings, come in a variety of flavors. Some women are warriors by any measure you choose—they wield a sword, fire a weapon, drop a bomb, or throw rocks down from the wall of a besieged city. They get their hands dirty. But once you move away from the front line and look at commanders, the story becomes more complicated. A woman who leads a charge is a warrior. A woman who puts on a girly uniform (or feminized suit of armor) to inspire the troops is not, at least in my opinion—even if she gives a speech that goes down in history.* There were a lot of women who fell somewhere in between those two poles.

For purposes of this book, I have included female commanders who have taken a role David Hay describes as "roughly analogous to what the United States' armed forces now denote by the term 'combatant commander': one who remains in the theatre of war, near the front lines, giving orders, planning operations and making command decisions, but someone who is not expected to lead the charge personally."[6]

By that definition, Matilda of Tuscany makes the cut. So does Isabella of Castile. To my sorrow, the Empress Maud and Harriet Tubman did not. Neither did Maud's contemporary, Tamar of Georgia, even though Tamar traveled with her troops and appeared on the battlefield. As best I can tell, she was a speech giver, not a strategy

---

* My favorite example of this is Elizabeth I of England at Tilbury in August 1588. Expecting an assault by the Spanish Armada, the fifty-something queen rode before her troops on a white horse, wearing a silver cuirass over a white velvet gown. (Probably not "boob armor," but we don't really know.) Her speech, intended to raise morale in wartime, is best remembered for the line, "I know I have the body of a weak and feeble woman, but I have the heart and stomach of a King, and of a King of England too." She went on to say: "Rather than any Dishonour shall grow by me, I myself will take up arms. . . . In the meantime my Lieutenant General shall be in my stead." It's heady stuff. And while I have no doubt she would have picked up arms if required, she didn't. She sent a proxy.

planner. It's possible that Tamar did command her troops, but if she did it is buried in sources that I can't read and don't have access to.

Which brings me to:

3. The question of sources

The historian who chooses to grapple with a topic across the artificial boundaries of academic fields inevitably finds herself dependent on secondary sources and translations of primary sources in languages she can't read. (And frustrated by hints about the stuff that has not been translated from Arabic. Or Chinese. Or Hungarian. Or Russian. Or—well, you get the picture.)

The problem is compounded by the nature of the sources that survive.* Sometimes women's stories make it into a historical footnote because they are attached to those of important men. Sometimes they are told as a good example or a horrible warning. Sometimes, as we will see in the case of Aethelflaed, Lady of the Mercians, they are left out of the official history for political reasons.† Often they exist only in fragments. Or take the forms of human remains, inscriptions, portraits, and other material evidence. Or were written a hundred years or more after the fact. And, as with all historical evidence, what we have is filtered through the assumptions of the (almost always) men who wrote them. Character assassination, salacious speculation, and hagiography are all present—and occasionally warranted.

Which brings us to:

4. Writing about war and warriors

There is a long tradition of collective biographies of notable women, warriors and otherwise, that emphasize the heroic aspects of individual women's stories. A growing number of these books are aimed

---

* The victor may write history in the short run (if by short run you mean over the course of three hundred to four hundred years, and assuming you write the kind of history in which there is a winner). In the long run, time itself "writes" history with the help of nibbling rodents, grinding sand, fire, water, and the occasional military rampage.

† In the case of Genghis Khan's daughters, they weren't left out of the historical record, they were deliberately removed. In the section of *The Secret History of the Mongols* that recorded Genghis Khan's spoken words in 1206, the text is cut away directly below the words "Let us reward our female offspring," leaving historians to grind their teeth and cobble together the extent of his daughters' achievements and rewards from traces in other sources. In Jack Weatherford, *The Secret History of the Mongol Queens: How the Daughters of Genghis Khan Rescued His Empire* (New York: Broadway Books, 2010), xi.

at adult audiences, but often they are written to provide female role models for girls. It's a worthy goal, but *Women Warriors* is not that kind of book.

Quite frankly, not all of these women warriors could be considered role models. We will see instances of lying, cheating, murder, and revenge, as well as defense of home, hearth, nation, or religious convictions—sometimes bound together in one woman's story. Gender confusion, love affairs, and rape are common. Some of the women included died in battle, were executed, or committed suicide. Many were maligned as witches or viragoes,* as sexually voracious, as sexually frigid, or as just plain crazy by the men who fought against them—and occasionally by the men who fought alongside them.[†]

Some of the stories I tell in *Women Warriors* involve simple acts of heroism, without regard to whether the war in which they fought was a "good war"[‡] or a pointless and bloody game of political dominoes. Some of the women I write about, like Queen Tomyris in the first chapter, can be seen as national heroines or archvillains depending on which side of the battlefield your ancestors stood on—or how you feel about women taking up arms. Some of the women I discuss led their nations into wars that were as bloody, stupid, and greedy as those instigated by their male counterparts. Others desperately protected their homes/towns/nations. There is a big difference between the poet Telesilla organizing the women of Argos to defend their city against invasion and Amina of Hausa leading her troops in wars of conquest against neighboring kingdoms. In my opinion, it is

---

* Originally a term for a vigorous and heroic woman warrior, today "virago" is an unabashedly negative term. A quick search for synonyms comes up with "termagant," "scold," "harridan," "shrew," "dragon," "she-devil," and "ogress."

† Disrespect, sexual slurs, and occasional violence from fellow soldiers (or sailors or marines) remain a problem in the military today, as demonstrated by the scandal surrounding the private Facebook group Marines United, in which male marines posted hundreds of explicit photos of female marines without their consent, accompanied by sexual threats. (On the upside, irate male marines were instrumental in taking the group down.)

‡ The concept of a "good war" is a tricky one. One woman's "good war" is another woman's imperial land grab. Attempts to define what makes a good war often come down to Supreme Court Justice Potter Stewart's statement about pornography: "I know it when I see it."

worthwhile to remind readers about women warriors from both ends of the spectrum—and all the shades of purple, green, red, and gray in between.

At the same time, anyone who writes military history—even those of us who write around the edges of the field rather than describing troop movements and armaments—must come to terms with the issue summed up in a statement attributed to Robert E. Lee at Fredericksburg: "It is well that war is so terrible—we would grow too fond of it." It is easy to grow numb to the horrors you describe. It is even easier to focus on individual acts of bravery without considering the losses/horrors that surround them and without weighing the larger issues of a specific war. I'll say it now, and I'll say it again at various points in various ways: war is ugly. No matter who is doing the fighting.

CHAPTER ONE

DON'T MESS
WITH MAMA

In 1488, Italian noblewoman Caterina Sforza (1462–1509), known as the Tigress of Forli, was besieged in the city's main fortress, the Rocca di Ravaldino. Members of the rival Orsi family had murdered her husband, Girolamo Riario, and held her children hostage.

The illegitimate daughter of Italian nobleman Galeazzo Maria Sforza, who would later be the Duke of Milan, Caterina had earned a reputation as a canny politician and an adept military commander four years earlier. Seven months pregnant, she seized the Castle Sant'Angelo and held it while she negotiated terms with the college of cardinals regarding her husband's landholdings of Imola and Forli after the death of his uncle, Pope Sixtus IV.*

Now she was once again immured in a seemingly impregnable fortress. She had tricked the Orsis into allowing her to go into the fortress to "negotiate" with the tower's commander.

---

* A contemporary observer reported "she wore a dress of satin with a train of two arms' length, a black hat in the French fashion, a man's belt and a purse full of gold ducats, a curved falchion at her side." Quoted in Sharon L. Jansen, *The Monstrous Regiment of Women: Female Rulers in Early Modern Europe* (New York: Palgrave Macmillan, 2002), 40. Apparently, the desire to describe what women political figures wore to the siege isn't new.

Finally realizing they had been tricked, the Orsis tried to lure her out by threatening to chop her children to pieces before her eyes. According to contemporary chroniclers, most notably Niccolo Machiavelli,* Caterina hoisted her skirts, flashed her genitals at the soldiers ranked below the walls, and shouted from the ramparts that she had the means to make more. Other witnesses claimed she was pregnant at the time and gestured at her belly as proof that she carried another potential heir.† Either way, the shock value, for her contemporaries and the modern reader alike, lies not in the gesture itself but in her decision to defend her fortress rather than her children. It derives a great deal of its gut-punching power from the fact that "motherhood" is as much a complicated cultural concept as it is a matter of biology.

Premodern cultures often treated mother and warrior as the definitive female and male roles. In such worldviews, "making a life" and "taking a life" are both necessary for the society's continued existence, both bloody—and fundamentally incompatible. It is no more possible for a mother to kill than for a warrior to give birth. The parallel nature of the two roles is made explicit in those cultures in which women who died in childbirth were equated with fallen warriors. For instance, the Aztecs believed such women shared the highest place in paradise with warriors. Similarly, Ashanti rituals for women who died in childbirth were almost identical to those for men who died in battle. And in ancient Sparta "it was not permitted to inscribe the names of the dead upon their tombstones, except for men who had fallen in war and women who had died in childbirth."[1]

In the modern world, the idea that mother and warrior are biologically ordained opposites has been expanded into a recurring theme of feminist theory, first formulated during the early days of the organized women's movement at the end of the nineteenth century: the

---

* Who was not there.

† In both stories, Caterina's defiance of the besieging army is heightened by the image of her pregnancy—potential in the first version and actual in the second. The image of a pregnant woman riding into battle is a potent symbol, whether used to demonstrate the toughness of the woman involved, her dedication to a cause, the desperation of a battle, or all of the above—and it is one that appears in many times and cultures.

idea that if women ran the world there would be no war.* The proponents of this theory argue that traditional "women's work" is devoted
to life: feeding, sheltering, nursing, tending the elderly, and, most im-
portantly, bearing and raising children. The violence of war not only
destroys that work but is antithetical to it. Fields are trampled into
blood-soaked mud. Homes are burned. Sons (and now daughters)
are killed or come home damaged in body and/or spirit. Over the
centuries, societies have used motherhood—actual and potential—as
the reason why women *should not* go to war; this brand of feminist
theory argues that motherhood (in its broadest possible sense) means
women *will not* go to war. Women are natural pacifists; therefore, the
world would be a more peaceful place if women were in charge.†

At its simplest, this argument is based on a series of assumptions
about the relative natures of men and women that is unflattering to
both. It is also counterhistorical. Empress Maud of Germany and
England, Catherine the Great, Golda Meir, and Margaret Thatcher,‡

---

* Last year I sat with the members of a seniors book club and listened to them tell
stories about growing up in the years soon after women got the vote in the United States.
More than one remembered his mother telling him that now that women had the vote,
the United States would never go to war again. Obviously things didn't work out the way
they expected.

† Antifeminist thinkers turn this theory on its head and question whether women
are tough enough to make hard decisions in times of war—a position exemplified by political opponents who asked 1984 vice presidential candidate Geraldine Ferraro whether
she would be able to "push the button" if necessary.
The reasoning goes like this:

1. Women are not allowed to go to war because they are not physically strong
   enough or not emotionally strong enough, or are so distracting they will endanger the men around them. (It is apparently irrelevant that women have always
   experienced the horror of war firsthand, whether because they live in a war-torn
   region or because they must endure war's impact on the men in their lives.)
2. People who never fought in a war are inherently incapable of making decisions
   about war.
3. Therefore, since women are not allowed to go to war, they (or should I say we?)
   are unqualified to hold an office that might require them to make decisions
   about war.

Can you say "Catch-22"?

‡ Thatcher answered critics who subscribed to the "women aren't qualified to make
decisions about war" theory with the argument that her practical skills as a homemaker
transferred perfectly to running a war. This was not a new idea. In medieval Europe, supply and logistics were a standard part of "house-keeping" as practiced by noblewomen.

to name only a few, all pulled the trigger on war, even if they didn't personally lead their troops into the field. At the other end of the power spectrum, we find the story of the Spartan mother who killed her own son after he survived a battle in which all his comrades died. She saw his survival as a maternal failure.

Mothers as natural pacifists? Maybe not.

DEFENDING HER CUBS

The belief that giving birth brings with it a biological imperative to protect also fuels the widely held idea that mothers of all species—sparrows, bears, and tigers, as well as humans—will fight to protect their children against external threats.* Taken to its logical extreme, the idea that a mother will fight against all odds to protect her children leads us from a mother who fights to defend her children from a threatening individual to one who fights to defend her children against a threatening army. Not surprisingly, most stories about women who fought for home and children center on defense.† Historically, mothers who fought to protect their children in time of war typically did so from a defensive position—often literally a last-ditch effort. Women guarded the wagons in an army's baggage train. They dug trenches, rebuilt fortifications, and carried weapons and water to those who fought. They formed home guard defense units, training alongside men too old and boys too young to join the

---

* This idea seems to be a specifically Western one. Such stories do not appear, for instance, in China, where filial piety trumps mother love as a fundamental virtue. Instead of stories of ferocious mothers we find tales of ferocious daughters: women driven to violent acts to avenge or save a parent. Same song, different verse?

† Sometimes the line between defense and offense is thin indeed. In 1119, Juliana of Fontevrault, the illegitimate daughter of King Henry I of England, shot a crossbow at her father. At the time, he was besieging her in her husband's fortress at Breteuil, but her attack was fueled in part by her father's earlier involvement in the blinding and mutilation of her young daughters—his granddaughters, in case you missed that—while they were held as hostages by one of his liegemen during a disagreement over the ownership of a strategically important castle.

Juliana was by no means an innocent party here. She and her husband held the liegeman's son in the other half of the hostage swap. (This was a common arrangement in disputes between European nobles and royals, intended to ensure good behavior, or at least to reduce bad behavior, by both parties—often with disastrous results for the hostages.) For reasons that are unclear, Juliana and her husband blinded the liegeman's son while he was in their care. Henry allowed the injury to Juliana's daughters in retaliation.

regular army. When necessary, they stood on the walls of besieged cities or fortresses and repelled invaders with rocks, boiling oil, gunfire, and defiant words.

The story takes a different turn when Mom goes to war at the head of an army, as we see when we look at the cases of three female rulers of small kingdoms who took on the greatest empires of their times in order to protect or avenge their children.

"MORE BLOOD THAN YOU CAN DRINK"

The story of Tomyris, the warrior queen of what is now Kazakhstan, demonstrates that the strength of a mother's rage does not end when a child becomes an adult.

In 530 BCE, Cyrus the Great of Persia ruled over what was then the greatest land empire of all time. It stretched from the Caucasus to the Indian Ocean, from the Mediterranean Sea to the Indus River. Over the twenty years of his reign, he had defeated the Medes, conquered the fabulously wealthy King Croesus of Lydia, subjugated the Greek colonies of Ionia, and seized the city of Babylon, bringing an end to the great Chaldean Empire.

His obvious next move was northeast to the steppes of Scythia, the reported home of the legendary Amazons, where Tomyris ruled the confederation of hard-riding tribes known as the Massagetae.* Unlike women in many of the neighboring territories, Massagetae women fought on horseback alongside their men, held property in their own names, and enjoyed considerable sexual freedom.† They also had a tradition of women rulers.

---

* Herodotus is the primary source for what we know about Tomyris, if we use the term "primary source" loosely. Writing roughly one hundred years later, Herodotus included her story in his history of the Greco-Persian Wars. Herodotus, a Greek writing the history of a long conflict between his own people and Persia, takes the perspective that "the enemy of my enemy is my friend" and treats Tomyris as a heroine. Or at least as the leader of the good guys. Other sources, most notably the Old Testament, represent Cyrus as a generous and merciful conqueror and don't mention Tomyris at all. The question of who tells a story and how the biases of the teller shape that story is always an interesting one.

† Some authors have interpreted Herodotus to say that the Massagetae practiced polyandry, in which women take more than one husband at a time. Whether or not Massagetae women had harems of husbands, they certainly had more freedom than women in the Persian Empire—or the women of Herodotus's Greece for that matter.

Seeing that Tomyris ruled alone, Cyrus first tried to win her territories with an offer of marriage, a time-honored means of annexing a kingdom, especially in cultures in which women are seen as the property of their fathers or husbands.* Tomyris knew Cyrus was courting her solely for her kingdom. She refused his proposal like the poisoned apple it was and demanded Cyrus leave her people in peace, saying, "Rule your own people and try to bear the sight of me ruling mine."[2]

In response, Cyrus marched his troops toward the border between his empire and the Massagetae lands. When he reached the Araxes River, he ordered his men to build bridges across it. It was obvious he did not have peace in mind.

Tomyris offered to meet him one-on-one if he would abandon his bridge-building and his invasion plans. The Massagetae would retreat three-days' march from the bridge and allow Cyrus to cross for a meeting. If he preferred, Cyrus's troops could retreat and Tomyris would come to him. Cyrus took the suggestion to his war council, where it was shouted down on the grounds that it would be "an intolerable disgrace for Cyrus, son of Cambyses, to give ground before a woman."[3] The presumably greater shame of defeat at the hands of a woman apparently never occurred to them as a possibility.

With the failure of Tomyris's attempt at diplomacy, the two countries went to war. At first Tomyris fought only to defend her borders against the Persian invasion. Then her son Spargapises and the men under his command fell into a Persian trap.

Cyrus's trap depended on one fact: the Massagetae, like other Scythian tribes, drank milk rather than wine.† He ordered an elaborate banquet to be laid out in his tents, complete with large quantities of wine. Then he faked a retreat, leaving some of his less-skilled soldiers behind to "defend" the camp. The seemingly abandoned feast caught Spargapises and his troops as effectively as peanut butter in a mousetrap. The Massagetae ate and drank themselves into

---

* The flip side of this was that annexation of a kingdom often included the sexual annexation of its queen, with or without her consent. Sometimes they were taken as wives or concubines. Sometimes they suffered a literal enactment of Susan Brownmiller's definition of rape as "the vehicle of his conquest over her being." See *Against Our Will: Men, Women and Rape* (New York: Simon & Schuster, 1975), 14. There's a reason defeated queens often committed suicide when the enemy was at the gate.

† Not as innocent as it sounds. I'm told fermented mare's milk (*koumis*) packs a punch.

a stupor. When they were too drunk to be dangerous, the Persians returned. They massacred most of the Massagetae forces, taking Spargapises prisoner.

Spargapises may have been clueless about wine, but he understood power politics. He tricked Cyrus into removing his bonds, then killed himself so the Persian emperor could not use him as a bargaining chip against his mother.

With Spargapises's death, the nature of the war changed. Keeping the Persians at bay was no longer enough for Tomyris; she wanted vengeance. Tomyris sent Cyrus a message in which she denounced the Persian ruler as a coward and threatened him with revenge for the death of her son: "I swear by the sun our master to give you more blood than you can drink, for all your gluttony."

Cyrus did not back down.

Tomyris led the remainder of her army against the Persians in a battle so bloody that Herodotus, unable to imagine the scale of future atrocities, judged it "more violent than any other fought between foreign nations." The Massagetae did not bother to take prisoners. Instead they killed everyone in their path, from camp followers to Cyrus himself. When the battle ended, Tomyris and her soldiers searched through the dead until they found Cyrus's corpse. Tomyris hacked off his head and plunged it into a wineskin filled with blood—reportedly drained from Persian soldiers—and proclaimed that her decapitated enemy could drink his fill. Thereafter she used the empty skull as a goblet.*

Cyrus's death at Tomyris's hands did not mark the end of the Persian Empire—or even stop its expansion. His successors continued Cyrus's expansionist policies. But they left Tomyris and the Massagetae alone.

BOUDICA LEADS A REBELLION

In 61 CE, another empire pushed another mother too far. Boudica's rebellion, which lasted only a few months, came close to driving the Roman Empire out of Britain.

---

* This was not a piece of personal gruesomeness on Tomyris's part. Scythian warriors traditionally made bejeweled goblets from their enemies' skulls. For that matter, the Romantic poet Lord Byron is said to have kept a skull goblet around, though it was not made from the remains of someone with whom he was personally acquainted.

The Roman presence in Britain was relatively new in 61 CE, but it already consisted of more than just barracks and soldiers. Military men and merchants alike brought their families to live with them and established enclaves in which they could live in a primitive version of Roman comfort—Rome away from Rome as it were. The Romans built towns and cities, spas, and temples. As was typical in the regions Rome colonized, they established "client" relationships with local rulers. (King Herod in Palestine is the most famous example of this arrangement.) These client-kings put off their kingdoms' inevitable absorption into the empire for a generation or two by accepting an unequal alliance with Rome.

Boudica's tribe, the Iceni, voluntarily formed an alliance with Rome when imperial troops invaded Britain in 43 CE, but the relationship was never an easy one. In 49/50 CE, the Iceni led a consortium of tribes in rebellion against Rome—triggered, ironically, by a Roman governor's decision to disarm his local allies in anticipation of a possible rebellion. After the rebellion was defeated, Boudica's husband, Prasutagus, emerged as the leader of the Iceni and client of Rome.

Boudica entered the historical stage eleven years later, with Prasutagus's death.* Roman law provided that when client-rulers died their kingdoms became the property of the emperor. Prasutagus attempted to sidestep this ruling with a legal device Roman nobility often used to protect their families' inheritances from imperial greed. His will divided his possessions among his two daughters, with Boudica serving as regent on their behalf, and the Roman emperor Nero, who was not known for his willingness to share.

---

* As with Tomyris, we know Boudica's story through a limited number of sources, with a few assists from modern archaeology. Unlike Herodotus and Tomyris, the men who told Boudica's story wrote from the perspective of her enemies. The Roman historian Tacitus, who was born five years before the revolt, wrote two separate accounts of Boudica's rebellion. He could at least claim secondhand knowledge of the events on which he reported: his father-in-law served as a member of the Roman governor's staff during the revolt, and there is evidence that Tacitus interviewed other veterans of the rebellion. Our only other source is a fragment of an account written roughly a hundred years later by Dio Cassius, which appears in a selection of readings compiled by a Greek monk in the eleventh century CE. Such are the tattered scraps from which history is pieced together. Quotations from Tacitus are from *The Annals of Imperial Rome*, trans. Michael Grant (London: Cassell, 1963), 317–21. Quotations from Dio Cassius are from *Dio's Roman History* 8, trans. Earnest Cary (Cambridge, MA: Harvard University Press, 1925), 83–105.

Prasutagus's attempt to provide security for his family and his kingdom failed. Probably acting under orders from Nero himself, Catus Decianus, the chief procurator,* not only claimed Prasutagus's kingdom for Rome but sent imperial soldiers to seize the former ruler's personal wealth, along with that of the other leading Iceni. When Boudica protested, she was publicly flogged and forced to watch as Roman soldiers raped her daughters.

Inflamed by the outrage, and fearing worse to come, Boudica and the Iceni took up arms. Other tribes that had suffered injustices under Roman rule hurried to join them—so many that Tacitus claimed the entire island of Britain responded when Boudica called for their aid.[†]

Boudica first led her forces against the Roman city of Camulodunum (modern Colchester)—a former military outpost inhabited by Roman veterans who had taken British land and houses (with official approval) and treated the former owners as slaves. Experienced soldiers or not, the people of Camulodunum put more resources into building a temple honoring the deceased and deified emperor Claudius than in keeping their defenses repaired. Archaeological evidence shows the Romans leveled the original defenses and built houses over them. When Boudica attacked, the Romans retreated to the partially completed Claudian temple. The emperor-god turned out to be less protection than a good bulwark would have been. Defended by military retirees turned farmers and a small force of active soldiers sent by Catus Decianus, the besieged forces at Camulodunum held out for two days before Boudica stormed the walls and burned the city to the ground.

So far, Boudica's forces had met with little meaningful resistance. Shortly before Boudica and the Iceni rose up in rebellion, the Roman governor of Britain, Gaius Suetonius Paulinus, led the main Roman army on a search-and-destroy mission against the Druid sanctuary at Mona (Anglesey) in Wales, where Suetonius believed the priestesses were harboring dangerous rebels.[‡] When he received reports of Boudica's uprising, Suetonius raced south with a legion of Roman soldiers.

Boudica and her allies headed toward Londinium, which was already a wealthy commercial center. Suetonius reached the city first.

---

* Essentially the CFO for Roman Britain.

† In fact, not all Britons joined Boudica's uprising. Dio estimated Boudica's force at 120,000, a more modest number, but still substantial.

‡ *Other* dangerous rebels—not related to Boudica's uprising.

He found Catus Decianus had fled to Gaul, leaving the city with no defense. The wealthiest residents had also abandoned the unfortified city. Those who remained begged the governor to protect them. Suetonius told the inhabitants he was unwilling to throw his troops away in an attempt to defend a site that could not be defended and recommended they follow those who had already left.

Only those who were too poor, too fragile, or too stubborn to leave were still in Londinium when Boudica and her forces arrived. The Britons once again killed the inhabitants and burned the town—a sixteen-inch-thick layer of red ash below the streets of modern London testifies to the completeness of the destruction. Next they attacked the nearby town of Verulamium (St. Albans), home to Romanized Britons rather than Roman expats. Boudica ordered them killed as collaborators.

According to Tacitus, a total of seventy thousand died at the sacks of Londinium and Verulamium. Dio describes the brutality of the deaths with salacious detail: "They hung up naked the noblest and most distinguished women and then cut off their breasts and sewed them to their mouths, in order to make the victims appear to be eating them; afterwards they impaled the women on sharp skewers run lengthwise through the entire body"—a symbolic rape that Dio seems to find more horrific than the actual rape suffered by Boudica's daughters at the hands of Roman soldiers. Tacitus, less explicit, reported that the rebels "could not wait to cut throats, hang, burn and crucify."*

The night before what would be Boudica's final battle, both commanders went to their soldiers' campfires to encourage their troops. Suetonius told his troops they had nothing to fear from Boudica's army because it consisted of more women than fighting men. His soldiers may have found that less than comforting given the well-known practice of Celtic women fighting alongside, or ahead of, their men—a habit the Romans found disquieting. (Three centuries later, Roman historian Ammianus Marcellinus, who fought against the Celts in

---

* Unlike Tacitus and Dio, we should compare Boudica's slaughter of the inhabitants of Londinium and Verulamium with the Roman slaughter of the Druid priestesses of Mona, who were hacked down and burned in their own altar fires at Suetonius's order at roughly the same time as Boudica's sack of Camulodunum. War is ugly, whether perpetrated by men or women—a fact we will have cause to return to over and over in the coming chapters.

Gaul, reported "a whole band of foreigners will be unable to cope with one of them in a fight, if he call in his wife.")[4]

Boudica drove past the gathered tribes that night in her wicker chariot with her daughters—a vivid reminder of why they fought. Britons were accustomed to being commanded by a woman, but Boudica made it clear that for her the battle was personal: "I am descended from mighty men! But I am not fighting for my kingdom and wealth now. I am fighting as an ordinary person for my lost freedom, my bruised body and my outraged daughters.... Consider how many of you are fighting—and why. Then you will win this battle or perish. That is what I, as a woman, plan to do. Let the men live in shame and slavery if they will!"*

Suetonius met Boudica in the field with ten thousand Roman legionaries and allied Britons—a force much smaller than hers, even allowing for exaggeration on the part of our sources.† Despite the overwhelming superiority of Boudica's forces, fighting against Suetonius and his battle-hardened soldiers was a very different prospect than attacking underfortified and undermanned civilian towns. The men of the Fourteenth Legion were professional soldiers. They were armed with daggers, javelins, and two-foot-long swords known as *gladii* (as in "gladiator") and protected by body armor, helmets with neck protection, and carved wooden shields.

By comparison, Boudica's army was a family affair. Noncombatants sat near the baggage wagons at the edge of the battlefield, like spectators at a Little League game. Warriors, male and female alike, carried the long Celtic sword, which was designed for one-on-one combat between heroes. Only the highest-ranking wore helmets and carried shields. The majority wore no armor and little clothing. The Celtic army advanced with music and shouting in what would have

---

* Tacitus probably made this speech up. No Roman would have been close enough to hear Boudica rally her troops. And if a Roman soldier had strayed into the Celtic camp, he certainly wouldn't have been taking notes on one of the wax-covered writing tablets that served as Rome's version of a steno pad.

† Historians today are cautious about accepting premodern estimates of the sizes of armies and the numbers dead. The assumption is that at best the writer did not have access to accurate numbers and at worse he diddled the numbers to make a victory more glorious or a defeat less humiliating. Modern military historians adjust the numbers based on their own assumptions about the realities of the period in question, creating estimates that may or may not be more accurate than those in the original sources.

appeared as an undisciplined mob to Roman soldiers trained to fight in ordered ranks.

Suetonius chose the terrain for making his stand against Boudica and her allies with care. He located his troops in a defile with an open plain in front of them and a forest at his flank and rear.* Protected by the narrow valley, the Roman soldiers held their line against the initial Celtic charge, hurling their javelins against the enemy but not counterattacking. Once Boudica's forces had exhausted themselves, the Romans moved forward in a wedge formation, driving the Celts back until they were pinned between the Romans and their own wagons. It was a death trap. Roman soldiers killed not only defeated warriors but also unarmed women, children, and even pack animals. Tacitus estimated that eighty thousand Celts died, compared to four hundred Romans. (Again, we have to be careful about accepting the numbers. Sometimes it's best to think of them as a metaphor.)

According to Tacitus, Boudica did not die on the battlefield. Instead, she poisoned herself rather than fall into Roman hands. Given her previous experience of Roman brutality, it's hard to fault that decision. We do not know what happened to her daughters. We don't even know their names.

From the Roman perspective, the rebellion was a nightmare, made worse by the fact that the initial defeats came at the hands of a woman, which, according to Dio Cassius, "caused them the greatest shame"— not unlike the idea that it would be an "intolerable disgrace" for Cyrus the Great to give ground before a woman. The question of shame will appear again and again over the course of this book—both the shame attributed to men who were forced to concede to victorious women warriors and the shame often attributed to women who took up arms.

In the case of Rome, the sense of shame was rooted in fundamental cultural differences regarding the status of women in Celtic and Roman society. Celtic women enjoyed rights and freedoms unknown to their Mediterranean counterparts. Female leadership, on the battlefield and off, was common. By contrast, Roman women had few legal rights. From birth to death, a Roman woman belonged to her male relatives. She could own and inherit property under certain conditions, but had no legal rights to her children. She was officially a citizen but could neither vote nor hold public office—not so different

---

* As with so much else about Boudica, we are not sure exactly where her final battle occurred. Identifying the site has become an academic parlor game.

from the position of women in the United States and Great Britain prior to the twentieth century.*

It's not surprising that Romans did not know how to deal with foreign queens. The idea that a Roman woman would fight beside her husband was laughable. The idea that she could lead an army? Unthinkable.

HISTORY REPEATS ITSELF

Eighteen hundred years later, the widowed ruler of another small kingdom squared off against the greatest empire in the world to defend her child's right to inherit. Lakshmi Bai (1828–1858), the Rani of Jhansi, joined the rebellion against British rule—variously known as the Indian Mutiny, the Sepoy Rebellion, or the First Indian War of Independence—only when she had no options left.

Like the Romans before them, the British in India established relationships with client-kings. Beginning in the mid-eighteenth century, Indian rulers negotiated with the British East India Company for military support against other Indian rulers. By 1857, what had once been protection had become a protection racket. Rulers of the "princely states" enjoyed personal luxury and titular authority, but British political agents held the real power in their kingdoms through a combination of fiscal control and military threat. East India Company troops, made up of Indian soldiers with British officers and British weapons, were stationed in the princely states. These troops were officially a royal prerogative but they were also a sword over the royal head. Only the most powerful and/or lucky Indian states managed to retain their sovereignty in real terms.

Lakshmi Bai was the widow of Raja Gangadhar Rao Newalkar, the ruler of the kingdom of Jhansi, which had been a British client state since 1803. Several months before his death, the childless raja adopted a distant cousin named Damodar Rao as his son and made a will naming the five-year-old boy as his heir, with Lakshmi Bai as regent. He made sure he took all the steps needed to make the adoption legal.

---

* Some high-status women played behind-the-scenes roles in public affairs no matter what the rules said—Nero's female relatives being a good, or perhaps a really bad, example.

Adopted heirs were an accepted practice in Indian kingdoms—both Gangadhar Rao and his predecessor had been adopted. Unfortunately for Lakshmi Bai and her son, a new governor-general was in control and making changes. James Andrew Broun Ramsay, Lord Dalhousie, instituted an aggressive policy of annexing Indian states on what now (and to many Indians then) seem flimsy excuses, most notably the doctrine of lapse. The British already exercised the right to "recognize" (i.e., control) succession in the princely states with which they had client relationships. Dalhousie now declared that if the British government in India did not ratify the adoption of an heir to the throne, the state would pass "by lapse" to the British. Few adopted heirs were ratified. (Does this surprise anyone?)

When the raja died in 1853, Dalhousie refused to acknowledge Damodar Rao as the legal heir to the throne and seized control of Jhansi, replacing the raja with a British bureaucrat. Lakshmi Bai did not initially oppose the British takeover with violence. Instead she contested the decision in the British courts, with the support of the prior British political agent at Jhansi and the advice of British counsel. She continued to submit petitions arguing her case until early 1856. All her appeals were rejected.

Meanwhile, discontent was building among the Indian soldiers who made up the vast majority of the British East India Company's army. The British made a number of policy decisions that many Indians perceived as an organized attack on the religious beliefs of both Hindu and Muslim soldiers.* The final straw came when the company handed its Indian troops the hottest new weapon in the British arsenal: the Enfield rifle. Rumors spread that cartridges for the Enfield were greased with a combination of beef and pork fat. Since the cartridges had to be bitten open, such grease would make them abominations for both Hindus and Muslims. British officers, each certain that the troops under *his* command were too loyal to believe anything so foolish, were slow to respond to the rumors. By the time they assured their men that the cartridges were greased with beeswax and vegetable oils, the damage was done.

In May 1857, discontent turned to mutiny. Eighty-five sepoys at the army garrison of Meerut refused to use the new rifles. They were court-martialed and put in irons. The next day, the regiments

---

* In fact those decisions seem to have been the result of a profound lack of understanding about the people they ruled.

stationed at Meerut stormed the jail, killed the British officers and their families, and marched toward Delhi, where the last Mogul emperor ruled, at least in name.

The mutiny at Meerut was the spark needed to set off a revolt that was already loaded, primed, and ready to fire. Thousands of Indians outside the army had their own grievances against the British. Reforms regarding child marriage and the protection of widows were seen as attacks on Hindu religious law. Land reform in Bengal had displaced many landholders. Members of the traditional nobility resented the forcible annexation of Indian states and wondered whether theirs would be the next to go. Leaders whose power had been threatened rose up, transforming what had begun as a mutiny into a many-headed resistance movement. Violence spread across northern India.

On June 6, the East India Company troops stationed in Jhansi mutinied. Two days later, they massacred the British population of the city and marched out to join their counterparts in Delhi. Given Lakshmi Bai's conflicts with their government, the British were quick to blame her for the uprising in Jhansi, though there is no evidence for her initial involvement. In fact, she wrote to the nearest British authority, Major Walter Erskine, on June 12, giving her account of the mutiny and asking for instructions. Erskine forwarded her letter to Calcutta, with a note saying it agreed with what he knew from other sources. He authorized the rani to manage the district until he could send soldiers to help her restore order.

With the region in chaos, Lakshmi Bai soon found herself under attack by two neighboring princes and a distant claimant to the throne of Jhansi, all of whom saw the crisis as an opportunity to do a little empire-building of their own. In order to defend her kingdom, she recruited an army,* strengthened the city's defenses, and formed protective alliances with the rajas of nearby Banpur and Shergarh.†️ As late as February 1858, she told her advisors she would turn the district over to the British when they arrived.

Erskine's positive assessment of the rani's actions was not enough. The central government in Calcutta still believed Lakshmi Bai was responsible for the Jhansi mutiny and subsequent massacre. Her efforts to defend Jhansi only confirmed that belief.

---

* Unfortunately, her new recruits included known mutineers from the Jhansi garrison. Mistake number one.

† Both of whom had already raised the flag of rebellion. Mistake number two.

On March 25, Major General Sir Hugh Rose and his forces arrived at Jhansi and besieged the city. Threatened with execution as a rebel if captured by the British, Lakshmi Bai resisted. In spite of a vigorous defense, by March 30 most of the rani's guns had been disabled and the fort's walls breached. On April 3, the British broke into the city, took the palace, and stormed the fort.

The night before the final British assault, Lakshmi Bai escaped from the fortress with her ten-year-old son and four companions.* The next day, the rani and her small retinue reached the fortress of Kalpi. She was now an official rebel and threw herself into the fight.

Defeated again and again through May and into early June, Lakshmi Bai and the rebel forces retreated before the British. On June 16, Rose's forces closed in. The rani led the remnants of her army into battle. On the second day of fighting, she was shot from her horse and killed.

Roman historians demonized Boudica. The British response to the Rani of Jhansi was more complicated. British newspapers denounced Lakshmi Bai as the "Jezebel of India." But Rose compared his fallen adversary to Joan of Arc.† Reporting her death to his commanding officer, he said: "The Rani was remarkable for her bravery, cleverness and perseverance; her generosity to her subordinates was unbounded. These qualities, combined with her rank, rendered her the most dangerous of all the rebel leaders. Although she was a lady, she was the bravest and best military leader of the rebels. A man among the mutineers."‡

Despite the praise of her enemies, Lakshmi Bai failed to obtain the only thing she wanted from the British: her adopted son received

---

* Popular accounts claim she rode off with her son strapped to her back. It's a powerful image of a mother at war, but not believable. As anyone with personal experience of a ten-year-old boy will tell you, he would be too active, too independent, and definitely too heavy to carry this way. On a saddle behind her holding on tight? Sure.

† An odd accolade given that a British court condemned Joan of Arc to death after she successfully led French troops against the British in the fifteenth century. It's probable that Rose did not intend to evoke all the implications of the Joan of Arc comparison. By the nineteenth century, "Joan of Arc" had become shorthand for a gallant national defense led by a woman—an idea we'll see again.

‡ A compliment that will feel familiar to any woman who was ever praised for "thinking like a man" or chafed at having "like a girl" used as an insult. Quoted in Joyce Lebra-Chapman, *The Rani of Jhansi: A Study in Female Heroism in India* (Honolulu: University of Hawaii Press, 1986), 114.

a pension, but was never recognized as the ruler of Jhansi, which was absorbed into British India.

The combination of war, motherhood, and motherland produces powerful symbols.

Over time, Tomyris, Boudica, and Lakshmi Bai became national heroines. In the late nineteenth century, Great Britain claimed Boudica as a predecessor to Queen Victoria.* The Indian independence movement adopted the Rani of Jhansi as a nationalist icon in the early twentieth century. Uzbekistan, Kazakhstan, and Azerbaijan, in search of national identities in the post-Soviet era, all claim Tomyris as their own.†

In the late twentieth century, liberation movements in Africa, Asia, and Latin America often adopted the image of a mother holding a child in one hand and a rifle in the other as a symbol of patriotism. This symbolism took explicit form in Nicaragua, where Sandinistas used the protection of children as a constant theme in their efforts to recruit women to join defense units. One iconic photograph of armed women in uniform crossing a river was captioned "'No more crimes against our children!' This is the combative shout of Nicaraguan women that was raised by thousands of female soldiers . . . in the reserve battalion."[5]

Today, American mother-soldiers have claimed the power of this imagery for themselves with controversial photographs of servicewomen breastfeeding while in uniform. Their position is summed up in a challenge coin produced by the organization Breastfeeding in Combat Boots,‡ which provides information and support for mothers in the military. A modern military emblem for mothers at war, one

---

* The phonetic roots for "Boudica" are related to various Celtic words for victory. Nineteenth-century scholars connected the dots and pronounced the Celtic warrior the first Queen Victoria.

† Heroism is in the eyes of the beholder. Tomyris is also a national bogeyman. When I tweeted that I was working on Tomyris, one Twitter correspondent responded, "Tomyris was a bitch. Any Iranian will tell you that." Apparently, two and a half millennia later, it is still an intolerable disgrace for Cyrus the Great to suffer defeat at the hands of a woman.

‡ Challenge coins are small medallions that carry an organization's insignia. They are traditionally given to members of a military unit and produced on demand to prove membership.

side of the coin shows two breastfeeding servicewomen—one an officer, one an enlisted woman—surrounded by the slogan "Giving the Breast for Baby and Country." The obverse shows a pair of combat boots with the words "Protect, Promote and Support." The message is clear: mother-soldiers will defend child and country alike. In other words, don't mess with mama.

CHAPTER TWO

HER FATHER'S DAUGHTER

The Chinese heroine Hua Mulan is one of the oldest and most enduring examples of a woman who becomes a warrior because of her role as a daughter.*

Scholars have argued for centuries over whether or not Mulan was a historical figure. At some level, it doesn't matter as far as piecing together her story is concerned. The available information about her life is scarce to nonexistent, even by the often-shaky standard of what we know about other women warriors of the ancient world.

Our oldest source for her story is the "Poem of Mulan," which appears in a twelfth-century poetry anthology compiled by Guo Maoqian,† who attributes it to a sixth-century collection that no longer exists. The poem is anonymous, undated, and three hundred words long. A few details, such as the use of the title "khan" rather than "emperor," suggest the poem dates from the Northern dynasties period (386–581 CE).‡

---

* Also known as Wei Hua Hu, Fua Mulan, or Wei Mulan. Names don't always travel well across time, space, and transliteration.

† Who is known to history primarily for said anthology. Women aren't the only people who leave thin trails in the dusts of time.

‡ Just to make it clear how vague all this is: there are scholars who disagree and place the poem, and therefore Mulan, in the Sui dynasty (581–618 CE). Imagine how difficult it would be for future historians to write about Abigail Adams if they didn't know whether her letters dated from 1776 or 1976.

For the most part, I chose not to discuss the stories of mythical women warriors, because there are plenty of historical examples to consider.* But Mulan is a special case. She is as well known in China as Joan of Arc is in the West. Despite the absence of biographical details in the original source, several regions of China claim her as their own folk heroine.

Mulan's story is familiar to American audiences thanks to the 1998 Disney film *Mulan*.† But the Walt Disney Company is simply one in a long tradition of Mulan adapters, and by no means the most fanciful in its interpretation. Over a period of 1,500 years, Mulan's story has been told in Chinese operas, plays, folk tales, and now video games.

While the versions differ in the details, the basic structure of the story remains the same: Threatened by invaders from the north, the emperor (or the khan) conscripted soldiers to defend the country. Because her father was too old to fight and her brother too young, Mulan purchased a horse, weapons, and armor; disguised herself as a man; and joined the army to fulfill the family's conscription obligation.

The original poem gives us a brief, vivid impression of Mulan's life as a soldier, but no details:

> She did not hear her parents' voices, calling for their daughter,
> She only heard the whinnying of Crimson Mountain's Hunnish
>   horsemen.
> Myriads of mile: she joined the thick of battle,
> Crossing the mountain passes as if flying.
> Winds from the north transmitted metal rattles,
> A freezing light shone on her iron armor.
> A hundred battles and the brass were dead;
> After ten years the bravest men returned.[1]

This is war from the common soldier's viewpoint, stripped down to misery and poetry. Later versions of the story fill this space with heroic deeds, gender-problematic romances, and, in the Disney version, a smart-mouthed dragon sidekick.

---

* No Amazons, except once or twice in passing.

† Disney's *Mulan* wasn't the first appearance of the Chinese woman warrior in American popular culture. Under the name Fa Mu Lan, she is a central image in Maxine Hong Kingston's *The Woman Warrior: Memoirs of a Girlhood Among Ghosts.* Published in 1976, Kingston's book opened the genre of memoir to women and minority writers in the United States.

At the end of their tour of duty, Mulan and her comrades met with the emperor, who offered them honorary ranks, appointments at court, and rewards "counted in the millions." (In one late version, the emperor discovers her gender and offers to make her his consort. She tells him she would rather die.) Mulan refused everything; all she wanted was a fast horse (or sometimes a camel) to take her home. Once there, she went into the house and put on a woman's clothing and makeup. When she came back out, her army buddies were flabbergasted by the truth. During the ten (or sometimes twelve) years she served in the army, none of her fellow soldiers suspected she was a woman.*

In Mulan's story, the link between being a daughter and becoming a soldier is direct and irrefutable. Chinese readers/listeners/viewers would understand her action as an extreme act of filial piety. In fact, in one version of the story she receives the posthumous title Filial-Staunchness. Filial piety—respect for and obedience to one's parents—is the foundation on which Confucian society stands. Children are loyal to their parents. Wives are loyal to their husbands. Subjects are loyal to the ruler. The ruler is loyal to the kingdom itself. If everyone performs their duties to those above them in the hierarchy, society flourishes. If duties are not faithfully performed, chaos reigns, the emperor loses the mandate of heaven, and dynasties fall. It is an alien concept for those of us who grew up in a culture defined in terms of rights rather than social duties. But it is as powerful a fundamental social principle as "all men are created equal."

Seen through this lens, Mulan became a warrior in order to protect her father, her family, and the social order as a whole. She preserved society's norms by stepping outside them.

Warrior daughters fought for a variety of reasons. Some, like Mulan, fought to preserve their society. Some fought to overturn it. Some fought simply to escape the narrow framework of what society expected of women. But whatever their reasons, most historical

---

* This is the major point at which the Disney version departs from the basic shape of the story. In Disney's *Mulan*, her fellow soldiers discover her deception when she is wounded and reject her—at least until she saves the empire. The change is powerful and reflects the historical experience of many women who fought disguised as men (except for singlehandedly saving the empire). Being wounded always brought with it the risk of exposure, a point we will discuss in more detail in chapter 7.

warrior daughters shared one common characteristic: they went to war as a result of their relationships with their fathers.

The warrior daughter is not an obvious outcome of the father-daughter relationship in most traditional societies, in which the male head of the family, extended or nuclear, exercised political, social, and economic power over other family members. While the details varied in different times and places, the basic outlines of the roles of fathers and daughters are remarkably consistent across those preindustrial societies for which data exists. Marriageable daughters were the ultimate trade good of the gift economy—an idea that survives in residual form in the ritual of "giving away" the bride.* Royal families exchanged daughters to cement power alliances or to establish peace between hostile nations. (In medieval England, such women were called "peace-weavers.") Wealthy merchants, cattle farmers, and plantation owners exchanged daughters to seal business alliances, consolidate holdings, or gain access to new markets. Well-to-do peasants and their urban counterparts included their daughters in the complex economic calculus that drove the exchange and/or acquisition of land, cattle, or other property. Whether payments took the form of a dowry, in which a bride brought goods or money into the marriage, or a bride-price, in which the groom's family paid the bride's family for a bride, at base these transactions treated women as commodities to be exchanged/given/taken/traded, based on their potential to produce children, food, status, connections, or domestic services.† In such societies, daughters were more apt to be "daddy's little asset" than "daddy's little girl." Even in places where the literal exchange of a daughter was a thing of the past, her legal identity was often an extension of her relationship first with her father and then with her husband. (As late as 1972, tennis star Billie Jean King could not get a credit card without the signature of her husband—an unemployed law student.)

By comparison, in traditional societies, past and present, sons have value in and of themselves. Families needed sons to carry on the name, the family business, the dynasty. (Henry VIII of England, who

---

* As anthropologist Gayle Rubin points out, "If women are the gifts, then it is men who are the exchange partners. And it is the partners, not the presents, upon whom reciprocal exchange confers its quasi-mystical power of social linkage." Rubin, "The Traffic in Women: Notes on the 'Political Economy' of Sex," in *The Second Wave: A Reader in Feminist Theory*, ed. Linda Nicholson (New York: Routledge, 1997), 37.

† A far broader category than housekeeping in the modern sense of the word.

married and remarried in his desire to father a male heir, is perhaps the most famous example of how far this perceived need could drive a man.) Men desired sons to perform religious rites in honor of ancestors, or carry on blood feuds to avenge a family's honor, or inherit the family farm.

In the absence of a son, a daughter could be used to "purchase" a son-in-law to serve as his successor. Or a nephew, cousin, or brother could step into the role that would otherwise be filled by a son. But in some cases, the lack of a son opened up opportunities for daughters. The chance to receive an education.* To inherit a business. To inherit a kingdom. In extreme cases, a son-shaped hole allowed, or forced, a woman to step outside her expected roles and go to war in place of her father, by the side of her father, or in emulation of her father.

PLUCKY PRINCESS LEADS A BAND OF REBELS

Several hundred years after Hua Mulan,† or perhaps a generation or two depending on which date you accept for the "Poem of Mulan," a woman warrior led a rebel army against the Chinese empire on her father's behalf and helped found the Tang dynasty, which is considered China's cultural and artistic golden age.

Princess Pingyang (ca. 598–623 CE) took up arms in the reign of the Emperor Yangdi, second (and last) emperor of the Sui dynasty.‡

---

* In her groundbreaking and controversial history of feminist thought, Gerda Lerner argued that prior to the seventeenth century, a woman was likely to receive an education only if she enjoyed three advantages: she was the daughter of a family with wealth or rank, her father was "enlightened on the subject of women's educability," and the family had no sons. See Gerda Lerner, *The Creation of Feminist Consciousness: From the Middle Ages to Eighteen-Seventy* (New York: Oxford University Press, 1983), 28.

† Assuming she existed anywhere other than the hearts and minds of her countrymen.

‡ With Princess Pingyang we are firmly in the land of historical records, though they may not always resemble history as we understand it. She appears in the "collected biographies" section of two Tang dynasty histories: *History of the Tang Dynasty*, written/collected by Liu Xo (887–946) and others, and *New History of the Tang* by Ouyang Xiu (1007–1072) and Song Qi (998–1061). (Once again we are dealing with history written long after the fact.)

No one denies Pingyang existed, though a number of later (non-Chinese) historians minimize the importance of her role in the rebellion. On the other hand, a few (even later) historians twist the evidence to suggest she led an all-female army. While we will see examples of all-female military units, this is not one of them.

Yangdi took the throne in 604, after assassinating his father and older brother. By 613, his ambitious and expensive imperial projects—including building the Grand Canal, expanding the Great Wall, creating a secondary capital in the western empire, and launching repeated military expeditions into Vietnam, Tibet, Central Asia, and Korea—made him unpopular with peasants and nobles alike. Disastrous military expeditions in 612 and 613 against the kingdom of Koguryo, in what is now North Korea and southern Manchuria, were two foreign wars too many for China's overburdened, overtaxed citizens. Peasants rose in revolt across the empire. The revolt soon spread to members of the aristocracy, many of whom controlled large personal armies. By 615, every province of the empire was in turmoil and the imperial army was engaged on a dozen fronts.

While his generals battled to contain the rebels, the emperor purged his government of any nobles whose loyalty he questioned. Pingyang's father, Li Yuan, was one of the nobles the emperor feared most. Li Yuan was a successful general and a powerful warlord. He controlled the region of modern Shanxi, a strong tactical position from which to attack the Sui capitals at Chang'an and Lo-Yang. That was sufficient reason for the beleaguered emperor to suspect treason, but the main reason the emperor feared him was less rational. In 614, a ballad that predicted the next emperor would be named Li became popular throughout China. In 615, a soothsayer took up the thread and warned Yangdi that someone named Li would soon become emperor. In 617, the increasingly paranoid emperor began to execute people with the Li surname—a step that ensured the prophecy was fulfilled. After Yangdi ordered the execution of another high-ranking general named Li, Li Yuan decided his best chance of survival was rebellion. He sent secret messengers to his son and to Pingyang's husband, Cai Shao, asking them to join forces with him to overthrow the emperor.

Li Yuan did not ask for help from Pingyang. He got it anyway.

Pingyang and her husband lived in the primary Sui capital, Chang'an, where Cai Shao was head of the Sui dynasty equivalent of the Secret Service, responsible for protecting the crown prince. When he received Li Yuan's message asking for his help, Cai Shao hesitated. On the one hand, he feared taking Pingyang with him would cause suspicions in the royal court and end the rebellion before it began. On the other hand, he feared that if he left Ping-yang behind she would be in danger once the emperor learned he had joined the rebellion. Pingyang, however, had no doubts about what they should do. She told her husband to join her father. She could take care of herself.

After Cai Shao left to join forces with her father, Pingyang fled to her family's estate in Shanxi. She found the region suffering from a severe drought and widespread starvation, which the imperial offi-cials were either unwilling or unable to alleviate.[*] She fed the starving from the family granaries, then sold what remained. With the family's wealth turned into hard cash, she assembled an army. Members of the families she had fed were the first recruits who joined what came to be called the Army of the Lady.[†] After arming her newly formed peasant force, she made alliances with groups of dissidents, bandits, and neighboring warlords, one of whom brought a personal army of ten thousand troops to fight under Pingyang's banner. Eventually she commanded a force of seventy thousand.[‡]

Dynastic histories emphasize that Pingyang kept strict discipline over her troops. Unlike many historical military leaders, she forbade looting, pillaging, and rape by her troops and punished offenders with a heavy hand. When her forces took control of a new area, she dis-tributed food to the local people, ensuring they greeted her army as liberators rather than conquerors.

After repeated victories against the emperor's armies in Shanxi, Pingyang joined up with her father and her husband. Together their forces encircled the Sui capital, which they captured within a year.

Yangdi fled the city and was later killed by his own men. Li Yuan became the first emperor of the Tang dynasty, which would rule China for three hundred years. Her father gave Pingyang the offi-cial title of princess, the honorific title *zhao*, meaning wise, and the military rank of marshal, which gave her the right to military aides

---

[*] Always a sign in Chinese history that the emperor has lost the Mandate of Heaven.

[†] Sometimes translated as "the Woman's Army," this is the phrase that leads excited revisionists to claim Pingyang commanded an all-female force.

[‡] At the risk of repeating myself, estimates of troop sizes in older primary sources are always suspect. In this case, what we can take from the numbers is that Pingyang led a rebel army, not a small guerrilla band.

and staff. Despite the rank and honors, she retired from military life, presumably because the national crisis had come to an end.[*]

Pingyang does not reappear in the dynastic histories until her death in 623 at the age of twenty-three. According to the official accounts, the struggle to win the throne for her father had exhausted her.[†] Her grief-stricken father, now the Emperor Gaozu, broke with tradition and insisted her funeral procession include a military band and other martial honors. The official in charge of court ceremonies remonstrated with the emperor because a military band at a woman's funeral was not an accepted practice.[‡] The emperor put him in his place, saying, "A military band plays military music; since the princess raised and commanded armies in the past in response to the righteous calls of dynastic change, she earned military merits.... The Princess's achievements matched those of a minister, and she should not be compared to ordinary women. How could her funeral have no military band!"[2] He then increased the size of the band to make his point.

IN HER FATHER'S FOOTSTEPS

On September 17, 1806, Nadezhda Durova (1783–1866) disguised herself as a man, sneaked out of her parents' home, and joined the

---

[*] It was not unusual for women to take up arms or even command armies in times of national crisis in traditional China, with the expectation that once the crisis was over they would return to their traditional roles as daughter, wife, and mother. For that matter, American women who stepped up to "man" factories, fly bombers from one airfield to another, or serve in the armed forces in World War II were expected to step away from the job after the war was over.

[†] An idea that we will see again in other times and places. The argument seems to be that because women are not designed to go to war, the few who succeed are so exhausted by the experience that it kills them. The medieval chronicle, *Life of the Queen of Queens, Tamar*, for instance, explained Queen Tamar's death in 1213 CE, after thirty years of constant campaigning, this way: "Woman's frailty could not remain unaffected in the course of continual campaigns and suffer no harm" In S. Qaukhchishvili, ed., *The Georgian Chronicle: The Period of Giorgi Lasha*, trans. Katharine Vivian (Amsterdam: Adolf M. Hakkert, 1991), 89. Evidently, in some cases it takes a few decades for exhaustion to catch up with them.

[‡] Ministers who remonstrate with emperors, often over much larger issues and at great personal cost, are common figures in Chinese history.

*A young Nadezhda
Durova in uniform.*

Russian cavalry.* By her own account, Durova enlisted because she
wanted the freedom and adventure of cavalry life, exemplified in her
mind by her father's military career. She served in the Napoleonic

---

* Our primary source for Durova's life is her own autobiographical writing. Published in her lifetime, with the help of noted Russian poet Aleksandr Pushkin, *The Cavalry Maiden: Journals of a Russian Officer in the Napoleonic Wars* (1836) and *The Notes of
Aleksandrov (Durova)* (1839) consist of edited excerpts from the journals she kept during
her ten years with the army. She later enjoyed a brief literary career as a writer of short
fiction, much of which draws on the same material. Durova is an unreliable narrator. She
claims she joined the Russian army when she was sixteen, though her military records
and other archival sources make it clear she was twenty-three. She fails to mention either
her marriage or the birth of her son on January 7, 1803. (An eleventh-century biographer
of Matilda of Tuscany similarly omits a husband and child from the story. In both cases,
the author replaces the reality of a woman who abandoned her husband with the image
of a warrior maiden—apparently there are limits to how many social norms a woman is
allowed to flout and still remain the story's hero.)

Wars and was the first woman to receive the Cross of St. George, a military decoration given to soldiers, sailors, and noncommissioned officers in the Russian imperial army for acts of "undaunted courage."

Durova was the eldest child of a hussar captain and the daughter of Ukrainian gentry. Both hoped their first child would be a son. They dealt with their disappointment in different ways, summed up by Durova's account of one dramatic incident. After a sleepless night caused by the infant Durova's sobs, her frustrated mother threw the still-crying four-month-old out of a moving carriage as they traveled to their next military post. Her father rescued their daughter and cradled her before him on his saddle until they halted for the night. Whether this incident is true, exaggerated, or fabrication, it illustrates a pattern of maternal rejection and paternal connection that would continue until her mother's death.

Following this event, her father turned Durova over to the care of one of his soldiers, the hussar Astakhov.* She spent her days with her father and Astakhov, who "carried me around all day, taking me into the squadron stables and sitting me on the horses, giving me a pistol to play with, and brandishing his saber while I clapped my hands and laughed out loud at the sight of the scattering sparks and glittering steel."[3] Back in her mother's room at night, Durova galloped around and shouted military commands she learned in the company of her father's hussars—actions that enraged her mother.

When Durova was five years old, her father left the army and took a position as the mayor of Sarapul, a district capital in the western foothills of the Ural Mountains. He decided it was time for Durova to leave the military as well. He returned her to the primary care of her mother, who wanted her to give up her "hussar ways" and replace them with appropriate activities for a Russian lady. She kept Durova inside and tried to teach her to make lace, sew, and knit. Durova had neither the inclination nor the skill for such pursuits. Everything she made ripped in her hands—not always by accident. In response, her mother would fly into a violent rage and whip Durova's hands. Durova says she might nonetheless have learned to be "an ordinary girl like the rest" if her mother hadn't combined the hated lessons

---

* According to Colonel A. A. Saks, one of Durova's biographers, it was common for personal orderlies to serve as attendants for officers' children in imperial Russia as late as the first decade of the twentieth century, suggesting the custom ended with the Russian Revolution rather than as a result of a revolution in childcare.

with the constant refrain that a woman's lot was not a happy one: "In my presence she would describe the fate of that sex in the most prejudicial terms: woman, in her opinion, must be born, live, and die in slavery; eternal bondage, painful dependence, and repression of every sort were her destiny from the cradle to the grave."[4]

Durova idealized her father, whose life seemed the antithesis of the narrow world her mother prescribed for her. In rebellion against knitting needles and social niceties, she hid a bow, a saber, and a broken gun in a dark corner of the garden, where she could practice with them whenever her mother's attention was elsewhere. At night, she sneaked out to the stable to ride a wild Circassian stallion her father purchased to tame as a saddle horse.* Her mother punished Durova whenever she caught her indulging in forbidden pastimes, but punishment was not enough to stop her. At the age of ten she planned an escape that depended on the ability to ride, skill with firearms, and a male disguise.

Durova put her tomboy dreams of escape on hold when she reached adolescence, a period when mothers and daughters often find themselves at odds. Her mother declared herself unable to control her daughter and sent Durova to live with relatives in Ukraine. Away from constant battles and her mother's unhappiness, Durova discovered it was fun to be a girl.

This brief period of familial happiness ended when she was called home by a family crisis brought on by her father's infidelity and her mother's subsequent collapse into grief-fueled depression. She found there was nothing she could do to help her mother, who had become a virtual recluse. Instead she filled her days riding with her father around the city. Pleased by her riding skill, he ordered a Cossack tunic tailored to fit her and gave her a fine saddle horse. He boasted she was the living image of him as a youth. If she had been a boy, the son he had dreamed of, she would have been the staff of his old age and an honor to his name.

---

* Rejecting feminine accomplishments and occupations in favor of traditionally masculine pursuits is a common element in accounts of women warriors from ancient China to the modern American military. In *The Warrior Queens*, Antonia Fraser dubs this the Tomboy Syndrome, in which the Warrior Queen, or more broadly the woman warrior, rejects dolls, needlework, or other feminine pursuits in favor of martial skills, hunting, or, in the modern world, team sports. Fraser claims the Tomboy Syndrome "demonstrates the perpetual need for reassurance which the emergence of a Warrior Queen seems to evoke: this woman is not like other women, runs the refrain" (Fraser, *Warrior Queens*, 12).

Distressed by her mother's condition and pleased by her father's attentions, Durova searched for a way to satisfy her childhood dream "to become a warrior and a son to my father and to part company forever from the sex whose sad lot and eternal dependence had begun to terrify me."[5]

Her chance came when a Cossack regiment arrived in Sarapul.

The Cossacks left Sarapul on September 15, 1806. On September 17, Durova cut off her hair, put on her Cossack tunic, slipped out of the house with her father's saber and three hundred rubles he gave her as a name-day gift, and rode through the night to the Cossack regiment's camp. She posed as a boy running away from home and convinced the Cossacks to allow her to ride with them until she could join a regular army regiment.

Durova traveled with the Cossacks for more than a month before they caught up with a regiment in Grodno, near the borders of modern Poland and Lithuania. The army was eager for men. Napoleon was advancing through Germany toward Russia's western border. Regiments needed new recruits to replace men lost in the Battle of Austerlitz ten months before. Even a runaway "boy" without papers was an acceptable candidate.

She began her career in a lancer regiment by training with other young soldiers: arduous drills with saber and lance that challenged her strength and skills. After several days of training, her captain asked her, with "paternal indulgence," what she thought of military life.* She replied she had loved military craft from the day of her birth and considered the warrior's calling the noblest of them all. The captain, who evidently had experience with enthusiastic young soldiers, predicted she might change her opinion after her first battle.

Once she completed her training, Durova was assigned to a combat squadron and ordered to the front. Before she left, she wrote to her father. She begged him to forgive her for running away and asked for his blessing. Not surprisingly, that didn't work out as she hoped. Raising a daughter as a tomboy was one thing; having her run away to join the army was something else again.

---

* Durova found substitute fathers more than once over the course of her military career, perhaps because of her perceived youth.

Durova saw battle for the first time on May 22, 1807, at Guttstadt in East Prussia, now divided between Russia and Poland, where Russian troops attacked French forces under Marshal Michel Ney. She found the battle exhilarating: "What a lot of absurd things they told me about the first battle, about the fear, timidity, and the last desperate courage! What rubbish!"[6] Over the next month, she went on to fight at Passarge, at Heilsberg, and at Friedland, where half her regiment fell to the enemy. Despite her claims of a military vocation, Durova bumbled through her first experiences of war—a fact she makes no attempt to conceal. At Guttstadt, where the regiment went on the attack squadron by squadron, she joined the attack with each new wave, "not from any excess of bravery, but simply from ignorance,"[7] gave up her horse to a wounded man, and lost her gear. While the regiment waited for orders to move out, she dismounted and fell asleep in the bushes. At Friedland she stopped to help a wounded man, separating herself from her regiment in the process and almost losing her horse a second time to a seemingly helpful band of Cossacks. At battle's end, the regiment's commander, General Petr Dem'janovich Kachowski, called her bravery scatterbrained and her compassion witless. He ordered her to the baggage train. When her immediate superior, who "loved her like a father," protested on her behalf, Kachowski explained he was sending her to the wagons to protect her until she had enough experience to use her daring—which now threatened to kill her with no benefit to anyone—for Russia's defense. The words of praise did nothing to lessen her shame over what she perceived as the worst possible punishment.[8]

On July 7, 1807, soon after the bloodbath of Friedland, Tsar Alexander I and Napoleon signed the Treaty of Tilsit. Russia and France were at peace, at least for the moment.

After her regiment settled into its garrison in Poland, Durova's commanding officer sent for her and told her to turn in her gear. She was wanted at headquarters in St. Petersburg.

With no further explanation, Durova was passed from one senior officer to another as she travelled from the Polish border to St. Petersburg, where she found herself in an audience with Tsar Alexander himself. The emperor took her hand and said, "I have heard that you are not a man, is that true?" Durova looked down at her feet. Looking up again, she saw Alexander blushing. Blushing in response, her hand trembling in his, she admitted she was a woman. He questioned her in detail about her reasons for joining the army. He lauded her as "an example to Russia," saying that her commanders had the highest praise for her and called her courage peerless. He awarded her the Cross of St. George because she had saved the life of a valued officer in one of the "witless" acts of compassion condemned by General Kachowski.

If Durova thought she was past the worst of it, she was mistaken. Her father had petitioned the tsar to find his runaway daughter and send her home. Now that peace allowed the emperor to attend to such small matters, the tsar intended to return Durova with honor to her father's house.

Durova didn't give him time to finish his sentence. As soon as she heard the words "return home," she fell to the floor, hugged the emperor's knees, and wept. She begged him not to send her home.

The emperor raised her to her feet and asked what she wanted.

She answered, "To be a warrior! To wear a uniform and bear arms! That is the only reward you can give me, sire!"[9]

Convinced by her passion, Alexander allowed Durova to remain a soldier on one condition: that she continue to hide both her identity and her gender. The Little Father of all Russians made her masquerade easier by giving her a new patronymic drawn from his own name, "Aleksandrov," a symbolic adoption that moved her from the care of one father to another.

When the fragile peace with France came to an end in January 1812, Durova's unit was posted on the Polish border.

She fought in the Russian rear guard, which was under constant attack as it retreated through Russia toward Moscow before the French. She fought at Mir, at Dashkova, at Smolensk, and at Borodino, where she received a contusion from a cannonball, which made it impossible for her to stand or ride without pain. Back on active duty some months later, she fought in the Prussian campaign of 1813, participated in the blockade of Modlin Fortress in Poland from August 10 to October 20, 1813, and served on Russia's western border after Napoleon's escape from Elba island on March 10, 1815.

As far as Durova was concerned, life on the battlefield was infinitely preferable to peacetime life in the garrison: "What a life! What a full, joyous, active life! . . . Every day and every hour now I live and feel alive. Oh, this way of life is a thousand, thousand times superior! Balls, dances, flirtation, music. . . . Oh God, what trivial and boring pastimes!"[10]

Durova's military career ended the same way it began, with the desire to please her father. In 1816, he demanded she leave the army to take care of him in his old age. A dutiful "son," she obeyed—perhaps aware her days of passing as a young man were numbered.*

For the next fifty years, Durova clung to the honorary masculinity she enjoyed during her ten years in the Russian army and the freedom it represented. Although everyone was aware of her masquerade, she wore men's clothing, used masculine parts of speech when referring to herself, and insisted others address her as if she were a man.† "He" was buried with military honors.

It would be a hundred years before another woman was awarded the Cross of St. George for her courage in battle.

NUN BIG COURAGE

In the mid-twentieth century, a Tibetan nun inherited her father's position as clan chieftain and led her people in armed resistance against Chinese rule.

Lemdha Pachen was born in 1933, the only child of the chieftain of the Lemdha clan in Gonjo in the Kham province of Tibet. She

---

* Throughout her ten-year military career, Durova posed as a soldier who was too young to grow the mustaches for which the Russian light cavalry was famous—a Peter Pan existence that Durova admitted caused speculation over time on the part of her comrades-in-arms. Vague rumors about the presence of a disguised "amazon" in the Russian army traveled through the ranks. More than once Durova heard inaccurate accounts of her own story—and on one occasion a report of her death—told by men who claimed to know someone who served with the woman or even to have seen her themselves. (Which, of course, they had, since she was sitting right there having a drink with the guys.)

† For the most part in this book I've been spared the conundrum of which pronoun to use to express the general condition. When I am writing about women in the collective, "she" is clearly the appropriate choice. The question of which pronouns to use becomes more problematic when talking about women who disguised themselves as men. It is difficult enough in the modern world, where sometimes the best, if uncomfortable, option is to ask someone how they identify themselves. But how do you choose the proper pronoun for someone in the past? In the course of this book, I took my cue from Nadezhda Durova. To the extent that I can do so without losing all clarity, I use masculine pronouns for anyone who chose to identify herself as male as a way of life. (You can see how tangled this gets.) In other words, I try to call them what they called themselves.

became a Buddhist nun and was given the name Ani Pachen—Nun Big Courage. It turned out to be appropriate.*

When Pachen was seventeen, her father arranged her marriage with the chieftain of another clan on the grounds she would need help governing the tribe after her father's death.† Unwilling to accept the marriage, she fled to a Buddhist monastery. Her father relented on the marriage plans. Six months later he called her home to learn her duties as a chieftain's heir. She obeyed, though given a choice she would have stayed at the monastery and continued her spiritual practice.

It was a troubled time. That same year the People's Republic of China invaded Tibet. Tibet had a small army, with no professional training. Its officers were members of the government bureaucracy who served a few months at a time in rotation. Tibet's citizen soldiers were no match for the forty thousand battle-hardened Chinese soldiers who poured across the border. It took the People's Liberation Army only two weeks to surround and capture Tibet's army, including the country's governor-general and his staff. With the army destroyed and no response to Tibet's appeals to the United States, India, and Britain for aid, the newly enthroned fifteen-year-old Dalai Lama sent a delegation to Beijing to negotiate. On May 23, 1951, the delegation reluctantly signed the Seventeen-Point Agreement for the Peaceful Liberation of Tibet, which accepted Chinese control over Tibet in exchange for promises to leave the Dalai Lama in control of the country's internal affairs and Tibet's religion and culture untouched—promises the Chinese broke almost immediately.

News of Chinese atrocities soon reached Kham province. Chinese soldiers entered Tibetan monasteries, stole their statues and sacred texts, and terrorized the monks and lamas. Children were forcibly

---

* The primary source for Ani Pachen's life is her memoir, *Sorrow Mountain: The Journey of a Tibetan Warrior Nun*, written in conjunction with Adelaide Donnelley and published in 2000. Donnelley describes the book as a story *based* on Ani Pachen's life, rather than a strict biography. The details must be taken with caution, especially reported conversations based on memory. But the broad sweep of the story is historically accurate.

† Pachen's case was not unique. A dear friend of hers, faced with parental plans for her marriage, was clear about their motivation: "If I marry who they choose it will strengthen our family." In Ani Pachen and Adelaide Donnelley, *Sorrow Mountain: The Journey of a Tibetan Warrior Nun* (New York: Kodansha International, 2000), 84. Giving daughters in marriage to cement political alliances continued in traditional societies well into the modern era. (And may still continue.)

taken from their families and sent to school in China. Tibetan men were pressed into service to help build roads into Tibet. Tibetans in other regions of the country were sent to labor camps or executed.

As tensions escalated, Pachen's father taught her to shoot. They stood on the roof and shot at a small wooden box on top of a post set in a field beside the house. The recoil of the rifle felt like a horse had kicked her in the chest, but she continued, eager to please her father. When she could hit the target, her father asked, "But if that were a Chinese? Would you dare to kill him?" She didn't know the answer.[11]

After Chinese soldiers beat a lama in the street and urinated over his head, Pachen's father began to meet with other local leaders on a regular basis to discuss tactics for dealing with the invaders. Pachen joined them at her father's request, though she never felt entirely accepted. They watched her when they thought she wasn't looking "with a mixture of curiosity, disbelief and dismay on their faces, as if they thought their meetings were no place for a woman."[12]

The Chinese confiscated property, killed landowners, set up communes in Tibetan villages, and brought in hundreds of Chinese peasants to settle in the sparsely populated regions of northern Tibet. In response, Tibetan leaders led thousands of resistance fighters against the Chinese camps. Things seemed to be at a stalemate.

The first bomb fell on the monastery at Lithang in the spring of 1956.

The lamas had refused to cooperate when the Chinese ordered them to provide a list of the monastery's possessions. Instead they called a meeting, where they urged the men in the village to take arms against the invaders. The villagers organized a raid on a nearby Chinese camp. Pursued by the Chinese, they took shelter in the monastery. The Chinese threatened to bomb the monastery if they did not surrender the villagers. The monks defied them.

The Tibetans lived secluded from the outside world. They knew nothing about the bombings of London, Dresden, and Tokyo. They had never even seen an airplane. When the first plane appeared in the sky above the monastery, the noise alone was terrifying. Then the bombs fell and the buildings exploded. There were six thousand people in the monastery; four thousand of them died.

In response to the bombings, Tibetans rose up in resistance across Kham province. By the end of 1956, tens of thousands of Tibetans had taken to the mountains: some fleeing the Chinese, some joining the armed resistance.

Pachen's father could no longer watch passively. He rode from village to village, meeting with local chieftains and lamas and making plans for resistance. He sent instructions to every family listing how many men, horses, swords, and guns they should contribute. He sent men from the clan to join the resistance fighters in the mountains.

When her father fell ill and died in 1958, Ani Pachen became the chieftain of the Lemdha clan and took up the task of organizing its forces. She had dreamed of a lifetime dedicated to prayer, but felt driven by duty to carry on her father's work. The only way to save Buddhist pacifism in Tibet was to go to war.

In early 1959, Pachen led six hundred resistance fighters from her clan into the mountains on horseback, armed with guns and swords.

They took advantage of the mountainous terrain to ambush Chinese convoys. They destroyed Chinese camps. At one point, a messenger rode into camp with a letter for her, written in Tibetan with a Chinese signature: "Return to your family and I will guarantee that nothing will happen to your possessions. Furthermore, if you surrender all the weapons that are listed . . . you will be awarded an appropriate rank for your deeds." Far from being tempted to surrender, she was outraged. "It's better to die than to surrender to the Chinese," she told the messenger. "Because I am a woman, they think I'll hand over the weapons of my people. It's an insult. Go back to them and tell them I will never surrender."[13]

Ani Pachen, her troops, and her family eluded the Chinese for two years. In 1960, the Chinese captured her as she fled over the Himalayas to India with her mother, aunt, and grandmother. In a speech later reported in the Buddhist magazine *Shambhala Sun*, she said, "When they arrested me, they bound my hands and feet and hung me upside down and interrogated me. They beat me continuously. I would pass out and they would throw water on me and beat me some more."[14]

Pachen spent the next twenty-one years in Chinese prisons, where she was shackled, tortured, and subjected to long periods of solitary confinement. She was released in 1981. Her orders were to return to Gonjo; instead she went to Lhasa, where she spent several years evading official notice and participating in demonstrations against Chinese rule.

In 1988, Pachen received word she was in danger of being arrested again. She fled to the Dalai Lama's headquarters in India. She continued to work as an advocate for Tibetan freedom until her death in 2002.

Pachen summed up her own career at the end of her memoir: "The story will go like this: She led her people to fight against the Chinese. She was present at the protests in Lhasa. She worked to save the ancient spiritual teachings. When I die, just my story will be left."[15]

If anything, the father-daughter relationship plays an even more important role today in the creation of women warriors.

In the past, it took a failure in the system to create a warrior daughter, whether that failure occurred at the family level or across society as a whole. Today, warrior daughters are a fact of life in the United States military—not because the system failed, but because it was transformed. In 1972, two new laws, the Equal Employment Opportunity Act of 1972 and the Education Amendments, known for the Title IX clause, threw the doors open to new opportunities (at least in theory), including the possibility of a young woman following in her father's military footsteps.

The idea of a military family, in which sons follow fathers, uncles, or grandfathers into the service of their country, is an old one, embodied in the United States military in the genealogical succession tables included in West Point's annual *Register of Graduates & Former Cadets*. The genealogical succession table in the 2010 *Register* is sixty-eight pages long; it lists every West Point graduate from 1802 to 2010 who was a descendent (or ancestor) of another West Point graduate. Women first appear in the *Register* in the class of 1980. Of the 119 women enrolled in that first class of cadets, sixty-two graduated.* Of those sixty-two women, five were daughters of former West Point graduates. Every graduating class since has included women who are the daughters, granddaughters, nieces, sisters, and, in one case, the great-great-granddaughter of former cadets. A new tradition began with the class of 2007, which included two women whose parents are both West Point graduates.

The West Point *Register* makes it easy to track how a particular version of the military family legacy applies to women in the modern American military, but that is one small part of the picture. Anecdotal evidence from publications with a military audience, such as *Military*

---

* The graduation rate for men in the same cohort was 62.3 percent—a difference of ten percentage points. Completing a degree at West Point is not for the faint of heart.

Times, and from the growing genre of memoirs by and about women who served in Afghanistan and the Middle East makes it clear a family history of military service inspires women to enlist in all branches of the service.*

In 2015, Time.com published a Father's Day article by Gayle Tzemach Lemmon, the author of *Ashley's War*. In it she discusses what she learned about the critical roles fathers play in raising young women who test their limits, particularly when it comes to the question of women in the military:

> I spent two years interviewing more than two dozen young women who volunteered in 2011 (when the combat ban for women was still in place) to be part of a U.S. Army Special Operations pilot program to put the fittest, finest and most capable women soldiers on the battlefield alongside tested special operations fighters. The hard-charging dad who encouraged his daughter to test every limit became part of nearly every story I heard from women who answered their country's call to join the kinds of combat missions seen by less than 5% of the U.S. military.[16]

What she describes is the modern counterpart of the father of earlier times who was "enlightened on the subject of women's educability": the feminist dad. To quote my own father: "The quickest way to believe in equal rights for women is to have smart daughters." Or athletic daughters. Or daring daughters. Or daughters who want to be warriors.

---

* Examples of this genre include Donna M. McAleer, *Porcelain on Steel: Women of West Point's Long Gray Line* (Jacksonville, FL: Fortis Publishing, 2010); Helen Thorpe, *Soldier Girls: The Battles of Three Women at Home and at War* (New York: Scribner, 2014); Gayle Tzemach Lemmon, *Ashley's War: The Untold Story of a Team of Women Soldiers on the Special Ops Battlefield* (New York: HarperCollins, 2015); and Mary Jennings Hegar, *Shoot Like a Girl: One Woman's Dramatic Fight in Afghanistan and on the Home Front* (New York: New American Library, 2017).

HER MOTHER'S DAUGHTER

In the fourth century BCE, Alexander the Great's older half-sister, Cynane (358–320 BCE—plus or minus a year or three in either direction), commanded Macedonian armies of her own.* Alexander and his (short-lived) empire became the stuff of historical legend. Cynane is largely forgotten.†

Cynane came from a tradition of women warriors.‡ Her mother, Audata, was the oldest daughter of King Bardylis of Illyria. When Philip II of Macedonia (aka Alexander the Great's father) defeated the Illyrians in 350 BCE, he received the Illyrian princess in marriage as part of the peace terms.§ In Illyria, noble women rode, hunted, and fought alongside their male counterparts. Audata trained her daughter as an Illyrian warrior princess, teaching her the same military skills learned by the young Alexander.

---

* Our main source for Cynane is the *Stratagems of War* by Macedonian historian Polyaenus, written well after the fact in the second century CE—leaving us with all the usual concerns that arise when our primary source isn't really a primary source. Despite the iffy nature of the source, no one suggests she didn't exist, or she didn't fight.

† Unless you play the history-based video game *Total War*, in which she is a playable commander with the moniker Cynane the Queen Slayer.

‡ Her name is derived from the Macedonian for "little she-dog." I assume being known as Little Bitch did not have the same implications then that it does now. But that might be wishful thinking.

§ Even warrior princesses were subject to the "let's make a deal" tradition of royal marriage. Philip would marry seven wives for political purposes, including Alexander's mother, Olympias.

Cynane earned a reputation as a talented military leader before she turned twenty. She commanded troops in the Macedonian expansion north into the Balkans, probably fighting on horseback like her Illyrian ancestors. Polyaenus credits her with defeating an Illyrian army, and with killing their queen Caeria in hand-to-hand combat.*

Around 337 BCE, Philip II arranged a marriage between Cynane and his nephew Amyntas, who held the Macedonian throne for a brief time as a young boy after his father's death.† The marriage was short-lived. When Alexander inherited his father's throne in 336 BCE, he killed off all his potential rivals, including Cynane's husband, whose claim to the throne was as strong as Alexander's own.

Widowed in her twenties, Cynane refused Alexander's attempts to marry her off for a second time. When Alexander set out to conquer Persia and other points east, Cynane remained in Macedonia, where she raised her young daughter, Adea (337–317 BCE), in the Illyrian tradition. Cynane returned to the historical narrative, and the battlefield, after Alexander's death in 323 BCE.

Alexander's untimely death left his empire without an obvious ruler. His wife, Roxane, was pregnant at his death and gave birth a few months later to a son, Alexander IV. Thanks to Alexander's ruthless extermination of male relatives with any claim to the throne, the only adult male family member left was his half-brother, Philip Arrhidaeus, whom contemporary sources described as mentally deficient.‡ With the choice between an infant and an incapable adult male, four of Alexander's generals cobbled together an awkward compromise that placed both heirs on the throne in a joint kingship, with the general Perdiccas as regent and the true power in the empire.

Perdiccas wasn't the only Macedonian commander who wanted to be the power behind the throne. Macedonia had no clear policy of succession. The qualifications were simple: a contender for the throne had to be male, a member of the ruling family, and competent and ruthless enough to take the throne and hold it against all comers.

---

* Perhaps the sole instance to date of a war with female commanders on both sides of the battlefield, thanks to the Illyrian connection.

† In other words, he ruled until Philip removed him from the throne. Unlike many usurpers, Philip did not kill the young man he displaced. Instead he raised Amyntas alongside his own children.

‡ Plutarch and others blame Philip Arrhidaeus's disability on a failed attempt to poison him, orchestrated by Alexander's mother, Olympias—though you could argue the poison succeeded if it left Philip incapable of competing with Alexander for the throne.

Cynane qualified for two out of three. Unable to seize the throne for herself, she decided to arrange a sword-point wedding between her daughter and the puppet king Philip Arrhidaeus, who was Cynane's half-brother.[*]

Less than a year after Perdiccas and his cronies formed the joint kingship, Cynane mobilized her troops and headed toward the imperial capital at Babylon. Perdiccas sent an army, headed by one of Alexander's generals, to stop her at the Macedonian border. She defeated him at the Strymon River, now the Struma, and crossed into Asia. Perdiccas sent a second army against her, led by his own brother, Alcetas, who grew up with Cynane. Perdiccas seems to have believed facing a childhood companion at the head of an opposing army would be enough to change Cynane's mind. It didn't. (Perhaps the boys didn't know her as well as they thought they did.)

According to Polyaenus, Alcetas's troops were awestruck at the sight of Cynane on the battlefield. (She was, after all, Philip's daughter, Alexander's sister, and the woman who defeated an Illyrian queen in hand-to-hand combat while still in her teens.) Undaunted by the size of his force, Cynane confronted Alcetas and reproached him for his lack of loyalty. Alcetas killed her in front of his army before she finished her speech. Bad decision. Seeing Cynane murdered by their commander, the Macedonian army mutinied and forced Alcetas to arrange the very marriage he was there to prevent.

With the mutinous army playing kingmaker, Adea married Philip Arrhidaeus and ruled for a short time in the coveted position of power behind the throne under the name Eurydice II.[†]

---

[*] Women in positions of political power often use the same tools as their male contemporaries. Even Isabella of Castile, who sidestepped being a political pawn in her brother's hands, used her daughters' marriages to build political alliances.

[†] Until Alexander's mother, Olympias, dethroned them in the name of her infant grandson, Alexander IV—an unsuccessful bid for power in the bloody game of musical chairs that followed Alexander's death.

CHAPTER THREE

THE WIDOW'S
RAMPAGE

A rtemisia II (fl. 353 BCE) entered the history books only because she was a widow.*

She ruled the Aegean state of Caria, a semi-independent Persian satrapy (or province) that controlled territory on and around the southwest coast of what is now Turkey, with her brother-husband, Mausolus.† When Mausolus died, around 353 CE, Artemisia succeeded him as the sole ruler. She built a magnificent tomb in his

---

* Not to be confused with Artemisia I, who fought on the side of Persia at the Battle of Salamis eighty years earlier. Our two primary sources for Artemisia II were both written in the first century BCE, long after the fact: Greek historian Diodorus Siculus's *Historical Library* and Roman engineer Vitruvius's *On Architecture*. Archaeological evidence, mostly in the form of sculpture and inscriptions, confirms some details. Some, though by no means all, classicists argue that Artemisia did not accomplish any of the actions the ancient sources attribute to her, except grieve for her husband. At least no one tries to claim she was a metaphor rather than a real person—an argument I've seen applied to both Boudica and the fifteenth- (or possibly sixteenth-) century Hausa queen Amina. After you read enough variations of historians arguing why a particular woman warrior didn't exist or fight, you grow a bit cynical.

† Seen from today's perspective, there is a serious ick factor to marrying your brother, but it was a common practice in royal families in the ancient Mediterranean and Pharaonic Egypt. (For that matter, the Hawaiian royal family practiced sibling-marriage into the mid-nineteenth century, when it became a hot button for Christian missionaries.)

61

memory* and, according to tradition, never recovered from her grief at his death. But while she may have been a weeping widow, she was not a wimpy widow.

Her ascension to the throne triggered a revolt by the island of Rhodes. Vitruvius claimed the Rhodians revolted because they "were outraged that a woman governed the cities across the whole of Caria."[1] Other sources suggest the revolt was an attempt by exiled Rhodian leaders to restore the island's independence. Whatever their motivation, Rhodes reached out to Athens for help. The famed orator, Demosthenes, who was a proponent of aggressive Athenian foreign policy, served as their spokesman. He predicted Artemisia would do little or nothing to counter Athenian interference in Rhodes. Demosthenes wasn't able to convince the Athenians to stick their noses into Caria's business. Perhaps his fellow Athenians were less dismissive of Artemisia's willingness to fight back. Perhaps they were wary of Caria's connection to Persia—messing with Persia never was a good thing for Greece. Whatever the reason, when Rhodes sent a fleet against the Carian capital of Halicarnassus (on the site of the modern city of Bodrum in Turkey), it was without Athenian support.

Warned the Rhodian fleet was near, Artemisia stationed archers along the city walls. She hid her ships, fully manned, in a secret harbor that was connected to the main bay by a man-made channel. Then she waited to spring the trap.

Acting on Artemisia's instructions, the townspeople of Halicarnassus greeted the invaders like a liberating force and invited them into the city. Meanwhile, the Carian fleet emerged from the hidden harbor and seized the empty ships. Then the archers stepped out of hiding and shot down the Rhodians in the marketplace.[†]

Artemisia wreathed the captured ships in laurel, the ancient sign for victory, manned them with her own troops, and sent them back to Rhodes. When the Rhodians greeted the ships as returning conquerors, the Carians seized the city without a fight. Artemisia ordered the rebel leaders executed. To commemorate her victory, she raised a statue in the captured city that depicted her in the act of branding Rhodes as a slave. A harsh reminder not to underestimate a widow.

---

* From which we derive the word "mausoleum."

† Personally, the part of the story I find hardest to believe is that the Rhodians did not anticipate archers on the city walls—not a new technique in the fourth century BCE.

When war and widows are mentioned in the same sentence, it is usually in some variation on the phrase "war widow": a term that is built on the recognition of emotional, social, and economic loss. It was true in the mid-nineteenth century, when social reformers created charities for the support of war widows and orphans after the American Civil War. It is true today in media coverage of the wars in Afghanistan and the Middle East—divided between reports of Muslim widows left destitute by the deaths of their husbands and sons and American widows forming support groups to deal with the emotional and social impact of their own losses.

The emotional power of the phrase rests in part on the assumption that widows are often socially and economically disadvantaged in comparison to the status they enjoyed in their married lives. It is an old idea: the phrase "the widow's mite" has long been used to denote a financial offereing from the poorest of the poor.

In addition to relative poverty, many widows suffered from the common cross-cultural perception that they were an economic, sexual, or social threat. Women from privileged backgrounds, or backgrounds with aspirations of privilege, were encouraged, or in some cases compelled, to withdraw from society.* Often that meant a period of mourning and seclusion that could range from months to as long as three years in Ming China. In some times and places withdrawing from society meant retiring to a religious community—Buddhist, Catholic, or Russian Orthodox, voluntarily or involuntarily.† In nineteenth-century England, withdrawing meant viewing the world from behind a widow's veil and following a complex set of mourning rules, at least for those who could afford to do so. In some African cultures it meant a period of seclusion followed by a ritual cleansing. Well into the modern era, traditional Hindu families expected

---

* An attitude that is not entirely absent in modern America. Ask any youngish widow who still lives in the place where she spent her married years and you will hear stories of being excluded from social events organized like Noah's ark—guests are invited two by two or not at all.

† Not that joining a religious community ensured a widow would retire from public life. Hojo Masako (1157–1225), known as the "nun shogun," was the widow of the first Japanese shogun. She took vows as a Buddhist nun shortly after his death, and then became the power behind the "Hojo regency," which shaped Japan's power structure for seven centuries. For that matter, the widow's veil did nothing to stop Queen Victoria of England, who clung to her mourning weeds for forty years and remained the most powerful woman in the world.

high-caste widows to live as ascetics for the rest of their lives: don white mourning saris, abandon all personal adornment, and not only reduce the amount of what they ate but abandon a wide range of foods and seasonings that were considered to have aphrodisiacal properties. At its most extreme, widow-removal took the form of ritualized widow-suicide. The best-known example of this is the Hindu practice of becoming *sati*, in which a widow threw herself on the funeral pyre of her husband,* but India was not the only place where this act was encouraged. Widow-suicide was also a social ideal in Qing dynasty China, where it was referred to as "following in death."

Defined in terms of loss in all its forms, widows were a living metaphor for the meek and the weak, seemingly the polar opposite of women warriors. And yet . . .

THE WIDOW'S MITE OR THE WIDOW'S MIGHT?

When we look at individual cases, we find women who flourished within the bounds of widowhood, maintaining control over the family farm, business, or kingdom. Barbe-Nicole Clicquot, the widow who gave her name to the French champagne Veuve Clicquot, was only twenty-seven when she inherited the company she transformed into an international champagne powerhouse. Widowed queens or noblewomen in many societies served as regents for underaged sons, often chosen for the position on the not-always-accurate presumption that mother-love (or laws that prevented women from inheriting) would make a mother a safer choice than a power hungry uncle or maternal grandfather.† Lower down the social scale, middle-class widows without an adult son or son-in-law often found themselves the de facto manager of a business or farm. Each powerful widow may have been an exception in her own time and place, but together they create an alternate story that must be taken into account.‡

---

* Limited to a small minority of women, most of them from the higher castes.

† In fact, mother-love did not always trump a taste for power. Some queens regnant resisted turning over power when a son grew up.

‡ Today we have what political scientists sometimes refer to as the "widow's walk to power," in which a woman steps into a position of political power after the (often-violent) death of her husband. The assumption is such women will carry on the same policies and protect the same interests as the men whose size elevens they try to fill. Corazon Aquino and Sirimavo Bandaranaike (the world's first female prime minister) are prime examples of this.

Historical widows who maintained their independence or some degree of power necessarily fought at a metaphorical level. A surprising number of them became literal warriors as well.

Women who served as regents often had to fight to defend their sons' rights and property from uncles, brothers-in-law, and/or more distant male relatives, especially in societies where primogeniture was not the norm and any adult male with a drop of royal blood and a strong sword arm was a contender for throne or estate.* Blanche of Navarre (?–1229), Countess of Champagne, for instance, was close to nine months pregnant when her husband died. She ruled as regent for her son for twenty-one years and defended his right of succession against counterclaims from her brother-in-law's son-in-law in the Champagne War of Succession in 1215.

Some widows used the power they inherited from their husbands as a base from which to acquire more power: Ayesha (614–678), the youngest wife of the Prophet Mohammed, for example, led troops into battle against the Prophet's son-in-law, Ali, during the succession struggles that followed the death of Uthman, the third caliph, in 656. Some fought to avenge the death of a husband, like Jeanne de Clisson (1300–1359), the Lioness of Brittany, who took to the sea as a pirate and ravaged the French coastline after King Philip VI of France arrested and beheaded her husband because of his role in a succession struggle over the Duchy of Brittany. Others, like Xian in sixth-century China, Qin Liangyu in seventeenth-century China, and Aethelflaed in tenth-century England, shared military responsibilities with their husbands and succeeded them as military commanders after their deaths. Some women picked up their fallen husband's weapons and fought on. Nancy Ward (ca. 1738–1824), for example, whose "real" name was Nanye'hi or White Rose, rallied the Cherokees after her husband fell in battle against the Creek and led them to victory. As a result of her actions she was given the title Ghighua (Beloved Woman or War Woman)—the highest title and role that could be bestowed on a woman leader, which brought with it a voting position on the warriors' council.† Ward was the last Cherokee woman to hold this title.

---

* We tend to think of primogeniture as a natural element of traditional societies. In fact, it is a relatively late and largely Western idea. In many cultures, succession was a case of survival of the fittest, or perhaps the most vicious.

† She would go on to make a name for herself in the American Revolution when she warned American settlers of an attack by Cherokees who fought as British allies. Whether she was a heroine or a traitor depended on where you stood.

And in a few cases, warrior widows succeeded so well they over-shadowed the memories of the husbands whose power they inherited.

MAWIYYA TAKES ON THE ROMAN EMPIRE

In 364 CE, four centuries after Boudica rallied the Celtic tribes in Britain, a widowed Arab queen led her troops in a revolt against the Roman Empire.

Mawiyya, known in the west as Mavia, succeeded her husband as the ruler of the Tanukh confederation, an alliance of seminomadic Arabs who migrated into Roman Syria in the third century.[*]

When Mawiyya came to power, the Roman Empire was in crisis,[†] threatened with invasions on both its western and eastern borders.

Barbarian invasions on the western border had been a problem for more than a century, and were getting worse as nomads from the Central Asian steppes migrated west. Waves of displaced Goths, Visigoths, Vandals, and others invaded from the plains of Prussia and Hungary, drawn by the rich farmlands south of the Rhine—and the cushy jobs in the Roman army.[‡]

---

[*] As is the case with many women warriors, we have few sources for Mawiyya's life. They often contradict each other on the details, and later sources include romantic additions. For instance, one Byzantine history claims "Mavia" was a Roman Christian who was captured by an Arab sheikh who fell in love with her beauty and that she ascended to his throne at his death. As is also often the case, historians today squabble over the details of her story. At least one questions whether we have enough evidence to believe she existed at all and argues that even if she did exist, her revolt was no more than a border squabble. Most of what we know about Mawiyya comes from several Greek ecclesiastical histories written in the fifth century, all of which seem to be based on a lost history by a fourth-century bishop from Palestine. These sources focus on the religious aspects of her revolt, which they saw as an important moment in the conflict between the so-called Arian heresy and what would later become the Catholic and Orthodox churches. They cast Mawiyya as the heroine of the story—unlike the sources for earlier queens who rose up against Rome, who were described by Roman historians in terms of sexual rapacity (Cleopatra), savagery (Boudica), and territorial rapacity, murder, and cowardice (Zenobia, a third-century Syrian queen who rebelled against Rome and nearly split the Roman Empire in two. She was the target of some serious trash-talking by both Roman and Arab historians). One of these historians, Sozomen, hints at another missing source: Arab poetry celebrating her exploits. That would be a source worth having.

[†] Again, or maybe still. The third century had been ugly.

[‡] By the time the western half of the Roman Empire "fell" in 476 CE, a substantial part of its army was made up of Germanic auxiliaries and mercenaries.

To the east, Persia remained Rome's most serious opponent, as it had been since the destruction of Carthage at the end of the Third Punic War in 146 BCE. The rivalry between the two superpowers was often a cold war, played out in the buffer states between them. (Armenia was always a hot spot.) Rome depended on local troops familiar with desert warfare, like the Tanukh, to patrol the long and disputed border west of the Euphrates.

Under the rule of Mawiyya's husband, the Tanukh served as Rome's main buffer against Persia. Rome paid the Tanukh a subsidy to protect the frontier against raids by the Persians and by nonallied tribes. When Mawiyya's husband died, presumably without an adult male heir, the Tanukh treaty with Rome died with him.*

There is no obvious reason Rome could not have entered into a new treaty with Mawiyya if both sides were willing. Perhaps the local Roman officials were uncomfortable making a treaty with a female leader. Perhaps Mawiyya had doubts about continuing the relationship with Rome, which soured when the emperor Julian (r. 361–363) cut the subsidies to Rome's Arab allies in 363.

Whatever the problem with the treaty, our fifth-century sources agree that religious differences were the immediate cause of Mawiyya's revolt.† The main theological debate of the day was the Trinitarian controversy between the followers of Arianism, which held that the Son of God was created by and separate from the Father, and adherents of the Nicene Creed, who believed the three parts of the trinity were co-eternal and equal.

Differences came to a head in 364 when the newly anointed emperor Valentinian named his younger brother Valens his co-emperor, with the mandate to rule the eastern portion of the empire from Constantinople. Valentinian was committed to a policy of religious tolerance; Valens was a fanatic Arian, who exiled even moderate Nicene bishops and replaced them with Arians. When Valens

---

* We know nothing about Mawiyya's husband. Not even his name.

† For the first three hundred years of its existence, Christianity was a minor sect in the Roman Empire, practiced alongside an all-you-can-eat buffet of other religions, polytheistic and monotheistic alike. Christians were persecuted on an on-again, off-again basis depending on how much trouble they were causing and the beliefs of the reigning emperor. Christianity's status changed in 331, when the emperor Constantine I (r. 306–337) made it legal for Christians to practice their religion. By the end of his reign, Christianity had become the dominant religion of the empire.

attempted to install an Arian bishop to serve the Tanukh, Mawiyya and her tribes rebelled.*

The seminomadic Arabs were highly mobile. The Roman legions were not trained to fight against the hit-and-run raids and guerrilla tactics used by Mawiyya's forces. The Romans called them "Arabs Scenitae"—Arabs under tents, as opposed to the settled Arabs who populated cities like Palmyra.† The "Arabs under tents" withdrew from their camps and melted into the desert, leaving Valens with no fixed target to attack. With their Arab allies turned against them, the desert itself became an enemy the Romans were ill equipped to fight.

With no serious opposition from the Roman legions stationed in Syria, Mawiyya led her troops deep into Phoenicia and Palestine and into Egypt as far as the Nile. The unnamed general of the Roman troops stationed in Phoenicia sent for help from his superior officer, the commander in charge of the forces of the eastern empire (also unnamed). When the senior commander arrived from Constantinople, he scoffed at the warnings of the local military, who had already faced Mawiyya on the battlefield. He ordered the local general to "keep aloof from the combat" and led his troops into battle against Mawiyya without reserves. He escaped only with the help of the local forces, whose general disobeyed the order to stay off the field.[2]

As the historian Sozomen summed up the situation, "This war was by no means a contemptible one, although conducted by a woman."[3] In the end, the Romans were forced to sue for peace on Mawiyya's terms. One condition of the peace, perhaps the critical one, was the ordination of an Arab ascetic named Moses as their bishop—the first Arab bishop for Arab Christians.

Later that year, once again allies of Rome, Mawiyya and her troops came to the aid of Constantinople, which a group of Goths had besieged. At least one Roman historian, Amiantus Marcellianus, whom

---

* Mawiyya may well have seen herself as a defender of the Nicene Creed, but control over the appointment of bishops had political and financial as well as theological implications.

† While it was literally true that they lived in tents, the description was dangerously reductive. Like later nomadic nations, such as Genghis Khan's Mongols, the Tanukh confederacy was a sophisticated alliance of tribes and a force to be reckoned with despite its lack of permanent cities, royal palaces, and marble monuments. The capitals of such nations were the mobile cities that traveled with their rulers.

we previously met commenting on the ferocity of Celtic women warriors, claimed Mawiyya's Arabs saved the city.[*]

The last we hear of Mawiyya is an inscription recording her death in a town near Aleppo in the heart of the Tanukh territory, forty-seven years after defeating the Goths at Constantinople. Cleopatra and Boudica should have been so lucky.

"ENCHANTED WITH HER HEROISM"

In mid-eighteenth-century India, a four-and-a-half-foot-tall former dancing girl (or perhaps courtesan) inherited a mercenary army from her husband (or perhaps lover) and became one of the region's most successful mercenary commanders. (Not a small statement. The field was crowded.)

Farzana, later known as Begum Samru,[†] was born around 1750 in a small town near Delhi.[‡] Her father was an Arab merchant. Her mother (anonymous, as they so often are) was either a second wife or a junior concubine. When her father died, around 1760, her half-brother, the son of his senior wife (or concubine), refused to support them. Her mother fled to Delhi, where she probably became a

---

* Of course, he also claimed the Arabs terrified the Goths into submission by running shrieking into battle naked, and that they sucked the blood from the throats of their fallen enemies. Obviously a source to use with care.

† "Begum" is a title, not a name. It refers to a married woman of high rank, though, in fact, Begum Samru was neither.

‡ There is no doubt that Begum Samru existed. She charmed and fascinated many European soldiers, merchants, and administrators who passed through India in the late eighteenth and early nineteenth centuries. References to her are scattered throughout their letters, memoirs, and scholarly works. The most important of these include the following:

+ The memoir of James Skinner, a successful Anglo-Indian mercenary commander and sometime comrade-in-arms of Begum Samru.

+ British Orientalist William Francklin's contemporary biographies of the emperor Shah Alam and Irish-born mercenary captain George Thomas—two of the most important men in Begum Samru's life.

+ *Rambles and Recollections of an Indian Official* by Major General Sir William Sleeman, who interviewed members of the begum's Sardhana Brigade some years after her death.

Some of the most interesting and unexpected accounts of Begum Samru appear in letters written by the wives of British administrators in the early nineteenth century, when an invitation to visit the begum at Sardhana proved you were on the social A-list.

courtesan.* The first thing we know for certain about Farzana is that by the time she was fourteen she worked as a *nautch* girl in Delhi's Chawri Bazaar.†

It was a time of political anarchy. The great Mughal Empire was crumbling. The emperor in Delhi was a powerless figurehead, kept on his throne only with the support of regional warlords. The Sikhs had revolted against the empire in 1710 and established an independent kingdom in the Punjab. The Maratha confederacy carved out an independent state in the area around Pune in 1714. Regional governors declared themselves rulers in their own right while still acknowledging the emperor in Delhi as the supreme political authority—a convenient fiction. Local rulers fought over their own unsteady thrones. The British and French East India companies—bitter rivals over trade privileges, territory, and monopolies—took sides in Indian succession struggles. Dismayed to find their much larger armies defeated by the companies' European-led forces, Indian rulers hired European mercenaries as drill sergeants, tacticians, and commanders.

The best, or perhaps the worst, of the freebooters became commanders of their own mercenary armies. One such commander was Austrian mercenary Walter Reinhardt, known as Sombre—whether because of his coloring, his expression, or his disposition is unclear. The Indian sepoys under his command changed Sombre into Samru.

Reinhardt arrived in India in 1750. At first he worked as a sword for hire, moving from employer to employer as the mood took him. He took a step up to the commander of an independent brigade when the military commander of Purnea in northern Bihar hired him to recruit and train an infantry battalion on the European model. When Mir Qassim—the third puppet ruler of British-controlled Bengal in as many years—made a bid for independence and moved his court two hundred miles away from British bullying, Reinhardt joined up, gaining command of two battalions, a bad reputation as the Butcher

---

* A word that suggests greater luxury and more control over her circumstances than "prostitute." Whether it's accurate is unclear. The word choice may be a piece of romanticizing.

† "Nautch girl" is a term that covers a lot of ground. Women at the top of the profession were similar to Japanese geishas, trained as both performers and companions. At the bottom of the scale, prostitutes performed a bump-and-grind to attract paying customers. The basic measure of success was the same for all—attracting a patron to pay for their company—though the rate of the pay and the length of the relationship varied dramatically.

of Patna, and British enmity. He fled British retribution, finding sanctuary for himself and his brigade with the powerful Nawab of Awadh. He fought alongside the armies of the nawab, the deposed Mir Qassim, and the Mughal emperor Shah Alam against the British at the Battle of Buxar on October 22, 1764.

After Buxar, Reinhardt was given the task of escorting the Awadh begums and their possessions to safety in Rohilkhand. The nawab could not have chosen a less trustworthy escort. Anxious to move out of the reach of the British, who were eager to get their hands on the Butcher of Patna, Reinhardt stole the begums' jewels and cash and fled, along with his brigade, to the service of the Jat rajah Jawahir Singh.

Farzana and Reinhardt met when the mercenary commander rode into Delhi in January 1765 looking for an evening of entertainment. He ended up at the *kotha** where Farzana worked as a *nautch* girl.

By all accounts the young Farzana was beautiful and charming. Reinhardt soon moved her out of the *kotha* and into his household. Like her mother, she was a second wife or concubine. Unlike her mother, she was able to hold her own against Reinhardt's senior concubine, Barri Bibi, and her son, Louis Balthazar Reinhardt.

According to James Skinner, "Her talents and sound judgment became so valuable to [Reinhardt] as to gain a great ascendancy over him."[4] Farzana accompanied Reinhardt's troops into battle, carried in a palanquin†—on-the-job training in how to run a military campaign as a mercenary captain. Warren Hastings, who served as the British East India Company's first governor-general from 1772 to 1785, reported that she was carried "from rank to rank encouraging the men who were enchanted with her heroism."[5] It is unclear whether Reinhardt ever married his Farzana, but his troops gave her the courtesy title of Begum Samru, the wife of Sombre.

After nine years in the rajah's service, Reinhardt changed allegiance for the last time. When Mughal forces expelled the Jats from Agra, he defected to the army of the Mughal emperor, Shah Alam, taking with him a brigade of some three thousand men including two hundred self-styled officers who had left the battlefields, or perhaps the slums, of Europe for richer pickings in India.

---

* A combination bar, brothel, and entertainment venue—think a dance hall in an old western movie.

† No case of Tomboy Syndrome here.

In 1776, the emperor named Reinhardt the *jagirdar* of Sardhana, a large estate, roughly eight hundred square miles, located forty miles northeast of Delhi.* It was a mercenary's dream come true. Reinhardt did not get to enjoy it for long.

When Reinhardt died in 1778, the company backed Farzana's claim to both Sardhana and the brigade—which now numbered five battalions of infantry, three hundred European and Eurasian officers and gunners, forty cannons, and the fat oxen needed to pull them—rather than allowing command to pass into the hands of Reinhardt's wastrel son, who was considered unfit to lead. Presented with a petition signed by those of the brigade who could write and attested to by those who could not, Shah Alam formally named Begum Samru commander of the Sardhana Brigade.

Members of the Sardhana Brigade may have thought they were getting a softer leader, but Begum Samru proved to be an active commander in chief. She personally led her troops into battle, though she may have relied on her officers for technical matters related to artillery and siegecraft. She won often enough that some of her rivals claimed she was a witch—a calumny often directed at successful female commanders over the centuries.† The only way in which she proved to be "soft" was her decision not to follow the contemporary custom of executing or blinding Reinhardt's son, her rival for leadership of the brigade—a choice that would come back to bite her.

Reinhardt's command of the brigade had been marked by looting, pillaging, and restlessly moving from one employer to another. The begum's leadership was marked by good stewardship and loyalty. She cultivated her relationship with the emperor, who was the source of economic stability for herself and the brigade. She developed the fertile land of the *jagir*. She supported the widows and children of fellow mercenaries—including Reinhardt's senior wife, who had slipped into senility.

Begum Samru saved the emperor's life and his throne more than once. Her first opportunity came in 1787, when the Rohilla general Ghulam Qadir marched on Delhi. Two days later, Begum Samru and

---

* Instead of paying their troops directly, the Mughals funded their armies by granting a military leader tax-free rights over an estate (or two, or ten), known as a *jagir*. The *jagirdar* passed on a percentage of the collected revenue to the imperial treasury and used the balance to pay his troops and line his pocket.

† What other explanation could there be for a female commander defeating a male opponent?

the Sardhana Brigade arrived in response to a distress signal from the emperor. Ghulam Qadir offered the begum an equal share of the plunder if she joined him. If Reinhardt had been alive, he might well have taken the bribe. Begum Samru, preferring an emperor in the hand to a usurper in the bush, refused the bribe, and drove the Rohilla commander back across the Jumna River.

When Ghulam Qadir returned the following year, Begum Samru once again marched to Shah Alam's defense, though she was not in time to prevent Ghulam Qadir from blinding the emperor, ransacking the palace in search of nonexistent treasure, and forcing the imperial princesses to leave the protection of the *zenana** and dance for the Rohilla troops. Ghulam Qadir made a run for it, but the Sardhana Brigade joined the Maratha army in tracking him down. They hung the Rohilla leader for two days in a specially constructed cage, then mutilated him in retaliation for his treatment of the emperor. His captors, among other tortures, scooped his eyes out of their sockets and sent them to Shah Alam in a box, so the blinded emperor could fondle them.

In recognition of her acts on his behalf, Shah Alam granted the begum a robe of honor—serious business in Mughal India—as well as an additional *jagir* for the support of her troops. He gave her the titles "daughter of the emperor" and "ornament of her sex"—a big step up for a dancing girl/prostitute from the Calcutta slums.

In 1792, Begum Samru broke the first rule of remaining a powerful widow, warrior, or otherwise: she remarried. She compounded the problem by marrying one of her own soldiers, the French artillery maker Pierre Antoine Levassoult, who was neither popular with nor respected by his fellow officers. Levassoult immediately attempted to take over the command of the brigade, alienating officers and sepoys alike.

When the begum failed to rein in her new husband, the unthinkable occurred: the Sardhana Brigade mutinied in the name of Walter Reinhardt's "worthless" son, Louis Balthazar. They planned to install Louis Balthazar as a puppet commander and run the brigade in his name, much as the Marathas ruled the empire in the name of the puppet emperor Shah Alam.

---

* The inner apartments of a wealthy Hindu or Muslim home where the women of the family lived.

Getting wind of plans to seize the couple, Levassoult convinced the begum to flee with him toward British territory. Most contemporary accounts say the two agreed to commit suicide if they were captured. Sources vary about what happened next. The most dramatic versions describe a Romeo and Juliet scenario, in which Levassoult committed suicide because he believed Begum Samru was dead. (At least one source suggests the begum and her maid faked the apparent death as a way to dispose of the inconvenient husband.) Modern historians speculate he was killed by one of their pursuers—most of whom despised him and all of whom were used to killing up close and personal on the battlefield. Whatever the details, their flight ended with Levassoult dead and Begum Samru a captive of her former troops.

She was rescued by a small force headed by George Thomas, an Irish mercenary who previously served with the Sardhana Brigade and may well have been a former lover. With a combination of threats, bluffs, and bribes, Thomas reinstated Begum Samru at Sardhana and took Louis Balthazar back to Delhi.

While Reinhardt and Begum Samru defended the Mughal emperor against those who wanted to depose or control him, the world around them was changing. The British East India Company had transformed itself from merchants and mercenaries to kingmakers and empire builders. On September 23, 1803, Begum Samru faced the British for the first time at the Battle of Assaye. Five battalions of the Sardhana Brigade fought on the side of Scindia and the Marathas against the East India Company's army, which was under the command of acting Major-General Arthur Wellesley, who would later become the Duke of Wellington. The battle was Wellesley's first major victory; he would later describe it as "the bloodiest for the numbers" that he ever saw.[6] (Quite a statement for the victor of Waterloo.) It was certainly the bloodiest battle Begum Samru took part in. Reinhardt had taught her that a mercenary's best strategy could be found in the line "He that fights and runs away, may live to fight another day." At Assaye, she stayed on the field and lost a quarter of her men.

The battle was the turning point in the war between the British and the Marathas, and the end of Maratha primacy in Delhi. The British replaced the Marathas as Shah Alam's primary protectors and Sardhana came under British control. Begum Samru successfully negotiated to keep possession of Sardhana, with all the rights and privileges she had previously enjoyed, and to maintain nominal command of the Sardhana Brigade. She was one of only two mercenary commanders who retained their forces under the British.

Begum Samru spent the next thirty years ruling Sardhana, while the brigade served as an irregular unit for the East India Company's forces. She led her troops for the last time at the British siege of the Jat fortress of Bharatpur in 1825. She pitched her tent next to that of the British commander in chief, and proceeded to charm him as she had charmed so many others over the course of a long career.

MRS. CHING CAPTURES THE SHIP

Cheng I Sao (aka Hsi Kai Ching, Ching Shi, Lady Ching, or Mrs. Ching, depending on the vintage of the account) terrorized the South China Sea in the first half of the nineteenth century—a time when many Chinese women were literally hobbled by bound feet.*

Cheng I Sao (1775–1844) was a Canton prostitute who married the successful pirate Cheng I in 1801 and soon became his partner in building a successful confederation of pirates from competing clans.†

Piracy was a family business in nineteenth-century China. Pirate clans lived on their boats—some of them spent their entire lives without setting foot on land. Within the world of the pirates, some women held rank, commanded ships, and fought shoulder to shoulder with their male counterparts.

The scale of Chinese piracy grew as a result of the Tay Son rebellion against Nguyen rule in Vietnam. The rebellion began in 1771 as a local insurrection in what is now the Vietnamese province of Binh Dinh. It quickly became a national movement, fueled by a broad base of support among the peasant and merchant classes. By 1792, the leaders of the rebellion needed more manpower, so they recruited

---

* They were also barred from holding public office and had limited opportunities for education and employment, but that didn't make China unique.

† Most of our information about Cheng I Sao and Chinese pirates in general comes from two English-language sources: The first is an unofficial history written by a Chinese government employee, Yuan Yun-lan, who knew several officials who died in combat with Cheng I Sao's pirates. Based on firsthand accounts, Yuan Yun-lan's work was published in Canton in 1830 and translated into English the following year by German orientalist Karl Friedrich Neumann as *History of the Pirates Who Infested the China Sea from 1807 to 1810*. The second, *A Brief Narrative of My Captivity and Treatment Among the Ladrones*, is a firsthand account by East India Company officer Richard Glasspoole, who was captured by Chinese pirates (*ladrones* in Portuguese) along with seven other British seamen.

pirates from the southern coast of China, including the Cheng family, to serve as an informal navy.* With the financial support of Vietnam's Tay-Son rulers, pirates organized themselves into associations made up of several dozen junks manned by hundreds of people—a far cry from the anarchic crews of Western pirate lore.

In 1802, the Nguyen regained power.† On July 16, 1802, the Nguyen navy defeated the pirates, who fled back to China.

The Cheng family had flourished under Tay-Son patronage; now Cheng I and his wife emerged as the most important pirate leaders. Building on years of working as an informal military operation, they turned piracy into big business. The Chengs unified the rival associations that emerged under the Tay-Son into a confederation of six fleets, each with its own flag and commander. By 1805, their confederation numbered some four hundred junks and between forty thousand and sixty thousand pirates.

When her husband died unexpectedly in 1808, Cheng I Sao took over. She avoided succession struggles by appointing her adopted stepson, Chang Pao, as her second in command.‡

Cheng I Sao transformed the confederation from an affiliation of personal relationships into what could be termed a pirate nation, including a strict code of law with penal sanctions and elaborate provisions for sharing booty, developed by Chang Pao.

At the height of her success, Cheng I Sao controlled a total of fifteen hundred ships and between seventy thousand and eighty thousand men. Her fleets attacked ships of all kinds, from small trading vessels to imperial war ships; collected protection money from coastal villages and trading ships; raided mandarin estates; and convoyed government salt fleets to the port city of Canton (modern Guanzhou). She set up offices along the coast where her financial agents could collect fees and transact other business.

By 1809, Cheng I Sao was powerful enough to threaten Canton. The Chinese government turned to the European powers for help, leasing the twenty-gun HMS *Mercury* from Britain and six men-of-war from Portugal. Big guns were not enough to defeat the

---

* Similar to the use of privateers in sixteenth-century Europe.

† With the help of French armaments. The first step on the slippery slope to French colonial rule.

‡ She later married him. This did not seem to cause the type of internal conflicts that Begum Samru unleashed with her second marriage, perhaps because Chang Pao was already a respected commander within the confederation at the time of their marriage.

pirate admiral. In 1810, the Chinese changed tactics and offered the pirates amnesty.

After the failure of the first amnesty negotiations, which Chang Pao led, Cheng I Sao decided it was in her best interests to negotiate peace terms with the Chinese empire herself. She arrived unarmed at the Chinese governor-general's headquarters on April 10, 1810, accompanied by a cadre of pirate women and children. She proved to be as effective at the bargaining table as she was on the deck of a ship. She successfully negotiated for universal amnesty for her pirates, the right to keep the proceeds of their piracy, and preferential access to jobs in China's military bureaucracy. Chang Pao received the rank of lieutenant and command of a fleet of junks. As for Cheng I Sao, she retired to Canton, where she reportedly lived a peaceful life until her death at the age of sixty-nine, "so far as [was] consistent with the keeping of an infamous gambling house."[7] (What? You expected her to take up knitting and mahjong?)

War widows still exist, and will as long as we continue to fight over borders, resources, religion, political philosophies, or the egos of political leaders. The classic widow-warrior does not. We have no modern equivalent of Mawiyya, Begum Samru, or Cheng I Sao. In the modern world (loosely defined), widows go to war on a smaller, more personal scale—from rage, or grief, or fear.* Consider the case of Maria Vasilyevna Oktiabrskaya (1905–1944), the wife of a Soviet army officer.

When Maria learned that her husband had been killed in action near Kiev in August 1941, she sold everything she owned to raise enough money to donate a T-34 tank to the Red Army. She made one condition: that she be allowed to drive it in battle. The army

---

* Not an entirely new idea. When we look beyond the rarified world of queens, countesses, and first ladies, we find earlier examples of widows who stepped up to the cannon, took up the sword (or automatic weapon), or cried out for revenge after their husbands' deaths. "Mad Anne" Hennis Trotter Bailey (1742–1825), for example, decided to fight the British and Shawnee after her first husband, Richard Trotter, was killed in a border skirmish with Native Americans in Lord Dunmore's War in 1774. She dressed in men's clothing and harangued her neighbors to take up arms. When the American Revolution began, she volunteered her services as a scout and messenger, leaving her seven-year-old son at home with a neighbor. She continued to act as a frontier scout and "Indian fighter" after the war.

recognized the publicity value of a grieving widow driving a tank in her husband's memory and agreed.

After five months of training as a driver and mechanic,[*] Maria was assigned to the Twenty-Sixth Guards Tank Brigade, deployed in the Smolensk area. When she arrived with her tank, the slogan "Fighting Girlfriend" painted on the side,[†] her fellow tankers treated her like a joke. She soon proved them wrong. In her first battle, on October 21, 1943, she took out an antitank gun and several machine gun nests, and was the first to breach the enemy line. When her tank was hit, she jumped out and repaired it under heavy fire. After the battle, she wrote to her sister that she was so angry that sometimes she couldn't breathe.

Promoted to sergeant after her first battle, she stayed angry until January 17, 1944, when she was hit in the head by flying shrapnel while once again repairing a damaged track on her tank on the battlefield. The wound proved fatal. She was posthumously awarded the Gold Star of the Hero of the Soviet Union, Soviet Russia's highest honor for bravery in action.

Sometimes the "widow's mite" turns out to be pretty mighty.

---

[*] An unusually long training period for a Soviet tank driver, most of whom were given the keys and pointed in the right direction. Presumably the Red Army didn't want its publicity stunt to blow up in its face. So to speak.

[†] Not that different than American test pilot Chuck Yeager painting "Glamorous Glennis" on the side of his plane in honor of his wife.

CHAPTER FOUR

THE MOST
POWERFUL PIECE ON
THE CHESSBOARD

Today, the queen is the most powerful piece on the chessboard. That wasn't always the case. The queen didn't even have a place on the board when Muslim invaders brought chess with them to southern Europe in the eighth century CE.

The chess queen gained the mobility that is her defining characteristic today during the reign of Queen Isabella of Castile (1451–1504), combining the powers of two other pieces, the bishop and the rook. (According to one contemporary commentator, she did not gain the powers of a third piece, the knight, "because it is uncharacteristic of women to carry arms on account of their frailty.")[1] The result was a new and controversial version of the game known as "mad queen's chess."

It is uncertain whether Isabella was the inspiration for the new power of her counterpart on the chessboard, but there is no doubt the Spanish queen was both powerful and mobile. She was a reigning queen at a time when reigning queens were rare. She transformed herself from a pawn in the power politics of fifteenth-century Europe into a key player with a brilliant combination of political savvy, military aggression, and bluffing.

Castile was at war for most of Isabella's reign. Her ascension to the throne touched off five years of civil war: Isabella's supporters fighting to defend her claim to the throne against that of her twelve-year-old niece, Juana.* Once Isabella's claim to the crown was secure, she declared war against the kingdom of Granada, the last Islamic kingdom in Spain.

Isabella and her husband, Ferdinand of Aragon, divided the responsibilities of military leadership soon after she took the throne.† Ferdinand acted as Isabella's general on the battlefield; Isabella directed the war effort in every other way. Isabella did not lead her troops on the battlefield (or at least not often), but she traveled with each campaign, even when pregnant, and plotted strategy and tactics for her generals. (On one occasion, during the ten-year war with Granada, she went into labor while at the council table.) She negotiated loans and requisitioned supplies. She calculated how many knights and foot soldiers each Spanish town was required to provide; the number of technicians, engineers, and laborers needed to build roads and bridges, construct siege machines, or otherwise support the war effort; and how many tools and weapons each man needed to supply. She studied the latest developments in heavy artillery, which had made its way west from the Islamic world, and hired experts from France and Germany to ensure that she bought the right guns and munitions. She outfitted a fleet to patrol the Mediterranean to prevent the arrival of reinforcements from Islamic North Africa. She developed an important innovation in military medicine: mobile field hospitals known as the Queen's Hospital. She was Castile's commander in chief, quartermaster general, and morale booster. Perhaps it's easiest to sum up her career in her own words: "Monarchs who wish to govern must also work."[2]

---

* Or, more accurately, the right claimed by Juana's much older husband, Afonso V of Portugal, who certainly did not intend to serve as consort while his child-bride ruled Spain.

† Isabella and Ferdinand were the fifteenth century's premier power couple. They ruled their two kingdoms together under the motto "tanto monta, monta tanto, Isabel como Fernando": "To stand as high, as high to stand, Isabella as Ferdinand." "Ferdinand standing as high as Isabella" would be closer to the truth. Isabella did not stand back while her brother bartered her hand away in the political marriage market. She chose her own husband and married him in secret. Ferdinand of Aragon was young, good-looking, and heir to a kingdom that was smaller, less wealthy, and less powerful than Castile. As part of the negotiations prior to their secret marriage, Isabella insisted on the fifteenth-century version of a prenuptial agreement that allowed her to govern Castile in her own right, with Ferdinand as her consort.

Isabella was the first of the extraordinary number of female rulers, regents, and consorts who dominated sixteenth-century Europe, including Isabella's granddaughter, Mary Tudor of England. Many of them led troops into battle, defended besieged castles and towns against attackers, or held fortifications while their husbands fought their way through the summer campaign season.

But the warrior queen long predates Isabella. As we have already seen, Tomyris and Artemisia II defended their kingdoms in the sixth and fourth centuries BCE, respectively. The Arab queen, Zenobia, rebelled against Rome in the third century CE and conquered the eastern third of the Roman Empire. Under her leadership, the desert city-state of Palmyra became the center of an extensive, if short-lived, empire that included Arabia, Egypt, and a chunk of modern Turkey. Cleopatra (69–30 BCE) commanded Egyptian naval forces in the great sea battle between Antony and Octavian—she was not just a pretty face. Several of the female Kushite rulers of ancient Nubia, known as *kandakes*, or *candaces*, led armies into the field. The best known of these was Amanirenas the Brave who, according to the Greek geographer Strabo, lost an eye in battle and defeated a Roman army in Egypt around 25 BCE.* In fourth-century China, during a period of turmoil as one dynasty dissolved and another rose to power, the Empress Mao led several hundred soldiers in a desperate attempt to fight off Yao Chang, the man who would become the new dynasty's emperor.† Raziya Sultan (d. 1210), named by her father as his successor, was the only female ruler of the Delhi sultanate in India. She was driven to the battlefield to defend her throne against an armed

---

* Fifteen years later, another *kandake*, Amanikasheto, defeated another Roman army. After a while you wonder why the Romans found the concept of a female warrior so difficult to fathom, since they fought against them with some regularity. And often lost.

† It was a classic "forlorn hope" operation. Although outnumbered, Mao and her forces managed to do significant damage before Yao Chang captured her. He wanted to make her his wife (or perhaps concubine)—a time-honored method of solidifying a conqueror's rule by extending his conquest to include his predecessor's wives. She responded with outrage at the idea that an empress would lower herself to be violated by a man she described as a bandit and an emperor-cide. Outraged in turn, he ordered her executed, along with two of the emperor's sons.

revolt by the Turkish nobility, led by one of her brothers.* In medieval
Europe, two of Isabella's own female ancestors, Urraca of Zamora and
her niece and namesake, Urraca of Castile, were warrior queens: the
first fought one brother on behalf of another brother, and the second
went to war with her own husband over control of Castile.

Et cetera, et cetera, et cetera.

Obviously it is not difficult to find examples of warrior queens.
Once you start looking, you stumble over examples of them in any
culture in which their male counterparts led troops into battle.[†]

THE KING'S WIFE OR A FEMALE KING?

But if warrior queens are a common thread through history, there
is little in the social and political theory of rule to account for their
existence.[‡]

While the practical and theoretical nature of kings has been and
continues to be explored at length, there is little work on the nature
of queenship.[§] A. M. Hocart sums up the general consensus among
political theorists on the subject of queens in his classic comparative
study of the nature of kingship: "The reason why the queen's nature is
vaguer than the king's is that, like all the other officers of state, she has
been absorbed into the king. She ceases to share with him the world.
When *he* becomes the universe *she* is reduced to be only part of him.
The creation of Eve from Adam's rib is the result."[3]

---

* A contemporary chronicler summed up her career with words that could apply to
many women warriors: "She was endowed with all the qualities befitting a king, but she
was not born of the right sex, and so in the estimation of men all these virtues were useless." In Minhaj-us-Siraj, *Tabakat-I Nasiri*, in *History of India as Told by Its Own Historians*, vol. 2, ed. H. M. Elliot and J. Dowson (London: Trübner and Company, 1869), 332.

† Which means pretty much every culture prior to the industrial revolution. The
exceptions seem to be those cultures in which the official ruler is a ritual figure and someone else, usually a warlord, governs in his name. The most dramatic example of this is
Japan, where the shoguns ruled in the name of the emperor, with a few exceptions, from
1185 until the Meiji Restoration in 1868. In cultures in which chiefs, kings, or emperors
do not go to war, there also are no warrior queens. Which is not to say there are no warrior women in such cultures. Two words: female samurai.

‡ The notable exception is Antonia Fraser's *The Warrior Queens*, in which she consid-
ers recurring themes in the stories of warrior queens.

§ In fact, none of the dictionaries scattered about the house include "queenship" as
a word.

Hocart's theoretical demotion of the queen to a mere appendage of the king is reflected in studies of historical queens. For the most part, queens are defined in terms of their relationship to kings rather than their relationship to kingdoms. A queen is depicted first as a king's wife and later as a king's mother. In fact, the English word "queen" is derived from the Anglo-Saxon word *qwen*, which is related to words in other early Germanic languages that mean wife—no king involved. No wonder some reigning queens claimed status as an honorary male and described themselves not as queens but as female kings—a tactic as old as Pharaonic Europe.

As we saw in chapter 3, queens often fought in their roles as king's mothers. Warrior queens also fought in their roles as kings' wives, typically in their husbands' absences. In both cases, as mothers and wives, warrior queens fought in the names of the kings from whom they derived their authority.

There is no similar theoretical discussion of the reigning warrior queen, who both ruled and fought in her own right rather than as a surrogate for a male relative. When historians or political theorists have considered the possibility, they invoke a one-two punch of exceptionalism. On one hand, there is the assumption that women engaged in warfare are, in John Keegan's phrase, "insignificant exceptions."[4] On the other hand, there is the assumption that a reigning queen is also an exception. Eighteenth-century historian Edward Gibbon, trying to make sense of the otherwise inexplicable reigns of Mary I (r. 1553–1558), Elizabeth I (r. 1558–1603), Mary II (r. 1689–1694), and Anne (r. 1702–1714), not to mention that of Mary, Queen of Scots (r. 1542–1567), came to the conclusion that "in hereditary monarchies, however, and especially those of modern Europe, the gallant spirit of chivalry, and the law of succession, have accustomed us to allow a singular exception; and a woman is often acknowledged the absolute sovereign of a great kingdom, in which she would be deemed incapable of exercising the smallest employment, civil or military."[5]

Trapped in the section of the Venn diagram where these exceptions overlapped, warrior queens justified their own existence—often at the working end of a sword.

THE ONLY WOMAN AT THE TABLE

Fifty years after Tomyris defeated Cyrus the Great of Persia, Artemisia I of Halicarnassus fought on the side of another Persian king,

Xerxes, in his war against the Greeks in 480 BCE.* Like her name-sake, Artemisia II,† she ruled the Carian city of Halicarnassus and the nearby islands of Cos, Calymnos, and Nisyros as a vassal of the Persian Empire. She commanded five ships on the Persian side at the Battle of Salamis—a battle the Persians lost in large part because Xerxes ignored her advice.

Ten years earlier, the Greeks had slaughtered a Persian army at the Battle of Marathon. Now the Persians were back for revenge, led by Xerxes himself.

In addition to a land army, reported by Herodotus to be the largest army ever assembled, Xerxes also put together a navy to fight the Greeks. Artemisia was the only woman in the fleet,‡ but she was not the only non-Persian to bring ships to the fight. Persia was a land power. Every ship in the Persian fleet was provided by an oceangoing Persian vassal state, including some places we think of today as Greek.

Herodotus reported that it was "a most strange and interesting thing" that Artemisia fought in the war against Greece.[6] She had a grown son who would have been the logical choice to serve as the Carian commander. Instead, Artemisia chose to command the Carian ships herself. According to Herodotus: "Her own spirit of adventure and her manly courage were her only incentives."§

Before Salamis, Artemisia distinguished herself in the Battle of Artemisium, which took place off the Greek island of Euboea (known today as Évvoia) at the same time the Persian army was forcing its way through the pass at Thermopylae. When the news came of the Persian victory at Thermopylae, the Greeks withdrew. Both fleets suffered heavy losses. There was no clear winner.

---

* As far as sources go, we're back to our old friend Herodotus. In this particular case, Herodotus (c. 484–425/413 BCE) almost counts as a primary source by modern standards. He was born in Halicarnassus a few years before the events in question. As one of his translators, Aubrey de Selincourt, speculates, he would have had ample opportunity to talk with men who took part in the events. Artemisia also appears in the writing of Pausanias, Polyaenus, and Plutarch, and in *The Persians* (472 BCE), written by the Greek playwright Aeschylus—who fought on the Greek side at Salamis.

† Who defeated an uprising by the island of Rhodes.

‡ That we know of. Women in later times disguised themselves as men and fought at sea as well as on land.

§ Not the last time we'll see brave women complimented by comparing them to men, I'm afraid. Not even the last time in Artemisia's story.

After his victory at Thermopylae, Xerxes marched across Greece and burned Athens to the ground. The Greeks abandoned Athens before the Persians arrived and rallied their navy off the coast, near the straits of Salamis. Now Xerxes had to make a decision. He could call it a win and go home. He could besiege the Greek cities until they sued for peace. Or he could meet the Greeks in a sea battle, hoping for another decisive win.

He called a war council with his fleet commanders, including Artemisia. Unlike the other commanders, Artemisia advised him not to fight the Greeks at sea. The Persian fleet was larger, but the Greeks were more experienced seamen. If Xerxes did not rush into a sea battle, the Greeks would soon disperse. But if Xerxes allowed himself to be sucked into another naval disaster it could mean the ruin of his land army as well as his navy.

Xerxes did not take Artemisia's advice. He decided the Persians had lost at Euboea because he was not there to oversee the battle in person. (Hubris much?) He ordered the Persian fleet to pursue the Greeks into the narrow channel between the island of Salamis and the Greek mainland. Artemisia may have believed the orders were a mistake, but when the Persian triremes rowed out of Phaleron Bay, her ships were among them.

The Battle of Salamis began on September 20, 480 BCE.

The triremes that made up the fleets on both sides were wooden warships that were state-of-the-art naval technology. In battle, when speed and maneuverability were at a premium, three banks of rowers powered the ships. The prow at the waterline ended in a ram: a timber core covered with cast bronze. (Do not forget the ram. It plays an important role in Artemisia's story.) Only amateurs—like the Persians—tried to board an enemy ship and fight it out on deck; experienced crews used the ram to strike another ship and then retreated before the enemy could fight back.

The narrow channel off Salamis turned Persia's superior numbers into a liability. The Persian fleet advanced in tight lines, similar to the formation of Persian troops in a land battle. The smaller, more maneuverable Greek ships soon gained the upper hand. At one point in the confusion of battle, Artemisia found herself pursued by an Athenian ship. She was blocked on one side by Persian ships and by enemy ships on the other. Desperate to escape capture by the enemy, she rammed another ship from the Persian fleet, which sank with its entire crew.* This maneuver convinced her pursuer that her ship was either under Greek command or had switched sides in midbattle— not an unknown situation in a fleet that was made up of ships provided by Persian vassal states with varying degrees of commitment to the empire.

The Greek commander's decision not to continue the pursuit was an expensive one. The Athenians had put a price on Artemisia's head, because they "resented the fact that a woman should appear in arms against them"†—ten thousand drachmas to anyone who captured her alive.‡

Xerxes watched the battle from the high land overlooking the channel. When an aide brought Artemisia's action to his attention, Xerxes made the not-unreasonable assumption that she had rammed an enemy ship, and declared, "My men have turned into women, my women into men."§

Artemisia made one last appearance in the history of the Greco-Persian wars. After the Battle of Salamis, Xerxes feared the Greeks would be emboldened by their victory and march against the Persian forces quartered at the Hellespont. One of his generals, Mardonius, suggested Xerxes return to Persia and leave Mardonius in command of an army of three hundred thousand men, with which he would subdue the Greeks. Artemisia advised the emperor to follow Mardonius's suggestion. If the Greeks won, Xerxes could blame Mardonius. If the Persian army defeated the Greeks again, Xerxes could take the credit. (A dubious management strategy by modern standards.) This time, Xerxes followed Artemisia's advice. He gave Artemisia the job of escorting his (illegitimate) sons to Ephesus.

---

* Some historians believe the ship she rammed belonged to a commander with whom she had quarreled previously. Perhaps he didn't think a woman's place was on the battlefield.

† Not unlike the Rhodians, who more than a century later were outraged that a woman, Artemisia II, should rule the cities and islands of Caria.

‡ The equivalent in modern dollars is best calculated as "a lot."

§ Antonia Fraser refers to this as the Shame Syndrome, in which men are shamed by being compared to women who are better "men." This double-edged trope is not limited to the distant past: both Indira Gandhi and Golda Meir were described as the "only man" in their respective cabinets. By describing powerful women as men, the trope effectively disguises the fact that Artemisia, and her successors, were the only women at the table.

We know nothing about Artemisia's life after she headed to Ephesus. Perhaps she went home to Halicarnassus and turned the reins of power over to her son. Perhaps her "manly courage" spurred her on to new adventures.

AETHELFLAED, THE LADY OF THE MERCIANS

In the tenth century CE, Aethelflaed, the Lady of the Mercians,* succeeded her husband as the ruler of the Anglo-Saxon kingdom of Mercia. She played a key role in reclaiming territory from the Danish Vikings, who had controlled a large part of England for forty years.

Aethelflaed (c. 870–918) was the eldest child of Alfred the Great (r. 871–899) and his wife, Ealhswith, a daughter of the royal house of Mercia.† Equally, if not more, important in terms of her role in English history, she was the sister of Edward the Elder (r. 899–924) who would unify England under the kings of Wessex, with a lot of help from his big sister.

Aethelflaed never knew a time when the Vikings weren't a threat. Beginning in 793, Viking raiders arrived in England each spring, as regularly as robins, and attacked the coasts and inland waterways of the British Isles. Over time, Viking raids evolved into permanent Danish settlements. By the end of the ninth century, the area known as the "Danelaw" covered a significant portion of England, from the north of Yorkshire to the Thames.

Alfred successfully defended the kingdom of Wessex against Viking attackers, but realized he could not drive them out of England

---

* Also known as Ethelfleda, because spelling was a chancy thing in the medieval world.

† You've (probably) heard of Alfred the Great, even if you know nothing but his name. The odds are you haven't heard of Ealswith unless you are a medievalist. Together, those two facts sum up a significant problem in adding women back into history—missing mothers. In her groundbreaking study of early modern queens, Sharon Jansen notes that royal family trees in political histories and biographies often leave out mothers, wives, and daughters, as if generation after generation of kings sprang full-blown from the heads of their fathers. When Jansen drew family trees that linked mothers, daughters, aunts, and nieces across generations, she discovered "networks of related women and patterns of connections between them"—networks that were not limited to blood ties. Such networks played an often-overlooked role in history—for instance, the importance of Aethelflaed's maternal connection with Mercia. See Jansen, *The Monstrous Regiment of Women*, 4.

entirely. In 886, he negotiated a partition treaty with the Danes, leaving northern and eastern England under Danish rule and returning West Mercia and Kent to Anglo-Saxon control.

Neither side honored the partition treaty, which at best slowed down action across the border for a few years. In order to consolidate their alliances against the Danes, Alfred arranged for Aethelflaed to marry his most important ally, Aethelred, Lord of Mercia. (It's beginning to sound familiar, isn't it?) She was no more than twenty at the time.

We know little about Aethelflaed's life until the first years of the tenth century, when Aethelred became ill. With no direct male heir waiting to inherit Aethelred's position, Aethelflaed became the effective ruler of Mercia during her husband's illness. When he died in 911, she succeeded him without opposition—the only female ruler in the Anglo-Saxon period in England and one of only a handful of women in early medieval Europe who ruled in their own right rather than as a regent for an underaged son or brother. (The fact that Aethelflaed was half-Mercian by birth may have played a role in the Mercians accepting her as their ruler.) She was the Lady of the Mercians, just as Aethelred was Lord of the Mercians, before her.*

Even before her husband's death, Aethelflaed began a program of fortress building designed to protect Mercia against sporadic Danish raids and to provide bases for Mercian military operations into Danish territory. She constructed ten fortified garrison towns over the course of ten years.

After her husband's death, Aethelflaed joined forces with her brother to protect their kingdoms against the Danes. She also sent a punitive expedition against the Welsh in 916, following the murder of a Mercian bishop, and led an alliance of Briton, Picts, and Scots rulers against a large group of Norwegian and Irish-Norwegian invaders, who crossed the channel from Brittany in 914.

In 917, the conflict between Anglo-Saxons and Vikings intensified. The West Saxon chronicles tell us Aethelflaed's brother, King Edward, occupied the Danish border town of Towcester, in modern Northamptonshire, shortly before Easter. In July, a Danish force

---

* Don't let the title fool you. Aethelflaed was a ruling queen by any standard. In fact, some scholars argue her title, *hlaefdige*, had connotations of political power that were absent in the contemporaneous title *qwen*.

counterattacked. By year's end, the Viking armies of Northampton and East Anglia surrendered to Edward.

The West Saxon chronicles leave out the fact that Aethelflaed led her own offensive against the Vikings at the same time. With Danish forces focused on her brother's army, Aethelflaed took Derby in a savage battle; it was the first of the five great strongholds of the Danelaw to fall to Anglo-Saxon forces. The following year she led her forces against the important Danish fortress of Leicester, which surrendered without a fight. Danish Christians in York, apparently tired of being ruled by a non-Christian Viking from Dublin who had seized control of their region in 911, approached Aethelflaed (*not* King Edward) with a formal promise of allegiance. Before she was able to finalize the treaty with the men of York, Aethelflaed died unexpectedly on June 12, 918, leaving Edward to win the final victory against the Danes.

After Aethelflaed's death, Edward seized the Mercian throne from her daughter, Aelfwinn, who was thirty-ish at the time of her mother's death. (In other words, not an underage child in need of a regent.) Six months after she succeeded her mother as Lady of the Mercians, Edward claimed her lands, uniting most of modern England under his control. According to one contemporary chronicle, she was taken into Wessex. Once in Wessex, Aelfwinn, daughter of Aethelflaed, disappears from the historical record.

It is only by chance that we know Aethelflaed as anything more than Edward's sister. Most of the surviving written sources for English history, most notably the *Anglo-Saxon Chronicle*, focus on Edward's kingdom of Wessex, which ultimately triumphed in the struggle for control of England. Those sources ignore Aethelflaed's achievements. They even omit her title of Lady of the Mercians. Instead she is referred to only as Edward's sister.[*]

---

[*] Referring to a woman primarily in terms of her relationship to a man rather than her own accomplishments did not end in the Middle Ages. According to Rachel Swaby, the *New York Times* obituary of Yvonne Brill in 2013 inspired her to write *Headstrong*. The obituary gave Brill the title of "world's best mom" because "she followed her husband from job to job and took eight years off from work to raise three children." To Swaby's disgust, "only after a loud, public outcry did the *Times* amend the article so it would begin with the contribution that earned Brill a featured spot in the paper of record in the first place: 'She was a brilliant rocket scientist.'" See Rachel Swaby, *Headstrong: 52 Women Who Changed Science—and the World* (New York: Broadway Books, 2015), xi. Unfortunately, the Brill obituary is not an isolated case. In some ways, we are still in the dark ages.

Luckily a surviving fragment of another chronicle, known as the *Mercian Register*, gives us a peek at the events of 902 to 924 from a Mercian viewpoint—and puts Aethelflaed in the center of the action.* The *Mercian Register* tells the story of three generations of Mercian noblewomen. It starts with the death of Aethelflaed's mother, Ealhswith, making it clear that Aethelflaed's links with, and claims to, Mercia predated her marriage. Thereafter, the chronicle focuses on Aethelflaed's actions as the Lady of the Mercians until her own death. The *Mercian Register* ends soon after Edward deposed her daughter in 918. The story of Aethelflaed and of Mercia itself is over, half-buried in the larger history of England's unification, and yet never entirely forgotten.

Writing two hundred years after Aethelflaed's death, English chronicler William of Malmesbury (1080–1143) described Aethelflaed as a warrior who "protected men at home and intimidated them abroad." He argued she "ought not to be forgotten, as she was a powerful accession to his [Edward's] party."[7]

HER MOTHER'S DAUGHTER, PART 2

The sixteenth- (or possibly fifteenth-) century Hausa queen Amina of Zazzau, now the province of Zaria in modern Nigeria, succeeded her mother to the throne, united Hausaland into a single state, and led her kingdom in expansionist wars for thirty-four years.[†]

The city-states of Hausaland, in West Africa, first appeared around 1000 CE. The region was made up of seven walled city-states, ruled by dynasties that claimed semidivine status, and seven "lesser"

---

* The *Mercian Register* is the main source for Aethelflaed's history, but it is not the only one. An Irish document, known as the *Three Fragments*, while considered less reliable than the *Mercian Register*, provides an appraisal of her achievements from a non-English perspective.

† Just because we've moved into the early modern period doesn't mean we've moved past the problem of "primary" sources produced long after the events they discuss. Much of what we know of Amina's rule—and early Hausa history in general—comes from the *Kano Chronicle*. Commissioned in the late nineteenth century by Sultan Muhammad Bello, ruler of the Sokoto Caliphate, in what is now northwestern Nigeria, the chronicle is a collection of oral traditions, written in the Hausa language using Arabic characters.

states, all of which were in constant competition with one another over territory, slaves, and access to the trans-Saharan trade with North Africa. With the arrival of Islam in the late thirteenth century, religious differences added a new layer of conflict between Hausa rulers who had converted and those who had not.

Zazzau first came to prominence among the Hausa city-states under the rule of Amina's mother, Bakwa Turunku, who was the twenty-second ruler of Zazzau and probably the first woman to hold the office. There are two different versions of how Amina came to power. In one, Bakwa Turunku named her sixteen-year-old daughter the heir apparent as soon as she became ruler and Amina succeeded her. In the other, a male relative named Karama ruled after Bakwa Turunku. Amina served as a general during his reign and became Zazzau's ruler after his death, in large part as a result of her military prowess.

In both versions, Amina came to power in her own right around 1576, united the Hausa states under her rule, and embarked on a career of territorial expansion. For more than thirty years, she led her army of fierce horsemen into battle, driving south and west to the mouth of the Niger, capturing the dominant northern cities of Kano and Katsina, and expanding the sub-Saharan trade routes into new territories. She built defensive earthenwork walls around her camp at every stop. Today ancient Hausa fortifications are still known as "Amina's walls."

Like her (probable) contemporary Elizabeth I of England, Amina refused to marry, but she never claimed to be a Virgin Queen. According to oral traditions, she took a new lover in each town she conquered: a dubious privilege since she ordered each lover beheaded in the morning as she left.*

---

* Such accounts must be handled carefully. Amina's treatment of her lovers echoes the framing story of the *Arabian Nights*—known in various forms throughout the Islamic world—in which the sultan took a new wife each night and had her beheaded in the morning. Moreover, Antonia Fraser points out the idea of sexual rapacity, which she calls the Voracity Syndrome, and its opposite, extreme chastity, are both common tropes in accounts of warrior queens. Such tropes are yet another way of claiming the warrior queen stands outside the world of ordinary women.

Today, Amina is a national heroine in Nigeria, complete with a postage stamp in her honor and the perhaps inevitable praise "a woman as capable as a man."*

KATHERINE THE QWEEN

When we think of Katherine of Aragon, we tend to think of her as Henry VIII's aggrieved first wife—worn out by miscarriages, humiliated by false pregnancies, and abandoned for a newer model because she was unable to satisfy Henry's obsession for a male heir. The battles we associate with her name are legal battles.

But in fact, in an earlier, happier time, Katherine of Aragon, Queen of England (and Queen Isabella of Castile's youngest daughter), successfully defended her adopted country against invasion by Scotland. The only reason she didn't lead an army onto the field was bad timing.

In June 1513, Henry VIII prepared to go to war against Louis XII of France alongside the pope and the Emperor Maximilian. In anticipation of his absence while on the continent, Henry named Katherine Regent and Governess of England, Wales, and Ireland. Her powers as regent included the authority "to fight and wage war against any of our enemies in our absence." She had the authority to assemble an army and "arm and equip them for war and to station, prepare *and lead them*" (emphasis mine).[8]

Katherine's regency was not a polite fiction. Government documents carried the official imprimatur "*teste Katerina Anglie Regina*" (witnessed by Katherine, Queen of England). Signing herself "Katherine the Qween" [*sic*], she ruled on appeals to pardon felons and signed warrants for payment of government expenses. She appointed minor officials. She settled questions related to the estate of the Countess of Somerset and a long-running dispute over ecclesiastical jurisdiction between the archbishop of Canterbury and the bishop of Winchester. And when Henry's brother-in-law, James IV of Scotland, mustered troops across the border in Scotland, Katherine enthusiastically organized England's defense.

---

* Quoted in S. J. Hogben and A. H. M. Kirk-Greene, *The Emirates of Northern Nigeria: A Preliminary Survey of Their Historical Traditions* (London: Oxford University Press, 1966), 218. "As capable as a man" is a concept we're going to grow very familiar with, and tired of, by the end of this book.

Writing to Thomas Wolsey, who was responsible for many details of the expedition to France, Katherine described herself as "horribly busy making standards, banners and badges"[9]—a description that hid the full range of her preparations for war behind a ladylike camouflage of needlework. Her mother had organized the Spanish war against Granada. Now Katherine proved herself to be her mother's daughter. She summoned able-bodied men to fight in England's defense. When the mayor and sheriffs of Gloucester ignored her letters asking how many men and horses they could supply, she followed up with a sharply worded order to answer within fifteen days. (They did.) She sent a fleet of eight ships with troops, heavy artillery, and gunners toward the Scottish border to reinforce the army, which was under the command of Thomas Howard, Earl of Surrey. She levied stores of grain, beer, and rope; suits of light armor; and the then enormous sum of ten thousand pounds, to be held by the abbot of St. Mary, near York, in case of need.

On August 22, James invaded England with thirty thousand men, backed by modern French artillery and financed by the French crown. He captured four English castles in quick succession and then settled into a fortified camp at Flodden Field.

Howard had been in the north since early August. Now he mustered his forces at Newcastle.

Concerned that James might defeat Howard, Katherine raised a second army from the Midland counties, then a third, which she intended to lead herself—as a strategist if not as a field commander.

On September 9, she moved out with what contemporaries described as "a great power" or a "numerous force." She carried with her two helmets, at least one of them decorated with "crown gold" by the royal goldsmith. She never had a chance to wear them.[10]

That same day, the Earl of Surrey defeated James IV at Flodden Field. King James was killed in the battle.

Katherine was in Buckingham, forty miles north of London, when she received the news, along with a portion of the Scottish king's surcoat, decorated with Scotland's royal arms. She sent the surcoat to Henry in France.

Traditional military histories of the battle take little notice of Katherine's role as regent and quartermaster and do not refer to her intention to lead her troops into the field. At most, they mention that she sent James IV's bloodied surcoat on to Henry in France as what one author condescendingly dubs "a handy souvenir."[11]

Her contemporaries were more generous. They acknowledged that she had played a key role in the war and pointed out that Katherine's defense of the home front was more important than anything Henry accomplished in his military adventures in France. Isabella must have been proud.

"A CUNNING AND PRUDENT VIRAGO"

For three decades, the seventeenth-century Mbundu queen, Njinga of Ndongo and Matamba,* defended her West African kingdom against the Portuguese with an in-your-face combination of warfare and diplomacy. In short, she was what one observer described, with admiration, as "A Cunning and Prudent Virago."†

When the Portuguese established a trading colony on the coast of what is now modern Angola in 1575, the kingdom of Ndongo was the second largest state in central Africa. Its population of roughly one hundred thousand people lived under the rule of local lords called

---

* Also known as Nzinga, Singa, Jinga, and Dona Anna de Sousa, depending on whom you talk to. Much of what we know about Njinga and her predecessors comes from accounts written by European eyewitnesses: Portuguese and Dutch colonial administrators, Catholic missionaries, soldiers, and merchants. The most important of these are two contemporary biographies, written by the Capuchin missionaries Giovanni Antonio Cavazzi and Antonio da Gaeta, both of whom lived in Njinga's court during her final years, where they served as her confessors and advisors. We also have diplomatic letters from Njinga to the various Portuguese governors and officials who served in colonial Angola during her decades-long reign, their Dutch counterparts in the 1530s, the Propaganda Fide (the Vatican agency responsible for overseas missions), and the pope himself. Dictated by Njinga to members of her court who were literate in Portuguese, these letters outline her dealings with Portuguese officials from her perspective.

† Before that term took a turn to the dark side. See John Ogilby, *Africa: Being an accurate description of the regions of Ægypt, Barbary, Lybia, and Billedulgerid, the land of Negroes, Guinee, Æthiopia, and the Abyssines, With all the Adjacent Islands, either in the Mediterranean, Atlantick, Southern, or Oriental Sea, belonging thereunto. With the several Denominations of their Coasts, Harbors, Creeks, Rivers, Lakes, Cities, Towns, Castles, and Villages, Their Customs, Modes, and Manners, Languages, Religions, and Inexhaustible Treasure; With their Governments and Policy, variety of Trade and Barter, And also of their wonderful Plants, Beasts, Birds, and Serpents. Collected and Translated from most Authentick Authors And Augmented with later Observations, Illustrated with Notes, and Adorn'd with peculiar Maps, and proper Sculptures*, vol. II (London: Printed by Tho. Johnson for the author, 1670), 654–55.

sobas, who owed their allegiance to the central ruler, the *ngola*,* who lived in the capital city of Kabasa.

At first, relations between the Portuguese and Ndongo were friendly. The ruler at the time, Ngola Kiluanji, welcomed trade with Europeans and his kingdom flourished in the early days of the Portuguese slave trade. By the time Njinga was born in 1582, Ndongo was at war with Portugal. The two states would remain in conflict for her entire life.

Njinga was a granddaughter of Ndongo's founder and the kingdom's fourth ruler. According to her biographers, she displayed intellectual and physical prowess as a child. She showed particular talent for wielding the battle-axe that was the royal symbol of Ndongo.† With her father's approval, she sat in on his judicial and military councils and studied the military, political, and ritual arts taught to the sons of Mbundu rulers. At the same time, as a privileged young woman at court, she paid careful attention to her appearance, which she would use as a weapon of another sort throughout her career. At some point during the reigns of her two immediate predecessors— her father, Mbande a Ngola, and her brother, Ngola Mbande— Njinga became a war leader in her own right.

In 1617, Ngola Mbande overthrew their father and named himself *ngola*. In order to consolidate his position, he killed all potential rivals, including Njinga's only son. To prevent the birth of new rivals, he ordered Njinga and her two sisters sterilized: a horrifying process in which oils combined with various herbs were thrown "while boiling onto the bellies of his sisters, so that, from the shock, fear & pain, they should forever be unable to give birth."[12] It appears to have worked: none of the three women gave birth thereafter.

With his position as ruler secure, Ngola Mbande set out to restore his kingdom to the wealth and power it enjoyed under his predecessors. He fought a losing battle against the Portuguese for four years.

---

* The Portuguese mistook the title of the ruler (*ngola*) for the name of his country. As a result, they called the kingdom Angola.

† The battle-axe was the preferred weapon of Ndongo's soldiers, men and women alike. They trained with them from early childhood, performing a rhythmic dance that fostered both speed and agility. Gaeta didn't meet Njinga until she was in her seventies, but he reported her ability to wield the axe and perform traditional military dances remained impressive.

In 1621, a new Portuguese governor, João Correia de Sousa, arrived in Luanda, in the colonial capital. Hoping a change of governor offered a chance for peace, Mbande sent Njinga to Luanda to negotiate a treaty with the Portuguese.

Fully conscious of the power of symbols, Njinga arrived with an impressive entourage of soldiers, musicians, slaves, and waiting women, and a new title, *Ginga Bande Gambole*—Njinga Mbande, official envoy.

Governor de Sousa was equally aware of the value of symbols in diplomatic situations. When Njinga entered his audience chamber, he greeted her from the governor's throne and gestured for her to sit on a cushion on the floor before him—the typical arrangement when African notables met with the Portuguese governor. Njinga refused to take the posture of a supplicant. She gestured for a female slave to come forward. The woman knelt on her hands and knees. Njinga sat on the woman's back as if she were a human chair. She was ready to negotiate, equal to equal.

Njinga remained in Luanda for several months and negotiated a peace treaty on her brother's behalf. For a brief time, her mission appeared to be a success, but neither side honored their agreements. Soon Ndongo and the Portuguese were at war once more.

In spring of 1624, Ngola Mbande died. Everyone agreed he was poisoned. The Portuguese said it was murder and pointed at Njinga. Angolan oral history claims he committed suicide in a moment of despair. Either way, Mbande made arrangements before his death for the care of the young son who was his heir. Recognizing the dangers of a child ruler, for both the young king and the kingdom, Ngola Mbande divided the responsibility in two parts. He named Njinga regent, with the power of governing Ndongo in the boy's minority. He put the boy under the guardianship of an ally named Kaza. In theory it was a brilliant solution to an age-old problem, but it didn't take into account Njinga's ambition. Njinga convinced Kaza to turn the boy over to her, using a combination of lavish presents and an offer of marriage. Once she had control of the child, she poisoned him, then pushed through her immediate election as the new *ngola* of Ndongo.

Njinga spent the next thirty years in warfare and diplomatic wrangling with the Portuguese. Between 1626 and 1655, the queen commanded her own forces against the Portuguese army. In 1630, she conquered a new kingdom, Matamba, which she used as a base for attacks on settlements under Portuguese control.

A new player entered the political and economic scene in 1641: the Dutch East India Company.

On April 20 of that year, twenty-two Dutch ships attacked and conquered the Portuguese colonial capital of Luanda. Njinga celebrated as soon as she heard the news, then sent ambassadors to propose an alliance. The Dutch were willing allies. Together Njinga and the Dutch almost brought Portuguese rule in Angola to an end.

By August 1648, Njinga and the Dutch seemed on the verge of driving the Portuguese out of Angola. But reinforcements were on the way from Rio de Janeiro in the Portuguese colony of Brazil. A fleet of fifteen ships and nine hundred men arrived in Luanda's port and bombarded the city with cannon fire. After a few days of heavy shelling, the Dutch East India Company surrendered all Dutch positions in Angola to the Portuguese.

With the Dutch defeated and in flight, Njinga retreated to her base at Matamba, from which she continued her guerilla campaign against the Portuguese and their African allies until 1654. According to one Portuguese observer, she launched at least twenty-nine invasions against *sobas* in Portuguese Angola and surrounding kingdoms between 1648 and 1650 alone.

Njinga was forty-two years old when she succeeded her brother as the *ngola* of Ndongo. In December 1657, when she was nearly seventy-five, she led her army into battle for the last time. Before the battle she prepared her soldiers—many young enough to be her great-grandchildren—by leading them in the customary war dance, a rigorous military exercise with arrows and spears.

When Njinga died in 1663, she left behind a thriving kingdom, which survived as an independent state until 1909, when the Portuguese finally succeeded in making it part of the colony of Angola.

In the 1960s, Angolan revolutionaries turned to oral traditions about Njinga for inspiration and celebrated her as a national hero who had united her people in an epic struggle against the Portuguese.

As armies became more professional in the eighteenth century, fewer rulers, male or female, led their troops into battle.* If it was unusual

---

* Military historian Barton C. Hacker argues this transformation also reduced the traditional support roles women played in European-style armies and contributed to their disappearance from the pages of military history.

for reigning kings to command troops in the twentieth century, it was unheard of for reigning queens to do so, much to the regret of Queen Wilhelmina of the Netherlands, who really, really wanted to join her forces at the front in the Second World War.

During the First World War, Wilhelmina, in conjunction with Prime Minister Pieter W. A. Cort van der Linden, maintained the Netherlands' long-standing policy of neutrality, to the extent of granting asylum to Kaiser Wilhelm II in defiance of Allied demands for his extradition as a war criminal. She changed her position on neutrality when faced with the Nazi threat. She warned government officials for years of the growing danger of Hitler and Germany, but they ignored her. In her memoir, she tartly remarks that "shortly before the war it was necessary for me to point out that Hitler had written a book, and that it might be of some use to examine its contents."[13]

Wilhelmina ascended to the Dutch throne in 1898 at the age of eighteen.* She was sixty when Nazi Germany attacked the Netherlands. She had spent much of the intervening forty-two years frustrated by the limits the Dutch constitution placed on her ability to influence government policy. Now she believed it was time to live up to the example of the ancestors for whom she had been named, William the Silent (1533–1584) and William of Orange (1650–1702), who had done great deeds in defense of their country.

Looking ahead to the possibility of a Nazi invasion, she planned to send the Crown Princess Juliana and her family to safety. She herself would travel south with her army, as Albert I of Belgium did when the Germans overran his country in the Great War. She was determined "to share the fate of the soldier and . . . to be the last man to fall in the last ditch."[14]

Germany attacked on May 10, 1940. German troops landed at three airfields surrounding The Hague, with orders to capture the queen and her cabinet ministers. Dutch forces beat them back, giving the royal family time to put their plans in action. By May 13, the Germans controlled much of the country. Informed the army could no longer guarantee her safety, Wilhelmina reluctantly left The Hague and boarded a British destroyer. Once aboard, wearing a life jacket

---

* She was not crowned, because the crown belongs to the Dutch people—a reminder that institutions that look similar at first glance may differ in important ways.

and a steel helmet,* she instructed the commander to set his course for Zeeland province, at the southwestern tip of the country, where Dutch and French troops were fighting the Germans. The British commander informed her the sea route to the southwest was too dangerous. His instructions were to go directly to England. She had no choice but to agree. Once she landed, she demanded an immediate return to Holland, and was politely refused. Clutching a gas mask and the steel helmet she had worn on the destroyer, Wilhelmina boarded the train to London.

Unable to join her troops on the battlefield, Wilhelmina found another way to fight. The queen, who had always been separated from her people by custom and her own stiff personality, became the heart of her country's resistance. Hours after the German attack began, she made her first radio broadcast against the Nazis, declaring over Dutch radio, "I raise a fierce protest against this flagrant violation of good faith, this outrage against all that is decent between civilized states."[15] She made her next broadcast the day after she arrived in Britain. Every day thereafter, the queen spoke to her people at the start of the Radio Orange program broadcast to the Netherlands by the BBC. Her radio speeches were passionate and personal; with one exception, she wrote them herself. Again and again she told her subjects the war was a struggle between good and evil. There could be no compromise with Hitler and his "gang of war criminals." She urged her people to resist the invaders and berated the Dutch "scoundrels" who cooperated with the Third Reich. The Dutch joked that the queen's grandchildren weren't allowed to listen to her broadcasts from their refuge in Canada because she used such foul language when she talked about the Nazis.

Late in World War II, Winston Churchill quipped, "I fear no man in the world but Queen Wilhelmina."[16] A ferocious chess player, he recognized the power of a queen in motion.

---

* Unlike Katherine of Aragon's, her helmet was standard issue and did not include a crown—which, after all, was the property of the Dutch people and not a personal emblem.

A QUEEN IN
ALL BUT NAME

The name Matilda means "mighty in war." The *gran contessa* Matilda of Tuscany (1046–1115) lived up to her name.* According to military historian David Hay, she was not only the most powerful woman of her time but was among the best European military commanders of her day—high praise for a woman who at best plays a supporting role in general histories of the period.[1]

Matilda was born in 1046, at the start of the "high middle ages," a period when Europe was beginning to recover from the political and economic chaos left behind by the unraveling of the Roman Empire in the West. She was the daughter of Margrave Boniface II of

---

* Unlike the lives of many women warriors of the medieval period and earlier, Matilda's life is well documented in primary sources from her own time period. Her actions are described in several contemporary chronicles as well as in diplomatic documents of the period. She also is referred to in numerous pamphlets, treatises, and other propaganda produced by the legal and political spin doctors she hired to justify her activities to a world uncomfortable with the idea of women leading armies. Another sort of army fighting on a different front. The most important, and weirdest, of the chronicles that reported Matilda's military campaigns is *On the Princes of Canossa*, also known as *The Life of Matilda*—an account in verse form written by the monk Donizo of Canossa. (The idea of writing history in Virgilian verse is daunting.) You have to use Donizo with care. Not only does he give the fortress of Canossa a speaking part, but he makes it clear his intention is to glorify Matilda's life. He glosses over a few details that don't fit his image of her. (A couple of marriages and a pregnancy, for instance—which I don't talk about in any detail either because they do not relate to her military career.) Adjusting for adulation, it is still a fair statement that Donizo was a better historian than he was a poet.

Canossa and his second wife, Beatrice, who was the daughter of the Duke of Upper Lorraine and a military commander in her own right. Through Beatrice, Matilda was a cousin of the Holy Roman Emperors Henry III and Henry IV.

Her father's assassination in 1052 and the subsequent deaths of her older siblings left Matilda the sole heir to extensive lands. She held much of the territory between northern Italy and Rome, including a system of fortresses that controlled access to the two main road systems across the Apennine Mountains. Although she was pressured twice into marriages that were politically advantageous to others, she kept control of her inheritance and the power that went with it at a time when it was not common for women to do so.

In 1076, a long-standing dispute between the papacy and the Holy Roman Empire* flamed into armed conflict. As the ruler of lands lying directly between the two greatest powers in Latin Christendom, Matilda was physically in the middle of things.

The Investiture Controversy was the culmination of several generations of conflict surrounding the relationship between religious and secular power in general and the relative power of the papacy and the Holy Roman emperor in particular.† The issue at the heart of the controversy was who controlled appointments to church offices—and the wealth and power church officials wielded.

Unresolved issues regarding lay investiture of bishops came to a head with the consecration of the reformist monk Hildebrand as Pope Gregory VII in 1073. Secular rulers had long claimed the right to appoint bishops and abbots in their realms and to perform the ritual that installed them in office. Gregory initiated reforms throughout the church, including a ban on simony, aka trafficking in ecclesiastical

---

* The Holy Roman Empire was a cobbled-together and shifting arrangement of semi-independent duchies, margravates, counties, and kingdoms in what is now Germany, Austria, northern Italy, and eastern France, best summed up by the eighteenth-century French philosopher Voltaire as being "neither holy, nor roman nor an empire."

† The relationship between popes and emperors was complicated. The king of the Germans did not become Holy Roman emperor until crowned by the pope. Without the papal nod, he was no more than the elected ruler of a confederation of interrelated states—first among almost-equals—and could be removed from office by his fellow German princes. At the same time, the Holy Roman emperors considered themselves the successors of Constantine and Charlemagne, responsible for protecting the church (including the papacy) from internal and external threats (including the pope). Head-butting over who was the boss of whom was inevitable and constant.

offices. Gregory expanded the definition of simony to include lay investiture of bishops. His ban on lay investiture of bishops was not just a religious reform. It also struck at the power of secular leaders.

The routine appointment of the archbishop of Milan in 1075 provided the spark for ten years of war. Local reformers in Milan had elected a new archbishop, but after initially accepting the local choice, Emperor Henry IV attempted to install the chaplain of his Saxon campaign in the position instead. Gregory ordered Henry to stop interfering in church affairs. In January 1076, Henry pushed back. He called a council of German bishops and convinced them to depose Gregory.* Gregory then excommunicated the emperor.† For good measure, he excommunicated Henry's most active supporters among the bishops.

The potential consequences for Henry were serious. In theory, excommunicating a monarch absolved his subjects from their obligation to obey him. In the Kingdom of Germany, where the monarch was elected by his peers, an excommunicated king could easily be deposed.

Henry discovered he had overestimated the strength of his position. Many of the German bishops backed away from Henry as fast as their ceremonial robes would allow and reconciled with the pope. With the validity of their oaths of allegiance in question, his newly pacified Saxon subjects rose once again in revolt, while his opponents among the German princes pressed for the election of a new king. His supporters won Henry a year and a day to free himself from excommunication before a new king was elected. He needed to grovel hard and he needed to do it fast.

In January 1077, Matilda and an armed force escorted the pope through her territory as he traveled toward Augsburg to meet with the German princes and bishops.‡ When Matilda and Gregory reached Mantua, where he was scheduled to meet his escort from Germany, they learned Henry was nearby. Matilda moved the pope from Mantua to her castle at Canossa—a fortress in the heart of the

---

* This was not the first time an emperor tried to influence who held the papal throne. Henry's father intervened in the choice of three popes in succession.

† Who was not technically emperor, since he had not been crowned by Gregory or his predecessor.

‡ Gregory and Matilda had reason to anticipate trouble on the road. The year before, a Roman nobleman, known to be pro-Henry, kidnapped Gregory from the altar during the papal mass on Christmas Eve. The outraged Roman populace forced the pope's release, but there were no urban mobs to protect Gregory on isolated mountain roads.

Apennine Mountains where she could ward off a small imperial force if necessary.

Matilda was prepared to defend the pope against attack, but Henry came to Canossa not as an aggressor but as a penitent.

Having crossed the Alps with a small escort, including his queen and infant heir, through what contemporary chronicles unanimously describe as unusually severe winter conditions, Henry presented himself at the gates of Canossa without any of the trappings of royalty. For three days he stood before the gates, barefoot and dressed in a plain wool robe, begging for the pope's mercy—sometimes in tears. Occasionally, he knocked on the door, but was not allowed to enter. On the fourth day, after negotiations in which Matilda played a key role, the shivering emperor was allowed into the fortress to beg face-to-face.

Gregory granted Henry absolution, but the emperor's humiliation at Canossa did not end his quarrels with the pope or his problems in Germany. Despite the fact that Henry had been reinstated in the church, his opponents back home elected a new king to replace him, Rudolf of Swabia. Both king and anti-king petitioned Gregory for his support.

At the Lenten synod of 1080, representatives of both would-be kings presented their petitions to Gregory in person. After hearing their arguments, Gregory excommunicated Henry a second time, on the grounds that he had not kept the promises he made at Canossa, and gave Rudolf his support. Henry convinced another council of German bishops to depose the pope. This time Henry's bishops elected an antipope, Archbishop Guibert of Ravenna, who took the title of Clement III (1080–1100).*

On October 15, 1080, Rudolf died in battle. No longer threatened by the existence of a rival candidate for the crown, Henry returned to Italy at the head of an army, to settle the question of the papal succession and his long-delayed coronation as Holy Roman emperor.

Matilda of Tuscany stood in his way.

Matilda had been an ardent supporter of church reform since childhood. She supported the monk Hildebrand before his election

---

* Not to be confused with the later Pope Clement III (r. 1187–1191). Keeping track of popes and anti-popes—not to mention kings and anti-kings—can be tricky. Some modern historical accounts describe Gregory VII as the anti-pope after 1080. All you can do is pick a side and stick to it. In this case, any pope of Matilda's is a pope of mine.

to the papacy in 1073 and continued to support his efforts after his investiture as Gregory VII.* While Henry and Rudolf faced off in their final battle, Matilda mustered troops to defend Gregory against Henry and Guibert. She would provide the main military support for Gregory and his successors in their struggles with Henry for the next twenty years.

The first battle of the Investiture Controversy took place in October 1080, as soon as word of Rudolf's death reached Italy. Henry's Italian supporters attacked and defeated Matilda's troops near her castle at Volta: the first of several defeats Matilda suffered at the hands of Henry's supporters.† Matilda was not yet a seasoned commander, unlike her younger cousin Henry, who had spent most of his adulthood on the battlefield. According to contemporary accounts from both sides of the conflict, she suffered heavy losses after Henry entered Italy in the spring of 1081. Bishop Benzo of Alba, a hard-core Henry supporter, mocked her as "wringing her hands and weeping for lost Tuscany."[2]

And yet there are signs Matilda was still a serious force in Italy. Henry felt threatened enough to convene a court that judged her guilty of treason for refusing to honor her feudal allegiance to him, placed her under "ban of empire," and stripped her of her title and her lands. Like Gregory's excommunication of Henry, this act released her vassals from their feudal obligations.

The ban was easy to pronounce but proved hard to enforce. Rather than meet Henry's forces on the battlefield, Matilda retreated to her fortress at Canossa.‡ While Henry's main army besieged Rome, Matilda's forces attacked Henry's supply lines and raided the holdings of his northern supporters from the protection of her network of mountain castles. She kept Gregory's communication lines open and provided him with information about Henry's movements—military

---

* At the time, rumors spread that Matilda and Gregory were lovers. Why else would a woman involve herself so closely in the political issues of the day?

Modern historians still bandy this accusation about—Matilda supporters and Matilda bashers alike.

† Many nobles in northern Italy supported Henry. Some doubtless shared his position on lay investiture, but others hoped for a portion of Matilda's vast holdings as a reward for their loyalty.

‡ Not an unusual choice for a medieval commander to make. Sieges and raids were the most common military actions in medieval warfare. Commanders took to the battlefield only when the potential for gain seemed greater than the risk of defeat.

and diplomatic. She exerted enough pressure on Henry's allies from her mountain stronghold that by 1082 his beleaguered supporters insisted he come north and campaign against Matilda in person.

After systematically ravaging the north, Henry besieged Rome itself. He captured the city on March 21, 1084. With Henry in control of the city, Guibert was consecrated as pope on March 24. Seven days later, on Easter Sunday, Guibert returned the favor and crowned Henry as Holy Roman emperor—which had to be a relief to Henry, who had ruled as king of the Germans since 1056 without papally approved imperial authority.

With the imperial crown on his head and a consecrated pope in his pocket, Henry left Rome on May 21, 1084. As he hit the road for Germany, he ordered his Italian allies to capture Matilda and destroy her fortresses, which would secure his lines of communication with Rome and gut the military strength of the papal reformists.

The combined troops of Henry's supporters marched along the Via Emilia, through the Po Valley—pillaging as they went. Matilda monitored their progress from the security of her Apennine fortresses. On the night of July 1, 1084, her opponents camped on the plain at Sorbara, close to one of Matilda's castles. Having crossed the valley from Parma to Modena unopposed, the invaders grew careless and did not set an adequate guard.

The next day, Matilda led a small force in a dawn raid on the sleeping camp of Henry's supporters*—the first time she met imperial forces in open battle in three years. Her troops broke through the camp's outer defenses, causing panic among the enemy ranks. They slaughtered large numbers of fleeing foot soldiers, captured a hundred knights, and took more than five hundred horses as part of their booty. Matilda lost a handful of her men and "no one of note"—the medieval assessment of a successful battle. Sorbara was a major victory in medieval terms and a turning point in the war, giving new hope to the reform party at the moment when Henry seemed triumphant.

For the next six years, Matilda was on the offensive against Henry's supporters. Pope Gregory's death in exile in 1085 did not end

---

* The Battle of Sorbara is an example of how difficult it is to pin down what women warriors actually did. We have four contemporary accounts of the Battle of Sorbara and the events leading up to it, one written by a possible eyewitness—practically live reporting on the evening news for the time. We know she planned the attack and gave the order. We know she commanded troops in a similar action in 1091. Nonetheless, scholars disagree as to whether Matilda personally led her troops into battle at Sorbara.

the conflict. Matilda became the secular rallying point for the reform cause and the armed supporter of two reformist popes in succession: Victor III, whose papacy lasted only four months, and Urban II, who completed Gregory's reforms, launched the first crusade, and left the papacy stronger than he found it.

In the spring of 1090, Henry mounted a counterattack. He seized Matilda's remaining lands in Lorraine, then invaded northern Italy. Over the next two years, he drove his armies toward Canossa. He took city after fortress after city with a combination of military victories and bribery. (The promise of imperial privilege, in which an autonomous town owed fealty only to the emperor, was a tempting offer to towns held in feudal tenure to a more-or-less local lord.) When she lost Mantua and Verona, the first to bribery and the second to betrayal, Matilda fell back south of the river Po. Henry continued to press her.

In September 1092, after a string of imperial victories, Henry offered Matilda generous peace terms if she would recognize Guibert of Ravenna as Pope Clement III. Against the advice of many of her supporters, she refused.

That October, Henry moved against Canossa, hoping to force Matilda to surrender by trapping her in her fortress. Warned of his approach, Matilda withdrew with an armed force to an outlying castle. After Henry exhausted his troops against Canossa, she attacked. Henry's siege turned into a rout, with Matilda's forces harassing the emperor's troops as they retreated in disorder across the Po.

Henry remained in Italy for the next three years, but the war was effectively over.

Whether or not Matilda actively fought, sword in hand, she was a "combatant commander" by any standard. Over the course of a forty-year military career, Matilda mustered troops for long-distance expeditions, fought successful defensive campaigns against the Holy Roman emperor (himself a skilled commander), launched ambushes, engaged in urban warfare, directed sieges, lifted sieges, and was besieged. She built, stocked, and fortified castles. She maintained an effective intelligence network. She negotiated alliances with local leaders. She rewarded her followers with the favorite currencies of medieval rulers: land, castles, and privileges.

Matilda fielded her last military action in 1114, putting down a revolt in the city of Mantua less than a year before her death. Mighty in war to the end.

CHAPTER FIVE

JOAN OF ARC OF
[FILL IN THE BLANK]

When I first told people I was working on a book on women
warriors, almost everyone responded the same way: "You mean
like Joan of Arc?"

Unlike many of the women warriors discussed in this book, Joan
of Arc is not forgotten. Her historical reality is not under dispute. The
documentation for her career is ample, at least by medieval standards.*
She is both the most famous woman warrior in European history, and
in some ways the least typical.† She is the example trotted out as the
exception to the rule that women don't fight. At the same time, she
is the model against which other female resistance fighters are measured. And on occasion a personal hero against which other female
warriors measured themselves: Isabella of Castile, for example, born

---

* The main source for Joan's career is the record of her trial, conducted between January 9 and May 30, 1431. Each day the chief notary of the court and his two assistants
recorded the back-and-forth of the trial in French. Every evening, the three compared
and corrected their work. Notarized copies of both the original and final transcripts still
exist. As a result, in addition to the testimony of many of her contemporaries, we have
Joan's actual words. Even though the trial transcripts are filtered through the male clerics
who recorded them and translated them from her native French into the Latin that was
the language of the law and government in the fifteenth century, her voice leaps from the
page. We also have Joan's letters to various movers and shakers of her world, dictated to a
scribe in a conversational tone rare in documents from the fifteenth century.

† The whole mission-from-God thing, complete with voices, makes her unique. Joan
of Arc was indeed exceptional, but not because she was a woman warrior.

The only picture of Joan of Arc that survives from her lifetime was doodled in the margins of the official records of the Parlement of Paris, next to the entry reporting her victory at Orleans. The clerk who drew it, Clémont de Fauquemberghe, never saw her.

twenty-one years after the Maid of Orleans's death, was an admirer of Joan of Arc and kept a chronicle of Joan's life on her bookshelf. Quite a testament at a time when even royalty owned few books.

Her story is an odd one, even in its most simple form.*

In 1429, France and England had been at war for almost a hundred years.† The French position looked bleak. Seven years after the death

---

* Her story is odder yet when looked at in a broader historical context that includes the bloody civil war that began with the assassination in 1407 of Louis, Duke of Orleans, at the instigation of his brother, the Duke of Burgundy; Joan's place in a lineage of female French mystics; and the internal politics of the French and British courts.

† Or more accurately, the French Valois dynasty and the English Lancastrian dynasty had fought over the throne of France since 1337, when Edward III of England claimed the throne of France through his mother.

of his father, King Charles VI, the Dauphin (also Charles) remained uncrowned while the British fought to hold France in the name of the infant son of Henry V. The English army and its Burgundian allies occupied much of northern France, including Reims, the city where French kings were traditionally crowned. Charles had taken refuge at the castle of Chinon, one hundred fifty miles southwest of Paris. The city of Orleans was under siege. If it fell, England's armies would have open access to Chinon, and to Charles—who, from the English perspective, was a rebel, not the heir to France.

Then a seventeen-year-old peasant girl from a village near the border of the Duchy of Lorraine appeared on the historical stage, claiming the voices of St. Michael, St. Catherine, and St. Margaret had told her it was her mission to put the Dauphin on the throne and save France from the English. Joan convinced the local commander at Vaucouleurs, Robert de Baudricourt, to send her to the Dauphin's court at Chinon, accompanied by six of his knights. With Baudricourt's help, Joan transformed herself from a peasant girl in a homespun red dress into a knight, complete with the expensive accoutrements of horse, retinue, standard, and armor. And not only into a knight—the epitome of male nobility—but a knight with a sacred mission. A crusader.*

Joan's career as warrior was brief. It lasted less than two years—thirteen months of which were spent in captivity.

She arrived at Chinon on March 6. The Dauphin, warned of her arrival, disguised himself as one of his courtiers. Joan picked him out of the crowd—an act seen as miraculous confirmation of both her mission and Charles's claim to the throne.†

A month later, Joan led the French army against the English forces outside Orleans. Once she was at the head of the army, things moved rapidly. In early May, she lifted the siege and forced the English out of the Loire Valley. In late June, at the head of a force of twelve thousand soldiers, she escorted the Dauphin across the dangerous countryside from Chinon to Reims. On July 17, Charles VII was finally crowned

---

* Crusades to the Holy Lands were long over, but the ideal of the Crusades was still very much alive in the fifteenth century as the Ottoman Empire moved west into central Europe. Joan believed in the crusading ethos, not surprising for a woman who heard the voices of saints.

† In a time when the faces of the British royal family are familiar to anyone with access to the internet or a newsstand, it is hard to understand in our guts how marvelous this seemed. Joan would never have seen a picture of Charles—not even on a coin.

in the cathedral at Reims with the Maid of Orleans in a place of honor at his side.

Joan was so successful that the English offered a reward for her capture, similar to the reward the Athenians offered for Artemisia nineteen hundred years earlier. The Burgundians took her at the siege of Compiègne in May 1430—a year after her initial success at Orleans—and sold her to the English for the reward. When the French failed to ransom her, the English turned her over to the Inquisition, which tried her at Rouen on charges of witchcraft, heresy, and dressing like a man.* She was burned at the stake as a heretic on May 30, 1431.

It would be another twenty-five years before the English were driven out of France.

The story of Joan of Arc has proved impossible to erase from history, but it has been rewritten and overwritten and scribbled on by people who insist on coloring outside the lines. Even the name by which we know her is someone else's invention: the name she chose for herself and preferred to use was *Jeanne la Pucelle*, Joan the Maid.

Over time, the phrase the "Joan of Arc of [fill in the blank]" has become shorthand for a (usually young) woman leading an army against an occupying foreign power.† The term has been applied to the solidly historical Ani Pachen of Tibet and the semi-mythical Trieu Thi Trinh of third-century Vietnam.‡ The *Women's Era*, a popular African American women's newspaper founded in 1890, called Harriet

---

* The offenses with which she was charged included five different charges related to her clothing: dressing like a man appears to have been as socially transgressive as witchcraft. It was certainly easier to prove.

† Leaving out the most critical parts of Joan's story: the voices, the religious conviction, the betrayal, and the burning at the stake.

‡ Trieu Thi Trinh's story is a cross between Cinderella and Joan of Arc. Orphaned as a young girl, Trieu Thi Trinh (ca. 222–247 CE) lived with her brother and his (possibly) Chinese wife. Her sister-in-law abused her and treated her as a servant. Finally Trieu Thi Trinh snapped. She killed her sister-in-law and fled to the hills, where she raised an army of a thousand men and women to fight against the Chinese occupiers. Trieu Thi Trinh won more than thirty battles against the Chinese and controlled an independent region for a brief time. When the Chinese defeated her forces, in 247 CE, she is said to have committed suicide, either by jumping in a river or having herself trampled by elephants. By the eighteenth century, Vietnamese nationalists and poets had turned Trieu Thi Trinh into a larger-than-life heroine, nine feet tall, with breasts three feet long, and able to walk five hundred leagues in a single day.

Tubman "the Black Joan of Arc."* Novelist Henry Miller heard the story of Greek nationalist Laskarina Bouboulina and asked, "How is it we don't hear more about Bouboulina? . . . She sounds like another Joan of Arc."[1] Even at the scale of a besieged city, we find a local heroine described as the "Joan of Arc of Braunschweig." Each of these women embodied to some degree what Halina Filipowicz describes as the central element of the "Joan of Arc cult": "a deeply felt need for a democratic hero of unflinching loyalty to a patriotic mission."[2]

The power of the image lasted well into the twentieth century: Soviet sniper Sergeant Vera Danilovtseva recalled that when Germany attacked the Soviet Union on June 21, 1942, "I, of course, immediately imagined myself in the role of Joan of Arc. Only to the front and only with a rifle in my hands."[3]

THE AGES OF REVOLUTION

Political coups, revolutions, and resistance movements against an occupying army or colonial government created women warriors in many times and places. Women fought in revolutions against Spanish control throughout Latin America in the early nineteenth century and against internal tyranny in the twentieth century. Female slaves battled for their personal as well as their national independence in the Haitian Revolution of 1802 to 1804. *Partisanas* took up arms in the Spanish Civil War and the anti-Nazi resistance movements in France, Greece, Italy, and Yugoslavia during World War II.† Women fought in the anticolonial wars that followed the Second World War.

---

* Tubman is best known for rescuing slaves and leading them north to freedom in the decade before the American Civil War, but she was also a highly effective scout for the Union army in the Department of the South. Although she was not a warrior in the technical sense, she was by any standard a leader of a resistance movement.

† A large percentage of the women involved in resistance movements in World War II were not warriors per se, though their jobs were as dangerous as those of their armed counterparts. Because women could move more freely, they carried out critical activities that allowed the armed resistance movements to function. They acted as couriers, collected intelligence, and arranged for food, supplies, and shelter for armed insurgents and downed Allied pilots. They transported weapons and ammunition and distributed illegal printed materials, sometimes using the trappings of pregnancy and motherhood to help them smuggle contraband under the eyes of German soldiers. Without them, the armed groups could not have carried out their actions, yet historians often describe their work as "passive resistance." They may not have been warriors as defined in this book, but they were not passive by any reasonable definition of the term.

In Vietnam, members of the so-called "long-hair army" were guerrilla fighters, served in antiaircraft artillery units, and fought in local militia units in Vietcong-controlled areas in South Vietnam. In the 1950s, Kikuyu women served with the forest combat forces of the Mau Mau rebellion in Kenya, and Muslim women fought in the Algerian wars for independence. Thousands of women joined the guerrilla armies of the late-twentieth-century revolutions in Africa, Asia, and Latin America—making up perhaps as much as 30 percent of these forces.* Beginning in 2014, between seven thousand and ten thousand Kurdish women joined the ongoing fight against ISIS in the Middle East. That same year, the so-called "invisible battalion" of women in the Ukrainian army became unacknowledged combatants in antiterrorist operations in the undeclared war with Russia.†

The one thing all these "Joans" have in common is a climate of national crisis.

"TWO SISTERS PROUDLY STOOD UP TO AVENGE THE COUNTRY"

In 39 CE, two young women led Vietnam in its first rebellion against China, which had then ruled the country for 150 years. They are often referred to as the Joans of Arc of Vietnam.

The Trung sisters, Trung Trac and Trung Nhi, were born in north Vietnam around 14 CE.‡ They were the daughters of a chieftain in

---

* Thirty percent seems to be the canonical estimate of the female component of any revolutionary force from the end of the eighteenth century through yesterday—suggesting it may be no more reliable than troop estimates in the ancient world. Perhaps it tells us as much about the desires and perceptions of those who report them as it does about the actual number of female combatants. To put this number in context, according to the *White House Project: Benchmarking Women's Leadership*, women on active duty made up 14.3 percent of the American military in 2008. Quoted in Rosemarie Skaine, *Women in Combat: A Reference Handbook* (Santa Barbara, CA: ABC-CLIO, 2011), 179. The percentages of women in the military in France, Germany, and the United Kingdom for the same year were 14.6, 8.3, and 9.3, respectively. See Irène Eulriet, *Women and the Military in Europe: Comparing Public Cultures* (Houndmills, UK: Palgrave Macmillan, 2012), 111.

† The "invisible battalions" became somewhat less invisible in 2017, with the release of an eponymous documentary film and companion report funded by the Ukrainian Women's Fund.

‡ Our earliest written accounts for the Trung sisters are Chinese. The sisters do not appear in Vietnamese accounts until the thirteenth century, by which time they were already semimythical figures. The modern historian is left navigating between hostility and disdain on the one hand and hagiography on the other.

A highly stylized image of the Trung sisters going into battle.

the Son Tay region.* We know little about their lives before 36 CE, when a new, more oppressive governor named To Dinh took over the province. He demanded bribes. He raised taxes on salt.† He imposed new taxes on the peasants, including one on fishing in the rivers. In short, he was the type of greedy and inept official whose actions typically trigger a rebellion in classical Chinese histories.

Trung Trac, together with her husband, Thi Sách, mobilized the local aristocracy to revolt. Learning of their plots and assuming Thi Sách was the driving force of the conspiracy, To Dinh had him arrested and executed, then hung his body from the city gates as a warning to other would-be rebels.‡

To Dinh's efforts to put down the rebellion backfired. Instead of giving up, the sisters raised an army of eighty thousand troops,§ most of them in their twenties and a large number of them women. Vietnamese sources claim that in one province alone, thirty-two of the

---

* Not to be confused with the Tay Son district, which would play a role in the career of Cheng I Sao more than a millennium later.

† Always a bad idea. Salt is more than just a condiment.

‡ According to one modern scholar, Keith Weller Taylor, Vietnamese scholars invented Thi Sách's death. He claims that Chinese evidence suggests Thi Sách lived and followed his wife into battle. I would love to believe this is true.

§ A number most historians take with a large grain of salt, for all the usual reasons.

army's sixty-nine generals were women, including the Trungs' elderly mother, who legend says trained the sisters in the arts of war.[*]

The Trungs and their untrained army drove the Chinese from Vietnam and created a new state that stretched from Hue in the south into southern China. To Dinh was so terrified he disguised himself by shaving off his hair and fled the country in secret.

For two years, the Trung sisters ruled their kingdom unchallenged. In 41 CE, the Chinese emperor Guang Wu Di sent one of his best generals, Ma Yüan, south to reconquer Vietnam. The sisters defended their borders against the Chinese for some time, but eventually they were overwhelmed by the empire's military and financial superiority. The Trungs fought their final battle in 43 CE, near modern Hanoi. According to Chinese sources, thousands of Vietnamese soldiers were captured and beheaded, and more than ten thousand surrendered.

The Trung sisters were not among those who surrendered. Some Chinese sources report Ma Yüan captured and executed them, then sent their heads to the Han court. Others state the sisters died in battle. Vietnamese sources—written centuries after the fact with a vested interest in portraying the Trungs as heroines—claim they committed suicide by drowning themselves in the Hat Giang River.

In the centuries that followed, a popular Buddhist cult developed around the sisters. Temples were built in their honor and individual villages celebrated the names and exploits of the Trungs' female followers. Anticolonial writers held up the Trung sisters as idealized examples of national courage in the struggle against first Chinese and later French domination.

Today they are remembered as national heroines in Vietnam, where the traditional anniversary of their suicides is a national holiday.

THE LIEUTENANT COLONEL

In July 2015, Argentina replaced the statue of Christopher Columbus that stood outside its presidential palace with one celebrating the

---

[*] Vietnamese accounts emphasize the large number of women in the army. By the nineteenth century, Vietnamese writers used this theme as a way to shame their male contemporaries for failing to rise up against first the Chinese and then the French. As one fifteenth-century Vietnamese poet put it: "All the male heroes bowed their head in submission; / Only the two sisters proudly stood up to avenge the country." Quoted in Keith Weller Taylor, "The Trung Sisters in the Literature of Later Centuries," in *Southeast Asian History: Essential Readings*, ed. D. R. SarDesai (Boulder, CO: Westview Press, 2013), 65.

country's war of independence. Instead of erecting a statue commemorating Simon Bolivar or José de San Martín, they chose to honor a woman warrior: Juana Azurduy de Padilla (c. 1780–1862).

The spirit of revolution that began with Britain's North American colonies and took new form in the first French Revolution in 1789 needed only a spark to ignite in Spain's Latin American colonies. In the spring of 1808, Napoleon's conquest of Spain and the forced abdications of first King Carlos IV and then his son and successor Ferdinand VII in favor of Napoleon's brother, Joseph Bonaparte, provided that spark. A few weeks after their abdications, rebels under the leadership of Simon Bolivar (1783–1830) fought to throw off colonial rule in country after country. Women fought alongside men in each country's war of independence and in the civil wars that often followed them.*

Juana Azurduy de Padilla was born in the area around the city of Chuquisaca (now Sucre, Bolivia), in what was then known as the Upper Peru region of the Viceroyalty of Rio de Plata. Accounts of her childhood vary, but they all agree on a few points: she was probably of mestizo origin, she received a convent education, and she was a rebellious student.

In 1805, she married Manuel Padilla, who would be her partner in fighting for her country's independence.

Four years later, on May 25, 1809, radicals took to the streets in Chuquisaca, making it the first city in Latin America to rise up against colonial rule after Ferdinand's abdication. The initial revolt ended with a decisive defeat of republican armies by royalist forces at the battle of Huaqui on June 20, 1811. The victory at Huaqui returned nominal control of Upper Peru to the royalists, but the region remained a central battleground between royalist and republican forces for the next seven years. By 1813 the surrounding countryside was dominated by six *republiquetas* (little republics) run by guerrilla commanders who continued to fight in the name of independence.

---

* Latin American specialist Catherine Davies reports historical accounts of at least ninety "prominent" women soldiers in those wars. See Catherine Davies, Claire Brewster, and Hilary Owen, *South American Independence: Gender, Politics, Text* (Liverpool: Liverpool University Press, 2006), 22. That number does not include the anonymous women who served as foot soldiers or camp followers in revolutionary armies. During the Mexican War of Independence, 20 to 30 percent of most rebel armies were women. (There's that number again!) While their primary function was grinding the corn that was the army's main food staple, they could and did pick up weapons and join their male comrades in battle.

Azurduy and Padilla, ardent supporters of the rebellion from the beginning, commanded the Republiqueta de La Laguna in the region of Potosí, from which they organized attacks against royalist forces and kept the road between Chuquisaca and Buenos Aires open for republican troops. Accompanied by a bodyguard of twenty-five women, known as the Amazons,* Azurduy commanded a group of male soldiers called the Leales (the Loyal Ones). She is known to have fought in at least sixteen major battles against the royalists and earned a reputation for daring on the battlefield.

The couple shared power and command of their *republiqueta* and their forces until Padilla's death in September 1816. Azurduy continued the fight without him, perhaps pursuing vengeance as well as liberty. She fled to Salta, in what is now northwest Argentina, where she and her troops joined forces with the local insurgent leader Martin Güemes, fighting under his leadership until he was murdered in 1821.

When Upper Peru won its independence in 1825, Azurduy returned to Chuquisaca.

The government of Buenos Aires recognized Azurduy's bravery on the field by awarding her the rank of lieutenant colonel in August 1816. She paid a high personal cost for that rank and for her country's freedom. Her husband died on the battlefield. Four of her five children died of malnutrition and disease in the guerrilla camps, where she gave birth to the fifth. The country she fought for promised her a pension, but never paid her. On May 26, 1862, Juana Azurduy de Padilla died alone and impoverished.

Today both Bolivia and Argentina recognize her as a national heroine.

LADY CAPTAIN

In the early years of the nineteenth century, wealthy shipowner Laskarina Bouboulina (1771–1825) commanded a fleet in the War of Greek Independence against the Ottoman Empire.†

---

* Just as women who led troops in battle are often described as the "Joan of Arc of wherever," Amazon (capitalized or not) is often a shorthand description for groups of women warriors. Perhaps the underlying thought is that a troop of women warriors must be a myth.

† Bouboulina left traces in contemporary accounts of the War of Greek Independence and in the archival records of the Ottoman Empire. Her personal documents and possessions are preserved at her home in Spetses, which is now a museum run by her descendants. She is also remembered in oral tradition and folk songs.

Bouboulina was the daughter of a Greek ship's captain from the island of Hydra, Stavrianos Pinotsis, and his wife, Skevo. Stavrianos was imprisoned for his participation in a failed rebellion against the Ottomans in 1769–1770. Bouboulina was born in the prison in Constantinople (modern Istanbul) where he was held. Her father died soon after. It is not unreasonable to assume she grew up with a grudge against the Ottomans.

After her husband's death, Skevo took her infant daughter home to Hydra. Four years later, she married again. Her new husband was also a sea captain, this time from the island of Spetses. According to some accounts, Bouboulina's stepfather encouraged her interest in ships and the family business—both the interest and the encouragement were unusual for the time and place.*

Like her mother, Bouboulina married twice: the first time at the age of seventeen to Dimitrios Yiannouzas and again at the age of thirty to Dimitrios Bouboulis. Both her husbands were Spetsiot sea captains. Both died in sea battles with the Algerian pirates who often raided the coasts of Greece.

The death of her second husband in 1811 left Bouboulina a wealthy widow with six children. Many women in her position would have relied on a male relative to manage their fortune. Bouboulina took over management of both of her husbands' mercantile shipping businesses. She proved to be a successful businesswoman.

In 1816, Ottoman officials gave Bouboulina a new reason to dislike the Turkish government: it tried to seize her fortune on the grounds that her second husband had fought on the Russian side in the Turco-Russian wars.† She retained her fortune, reputedly helped by the sultan's mother, who convinced her son to intervene on Bouboulina's behalf.‡

Bouboulina was not the only Greek to resent Turkish rule in the early nineteenth century. Greeks had been part of the Ottoman Empire for roughly four hundred years. For much of that time, they had enjoyed a privileged position. Educated Greeks dominated the

---

* A variation on the Tomboy Syndrome, with the male arena of ships and business replacing riding and weapons training.

† Not an unfounded accusation. The Russian government awarded him with the title of captain in the Russian navy for his services and made him an honorary Russian citizen.

‡ Popular accounts claim the sultana made her promise to defend Ottoman women when the opportunity came—a fairy-tale twist to the story with later real-life consequences.

Ottoman administration and Greek merchants held a near monopoly on trade in the Turkish Mediterranean. Privilege is not the same thing as independence, however.* In the late eighteenth century, vague discontent turned into Greek nationalism thanks to two international movements. Romantic Hellenism created an interest in ancient Greek mythology and literature throughout Europe, bringing with it a renewed sense of ancient Greece as the birthplace of democracy. At the same time, the revolutionary ideals of the American and French revolutions led nationalist groups across Europe to dream of new states based on shared languages and culture rather than imperial provinces shaped by the political maneuvering of the great imperial powers.†

In 1816, members of the Greek merchant diaspora in Odessa founded a secret society dedicated to liberating Greece from Ottoman rule, the Filiki Eteria. By the early 1820s, hundreds of wealthy and educated Greeks belonged to the society—intellectuals, shipowners and sea captains, members of the clergy, landowners, and merchants. Bouboulina purportedly became the only female member of the Filiki Eteria, though her name does not appear among the 1,093 names on the surviving membership lists.‡ Whether she was an official member of the organization, or an unofficial one-woman ladies' auxiliary, she devoted her fleet and her fortune to the independence movement.

Buying arms and ammunition in foreign ports and smuggling them into Spetses in her ships was risky enough, but Bouboulina also commissioned a Spetses shipyard to build a warship, the *Agamemnon*§—an in-your-face act of rebellion that brought Bouboulina to the attention of Ottoman officials once again. The Ottomans imposed strict limits on how large Greek-owned ships could be and the size and number of armaments they could carry. The *Agamemnon* did not meet those standards. The Ottomans accused Bouboulina of secretly

---

* Revolutions often begin among the relatively privileged who aspire to more rather than among the poorest of the poor.

† The Greeks were not the only ethnic group chafing under Ottoman control. The Serbs were the first to rise up, in a bloody and unsuccessful bid for independence that lasted from 1804 to 1813.

‡ Bouboulina may have been the only female member of Filiki Eteria, but she wasn't the only woman to fight for Greek independence. Manto Mavrogenous (1796–1848), the daughter of a wealthy Greek merchant, outfitted and commanded two ships in the war.

§ A provocative name for a Greek-owned ship. Agamemnon, the king of kings who led the combined Greek forces against Troy, was an unambiguous symbol of Greece unified in war.

building a warship—as in fact she was. She bribed the officials and completed the construction of the ship without incident. At 108 feet long, with eighteen heavy cannons, the *Agamemnon* was the first and largest ship in the Greek fleet.*

The War of Greek Independence began on March 25, 1821, with an unsuccessful raid into Moldavia by a band of Greek expatriates led by Alexander Ypsilantis, the head of Filiki Eteria. Two weeks later, the region known as the Peloponnesus, including the island of Spetses, rose in revolt.

Fifty-year-old Bouboulina paid for and commanded four ships in addition to the Agamemnon, and a small private army of Spetsiots. Her ships were captained by her sons and half-brothers, several of whom died over the course of the rebellion. She called her troops her "brave lads"; they named her Kapetanisa (Lady Captain).

Soon after the war broke out, Bouboulina blockaded the port at Nafplion, a key Ottoman stronghold. Nafplion was guarded by three fortresses and armed with three hundred cannons. "Everyone" considered the fort to be impregnable. Bouboulina proved everyone wrong. Nineteenth-century Greek historian Anargyros Hatzi-Anargyrou wrote an eyewitness account of her assault on Nafplion:

> On December 4, 1821, as I remember, on board her own vessel, she alone gave orders for the boats to attack the fort. They immediately sail forward but a rain of bullets and cannon fire from the seaside fortifications make her brave lads fall back for a moment. Like an angry Amazon, watching the battle over the side of her boat, she then shouts—Are you women then and not men?† Forward! Her officers obey, regroup and attack—they fight but die in vain, since the fort was impregnable by sea. For this reason, she herself lands with her forces and stays until the fall of the fort on 30th November 1822, leading her men in battle, spending her fortune."[4]

---

* To put this in context, HMS *Victory*, Lord Nelson's flagship at the Battle of Trafalgar, was more than 227 feet long and carried 104 guns. Even frigates, the smallest ships used by the British navy, carried between twenty and forty-eight cannons. By the standards of the time, the rest of Europe would have considered the *Agamemnon* an armed merchant vessel, not a war ship.

† A reminder that women warriors are not immune to the cultural assumptions of their times. More than one woman warrior has played the "if a mere woman can do this, so can you" card. In fact, Russia created an army unit made up entirely of women warriors on this principle in World War I.

In the following years, Bouboulina participated in other military engagements against the Ottomans. Her most famous action occurred in September 1821, after the Turkish position at Tripolis fell to besieging Greek forces. The fall of the city was followed by three days of massacre and looting that left thirty thousand dead. Bouboulina led her sailors into the town, where, at the risk of her own life, she defended the women and children who lived in the harem of the city's ruler—reportedly because of the promise she had made to the sultan's mother.

At the end of 1824, while war with the Ottomans continued, civil war broke out between opposing factions of rebels over leadership of the new Greek state. Connected by marriage to one of the rival leaders, Bouboulina was deemed a dangerous opponent to the Greek government and arrested twice. Finally, she was exiled to Spetses.

She remained in Spetses until her death on May 22, 1825, five years before the formation of an independent Greek state recognized by the European powers. Instead of dying in the battle for Greek freedom, she was killed by a stray bullet fired in a vendetta with another Spetsiot family. She was impoverished at her death, having lost her sons, her ships, and her considerable fortune in pursuit of Greek independence.

Greece gave her the honorary title of admiral after her death. (And yes, her image appeared on a Greek postage stamp in 1930, commemorating the hundredth anniversary of Greek independence.)

EMILIA PLATER

Polish nationalist Countess Emilia Plater (1806–1831) fought in the November Insurrection of 1830–31, a failed attempt to liberate Poland and formerly Polish territories in the Russian client-states of Lithuania, Belorussia, and Ukraine from Russian occupation.[*]

Plater was born in Vilnius, in what was then the Russian-held sector of partitioned Poland. She was a member of one of the oldest

---

* Much of what we know about Plater comes from *The Life of the Countess Emily Plater* (1835), a biography by her relative and fellow Polish nationalist Jósef Straszewicz (1801–1838). Published in 1835, the biography is shaped by Straszewicz's desire to promote the Polish cause in the west. Like Donizo of Canossa's biography of Matilda of Tuscany, Straszewicz's biography of Plater is told as the story of a heroic life, with inconvenient truths covered over with flowery prose.

and most powerful aristocratic families in the region. (Again, privilege is not the same thing as independence.)

The stories of Plater's childhood, filtered through Straszewicz's nationalist agenda, give us the picture of a woman raised to be a national heroine. Brought up by her mother after her parents separated, she received a classical education, unusual for a woman at the time, with a strong emphasis on Polish patriotism. She learned to ride and shoot. And she consciously modeled herself on heroines of the past, most notably Joan of Arc.*

The November Insurrection, also known as the Cadet Revolution, began in Warsaw. Tsar Nicholas I feared the revolutions that had broken out in France, the Papal States, and Belgium would spread across Europe, not unreasonable given the nationalist aspirations inspired by the first French Revolution in the subject peoples of Europe's great empires. On November 19, he ordered the Polish army to march west and reestablish order in France while Russian troops took their place in Poland. Polish nationalists saw the arrival of Russian troops as the first step in abolishing what little autonomy the kingdom of Poland possessed.†

As was the case in many European countries in the mid-nineteenth century, a secret organization of students, nationalists, and the socially discontented was in place and eager to take action. On November 29, before the Polish troops marched out, a group of nationalists attacked the Belvedere Palace with the goal of killing the Grand Duke Constantine, who was the tsar's younger brother and the de facto ruler of Poland. At the same time, cadets from the infantry officer school stormed the Russian army barracks. Neither attack succeeded, but the attempt inspired a popular uprising in the city. Civilian volunteers stormed the city arsenal, armed themselves, and took control of a portion of Warsaw. All but two of the Polish generals and most of the army joined the rebellion. So much for putting down the revolution in France.

---

* Presumably she took the heroic portion of Joan's story as her example rather than the hearing-voices and burned-at-the-stake parts.

† Not without reason. The Holy Alliance of Russia, Prussia, and the Hapsburg Empire had carved Poland into bits at the end of the eighteenth century. In theory, the (much-reduced) kingdom of Poland was an autonomous state, but since Tsar Nicholas was also the king of Poland, its autonomy was theoretical indeed.

When news of the uprising reached Vilnius in the spring of 1831, Plater joined the struggle without hesitation. She had always claimed she would someday be a soldier and now her chance had come. She cut her hair, put on a military uniform,* and organized a force of three hundred volunteers—including two of her cousins, who were cadets at the local military academy. Plater's volunteers fought in several skirmishes against Russian troops. She then joined forces with another insurgent unit, and took part in capturing the city of Ukmerge.

In June, a large force of Polish rebels under the command of General Dezydery Chlapowski (1788–1879) and a combined Polish-Lithuanian force under Antoni Gielgud (1792–1831) reinforced the Lithuanian rebels. As the newly appointed commander of the Lithuanian army, Chlapowski organized the insurgent forces into regular military units—never a promising situation for a woman warrior. He tried to convince Plater to go home. Plater refused and declared herself determined to fight until Poland was free. Impressed with her determination, he gave her the rank of captain and named her the commander of the First Company of the First Lithuanian Infantry Regiment. She fought in the capture of Kaunus on June 25, in which her company was decimated, and distinguished herself in a failed Polish attack on the garrison of Szawel.

The attack on Szawel was one of the last Polish actions in Lithuania. Faced with superior Russian strength, the Polish high command ordered its forces to retreat into Prussian territory, where they surrendered. Instead of retreating with the rest of the army, Plater decided to make her way to Warsaw, where rebel units continued the fight. She fell ill along the way and took shelter in a manor on the Polish-Lithuanian border, where she died on December 23.

Plater spent only three months in battle. Her actions did nothing to change the course of history, or even the course of the rebellion.†

---

* Durova explained in her memoir why she owned a uniform. No one says where Plater got hers. Did she have one hanging in her armoire, waiting for her chance? Did she borrow one from a male cousin?

† The November Insurrection was a disaster from the perspective of Polish independence. Many of the participants in the uprising were sent to Siberia; others fled to western Europe and the United States. The Polish army was disbanded. The Constitution of 1815 was replaced with a more restrictive charter, which abolished elected institutions. Freedom of the press was curtailed and Warsaw University was closed. Both Poland and Lithuania remained under foreign control until the end of World War I, when they enjoyed a brief period of independence before their occupation by Nazi Germany and subsequent return to Russian control as part of the Soviet Bloc.

JOAN OF ARC OF [FILL IN THE BLANK] 123

But those three months were enough to make her a symbol of Polish patriotism, both at home and abroad.* She was the subject of paintings, songs, dramas, and, most notably, a popular poem by fellow Pole Adam Mickiewicz, "The Death of the Colonel" (1832). (Mickiewicz not only promoted her from captain to colonel, but transformed her into a leader of the insurrection—something not even her biographer, Straszewicz, claimed.) In France, where the Polish insurrection was believed to have kept Russia from taking action against France's own uprising in 1830, Plater's story was compared to that of Joan of Arc, with Plater proclaimed another Joan of Arc. One author even claimed Saint Joan had sent Plater to fight for Polish freedom and crush *l'ignoble barbarie* of Russia—apparently not noticing that neither end had been accomplished.[5]

THE BATTLE WHERE THE GIRL SAVED HER BROTHER

In 1876, a Cheyenne woman named Buffalo Calf Road Woman took part in the so-called Sioux Wars, fought between the United States and the Native American nations of the American West—a war of conquest by any standard. As is so often the case, details about her life are scanty.† She was probably born in the 1850s. She was married to a Cheyenne warrior, Black Coyote, with whom she had two children. She made her mark on history at the battles of Rosebud River and Little Bighorn, where she fought alongside her brother and husband.

The road to Little Bighorn began in 1874, when American soldiers discovered gold in the Black Hills of South Dakota. Recent treaties with the United States government had guaranteed the tribes of the

---

* At least four other women are known to have fought in the insurrection, one of whom served as Plater's aide-de-camp. None of them enjoyed Plater's posthumous fame.

† For many years, most of our information about Buffalo Calf Road Woman came from accounts by two North Cheyenne women, Kate Bighead and Iron Teeth—oral histories collected in the late 1920s by amateur historian Thomas Bailey Marquis (1869–1935). In June 2005, male Cheyenne storytellers shared their version of Buffalo Calf Road Woman's story for the first time. Cheyenne storytellers gave a public presentation of their official oral traditions regarding the defeat of the Seventh Cavalry at the Battle of Little Bighorn—the kick-off for a Cheyenne oral history project. According to Cheyenne elder Frank Rowland, the Cheyenne took a hundred-year vow of silence about the events of 1876 for fear of retribution from the United States government (Martin J. Kidston, "Northern Cheyenne Break Vow of Silence," *Helena Independent Record*, June 27, 2005). Evidently North Cheyenne women didn't take the same vow of silence.

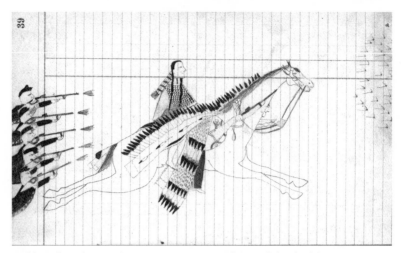

Buffalo Calf Road Woman's story as it appears in a Cheyenne ledger-book history, ca. 1889.

northern plains control of the region, which was prime hunting territory and sacred ground for the tribes. The discovery of gold changed everything—at least from the viewpoint of those who believed that the desires of white settlers took priority over treaty obligations. At first the United States Army made a half-hearted attempt to keep prospectors out, but as mining towns like Deadwood sprang up in the treaty territory, the focus shifted. Since the army couldn't keep the settlers out, it decided to remove the Native American tribes.

The United States government ordered all native peoples who remained in the Black Hills to relocate to the Sioux reservation in South Dakota by January 1876.* Any tribes who failed to relocate faced forcible removal by the army. This was a clear violation of the treaty.

Many Cheyenne refused to relocate to the reservation. Instead they moved to the area between the Powder and Bighorn rivers. Over time, the Cheyenne were joined by various groups of Sioux. By the summer of 1876, six separate tribal circles and their chiefs—a group estimated at between eight thousand to ten thousand men, women,

---

* A reminder: the tribes were independent nations, not subjects of the United States, and under no obligation to obey its orders.

and children—had set up camp together, including Buffalo Calf Road Woman; her husband, Black Coyote; their daughter; and Buffalo Calf Road Woman's brother, Comes-in-Sight.

General A. H. Terry, commander of the US Army troops in the area, devised a three-pronged campaign to drive the tribes from the disputed area. General George Crook was to head north toward the area surrounding Rosebud and Little Bighorn from his head-quarters at Fort Fetterman, in what is now Wyoming. General John Gibbon was to travel south along the Bighorn—a move designed to catch the tribes between his troops and Crook's. A third force, the Seventh Cavalry under General George Custer, would approach the lower Rosebud from the east, with the job of driving the tribes back toward Crook and Gibbon.

Two of the three forces made contact with the tribes, though not with the results General Terry anticipated. Buffalo Calf Road Woman took part in both conflicts.

Crook was the first to encounter the loose confederation of tribes. Crook's force was made up of forty-seven officers and a thousand enlisted men (cavalry and infantry alike) as well as sev-eral hundred Crow and Shoshone auxiliaries.* When the Chey-enne heard Crook was leading a war party against them, several hundred Cheyenne and Sioux warriors, including Buffalo Calf Road Woman, her husband, and her brother, rode out to stop them. They attacked Crook and his soldiers near Rosebud Creek on June 17. It was at this battle that Buffalo Calf Road Woman earned her reputation as a warrior.†

The battle lasted for six hours, fought back and forth across a field that extended for several miles along the Rosebud River. During the course of the battle, Comes-in-Sight's horse was shot down in front of Crook's infantry line. Buffalo Calf Road Woman charged through enemy gunfire to rescue him. Comes-in-Sight mounted behind her and she carried him to safety. Historians of the American West know

---

* The Indian Wars were never as simple as white settlers versus Native Americans. Rivalries and resentments between the different tribes added a layer of complexity to every engagement.

† Or more accurately, this battle is the first appearance of Buffalo Calf Road Woman in our sources. For all we know, she could have fought alongside the male Cheyenne for years.

the events of June 17, 1876, as the Battle of Rosebud River; the Cheyenne call it the Battle Where the Girl Saved Her Brother.*

Eight days later, Custer attacked the encampment at the Little Bighorn—an unplanned attack against a force that proved to be much larger than his scouts reported. A few women accompanied the men as they rushed onto the battlefield: they tended the horses, sang "strong heart" songs of encouragement, and watched for fallen or injured men.

According to both Kate Bighead (who was on the field that day) and Iron Teeth (who was not), only one woman went to the battlefield with the intention of fighting: Buffalo Calf Road Woman. Armed with a six-shooter and "plenty of bullets for it,"[6] she rode and shot alongside her husband throughout the battle. More recently, (male) Cheyenne storytellers credit Buffalo Calf Road Woman with delivering the blow that knocked Custer off his horse and attribute the general's subsequent death to the women gathered at the battlefield.†

The Cheyenne and Lakota won the battles of Rosebud River and Little Bighorn, but lost the effort to remain free of the reservation. In 1877, after two years of being hounded by the United States army, Buffalo Calf Road Woman and the other Northern Cheyenne surrendered with Crazy Horse at Fort Robinson. Instead of being sent to the Sioux reservation, as they expected, the Northern Cheyenne were relocated to Indian Territory (modern Oklahoma). After a year of starvation and disease, three hundred Cheyenne fled the Indian Territory, Buffalo Calf Road Woman among them.

The Northern Cheyenne Exodus began as an attempt to rejoin other Cheyenne in the northern plains; it turned into a running battle with the US Army across Kansas and Nebraska. Our only glimpse of Buffalo Calf Road Woman during this time comes from historian and novelist Mari Sandoz, who places Buffalo Calf Road Woman at

---

* Buffalo Calf Road Woman wasn't the only woman at the battle on the Rosebud River. A Crow woman named The Other Magpie worked as a scout for General Crook, reportedly seeking revenge for the death of her brother at the hands of the Sioux. Everything we know about The Other Magpie comes from an interview with Pretty Shield, published by Montana ethnographer Frank Bird Linderman in 1932 as *Red Mother*. Pretty Shield claimed all the women could tell this story but the men would not talk of it—a statement that sums up the treatment of women warriors in historical accounts across cultures.

† Frank Rowland ends this account with a small dig at both Custer and the Cheyenne women: "When he fell, he wasn't touched by the warriors because he was unclean. He was bad medicine." In other words, he wasn't good enough for the men to kill.

the Battle of Punished Woman's Ford in Kansas on September 17, 1878—"a gun in her hands, ready, the baby tied securely to her back."[7]

In the spring of 1879, they were captured and imprisoned at Fort Keogh, Nebraska, where Buffalo Calf Road Woman succumbed to the "white man's coughing disease"—probably diphtheria. Buried in the rocky hills outside Fort Keogh, she largely disappeared from history, erased not only by "white man's history" but by her male tribesmen's vow of silence.

Not all women who fight to liberate their country achieve the status of national heroine. For every Emilia Plater, there were other women who fought alongside her who are forgotten. For every Bui Thi Xuan,[*] Pearl Witherington,[†] or Teurai Ropa (Spill Blood),[‡] there were

---

[*] Bui Thi Xuan (d. 1802) led armies against the Nguyen dynasty in the Tay Son Rebellion in eighteenth-century Vietnam. She was enough of a threat to the Nguyen that they sentenced her to being trampled to death by an elephant after her defeat. Vietnamese nationalists later used her story as an emblem of resistance against the French and the Nguyen puppet court at Hue.

[†] Witherington (1914–2008) was a member of the British Special Operations Executive (SOE) and a leader of a French *maquis* during World War II. Parachuted into occupied France on September 22, 1943, she was assigned as a courier to an SOE network run by Maurice Southgate. When the Gestapo arrested Southgate in May 1944, Witherington and another operative divided the network into two sections. Witherington took over as leader of the new Wrestler network. Under her command, the group of two thousand *maquisards* were primarily engaged in sabotage, including attacking rail lines between Paris and Bordeaux and severing German telephone communications around Orleans in anticipation of the D-Day landing. She was so effective Germany offered a million francs for her capture—$29 million in 2016 dollars. At war's end, she was recommended for the Military Cross. Since Britain did not award that honor to women, she received a civil honor instead, the Member of the British Empire. She returned it, with a note stating she had done nothing "civil" in the war.

[‡] In 1973, Joyce Mugario Nhongo (b. 1955) changed her name to Teurai Ropa and joined the Zimbabwe African National Union (ZANU), which was waging a guerrilla war against Ian Smith's white supremacist regime. At eighteen, she was the only woman among a cadre of men who trained in using AK rifles and submachine guns. At twenty-two, she became the youngest member of the Central Committee and the National Executive of ZANU. Teurai Ropa was not just a political operative—she was an active combatant. When Rhodesian soldiers attacked her camp in 1978, she fought in its defense even though she was in the last stages of pregnancy. She gave birth to her daughter, Priscilla Rungano, three days later. A month after giving birth, Teurai Ropa sent her infant daughter to safety and continued to fight until Rhodesia (renamed Zimbabwe) gained independence in 1980. Unlike her nineteenth-century counterparts, Teurai Ropa played a role in her country's new government, including a ten-year stint as her country's vice president, from 2004 to 2014.

hundreds of women warriors whose service to their country is at best remembered as part of a collective. The Resistance. The Guerrilla Girls of Zimbabwe. The "long-haired army."

Those freedom fighters who are honored as national heroines have streets and schools and airports named after them. They are the subjects of heroic sculptures and commemorative postage stamps. Their stories are told in bowdlerized versions for school children.* A few with particularly colorful (i.e., blood-red) stories have found fame beyond their national borders as characters in history-based video games.

At the highest level, the memory of national heroines inspires new generations of national heroines. Joan of Arc is the most well-known example of this, but she is not the only heroine to inspire others.

In World War II alone, three different military organizations invoked the memories of earlier women warriors and thereby claimed their places in their national lineages of freedom fighters. The Emilia Plater Independent Women's Battalion was an all-female Polish combat unit formed of volunteers who had fled to the Soviet Union after the German occupation of Poland. Only a small number of the Polish women serving during the war were part of this battalion, but Polish military women on the eastern front were commonly known as Plateróki.† Laskarina Bouboulina was commemorated in the Bouboulina group—an underground resistance organization during the German occupation of Greece in the Second World War. Bouboulina's great-granddaughter, Lela Karagianni (1898–1944), whom German interrogators would describe as "the most dangerous spy in the Balkans," ran the organization.[8] And in Burma, the women's branch of the Indian National Army, a military organization dedicated to winning India's freedom from the British, was known as the Rani of Jhansi Brigade after the queen who won the respect of her military opponents, if not the right to retain her kingdom.

Each of these organizations looked back to a woman who had been acclaimed as the Joan of Arc of her time and place, making them, perhaps, Joan of Arc once removed.

---

* Many of their stories would not earn a PG rating without serious editing.

† There is a certain irony here, since Emilia Plater fought for Poland's freedom from Russia.

CHAPTER SIX

WO-MANNING
THE RAMPARTS

I n the fifth century BCE, the Greek poet Telesilla led the women of
Argos in a backs-to-the-wall defense of their city against the Spartan army.*

Sparta was the dominant power in Greece. The city-state had conquered or made alliance with most of the powers in the region. In 494
BCE, it attacked the last independent city-state—Argos. The Spartans quickly defeated the Argive army. The remaining Argive soldiers
fled, taking sanctuary in a sacred grove. The Spartans pursued them
and set the grove on fire. There were no survivors. With the Argive
army destroyed, the Spartan king, Cleomenes, led his forces to the
city of Argos, expecting the inhabitants to surrender. Bad call.

---

* Once again, our primary sources for the story are primary in the sense of being
our main sources, not in the sense of being eyewitness or contemporary accounts. We
have two major sources for Telesilla's story. The Roman historian Plutarch (26–120 AD)
included the story in a section of his *Moralia*, titled "Bravery of Women," which he wrote
after a conversation on the equality of the sexes with his friend Clea, a high-ranking
priestess at Delphi. The story also appears in a work titled *Description of Greece: A Travel
Account by a Second-Century Greek Geographer Named Pausanias*. Scholars believe that
both Plutarch and Pausanias got the story from an Argive historian named Sokrates.
Surprisingly, Herodotus, who usually loves a good tale about a woman warrior, does not
include the incident in his account of the battle between Sparta and Argos—perhaps
because he used Spartan sources, which may well have downplayed their defeat at the
hands of a group of women led by a poet.

Inside the city walls, the poet Telesilla called on the women of Argos to defend their homes and children. Under her leadership, they armed themselves with any weapons their men had left behind, plus the ceremonial weapons from the city's temples, and the Bronze Age equivalents of carving knives and cast-iron skillets. They followed Telesilla to the city walls, where they waited for the Spartan attack. When the Spartans broke through the city gates, the Argive women fought ferociously. Finally the Spartans retreated, "reflecting that victory, purchased by the slaughter of women, would be odious and defeat shameful."[1]

When the battle was over, the surviving Argive women buried their dead along the road to the city gate, adapting the custom of burying fallen warriors on the battlefield.

The Spartans did not attack Argos again.

According to Plutarch, Argos still celebrated the defense of the city by its women five hundred years later at an annual festival in which the women dressed as men and the men wore women's dresses and veils.* Other sources tell us the women's military success upset the social order in fundamental ways. The Argive women who had stepped outside the narrow bounds of appropriate behavior for Greek women of the time found it difficult to step back into them. As Americans discovered when soldiers returned to the United States after World War I, it's hard to "keep them down on the farm after they've seen Paree."

Chinese statesman and reformer Yang Shang (d. 338 BCE), author of a political and military treatise, *The Book of Lord Shang*, recommended military commanders use "the army of adult women" to help defend besieged cities by digging traps, building earthwork defenses, and burning the surrounding countryside, thereby freeing able-bodied men to fight the enemy. Besieged cities have instinctively followed his plan for millennia.

---

* J. G. Frazer (1854–1941), best known as the author of *The Golden Bough*, a study of comparative mythology, suggests in his edition of Pausanias's *Description of Greece* that "the story of the defence of Argos by Telesilla may have been invented to explain this festival"—because of course that makes more sense than the other way around. See Pausanias, *Pausanias's Description of Greece*, trans. J. G. Frazer, vol. 3 (New York: Bilbo and Tannen, 1965), 197.

Throughout history, women took to the walls or the fields with whatever forces they could muster to defend their homes, castles, and cities when a besieging army was at the door. For the most part, women played supporting roles: carrying food, water, and ammunition to the soldiers; boosting the morale of the city's defenders and/or mocking the besiegers; and helping to rebuild defenses or dig trenches. They threw stones,* hot water, hot oil, or, in colonial America, boiling lye on the heads of attacking soldiers who got near the walls. Some picked up scythes, or swords, or machine guns, or mortars, and fought.

Wo-manning the ramparts was seen as a last-ditch resort, often undertaken, as in the case of the women of Argos, in the absence of able-bodied men. For example, when Pyrrhus, king of Epirus,† attacked the city of Sparta in 272 BCE, the Spartan king and his army were out of town. The remaining men met to make plans to evacuate the women. The king's daughter, Archidamis, crashed the meeting, armed with a sword, and berated the men for thinking they could expect Sparta's women to leave. Instead of allowing themselves to be evacuated, the women helped defend the city. In addition to bringing men food and ammunition during the battle, they took on hard jobs, like digging an anti-elephant trench,‡ in order to free up men to fight.§

Women's involvement in defending their homes was also assumed to be inherently temporary. Even the spirited women of Sparta left the battlefield as soon as the army returned, "thinking it no longer decent to meddle in military affairs."[2] In short, don't make a habit of it, ladies.

And yet, over the centuries, women have made a habit of it. Women who fought to defend their city walls were the most common type of women warriors in the days before women were able to openly enlist in the regular military.¶ They outnumbered many times over the combined forces of queens, commanders, women who fought disguised as men, and women who fought undisguised alongside men on the battlefield. Their participation was not only welcome but often

---

* Or roof tiles in the ancient Mediterranean.

† Whose costly military victories gave rise to the phrase "Pyrrhic victory"—sometimes winning isn't worth the price.

‡ The ancient world's version of the antitank ditch.

§ An idea that would last well into the twentieth century—and is in fact still alive in some circles.

¶ In other words, for most of human history.

expected, whether they wielded a weapon on the walls or a shovel in the trenches.

ON THE CITY WALLS—AND SOMETIMES IN THE CITY STREETS

From the first cities of the ancient Middle East well into the eighteenth century, military success often depended on your ability to hold a fortified position and control the countryside around it. (Or, looking at it from the perspective of the besieger, success depended on seizing your opponent's castles or fortified towns, and thus gaining control of the countryside.) Siege technology changed over time. Bows, swords and axes, scaling ladders, siege towers, battering rams, and catapults that could throw a high trajectory stone ball over a castle wall—all used by besiegers in various forms from ancient Assyria through the fifteenth century—were replaced over time by muskets, explosives, and heavy artillery that could fire a projectile through a stone wall. City fortifications evolved from mud-brick city walls to stone keeps* to the elaborate five-pointed fortifications designed by military engineers of the eighteenth century.

But if the technology changed, the fundamental relationship between besieger and besieged did not. Sieges were a brutal form of total warfare. Besiegers suffered from exposure to the elements, the potential for inadequate supplies, and the possibility of being overtaken by the fresh soldiers of a relieving force. The besieged faced the possibility of starvation in a long siege and the threat of looting, rape, and murder if the walls fell. Civilians in a besieged city had the choice of being useless mouths to feed or active participants in the defense. Many, men and women alike, chose to fight, or at least provide support to those who did.

The most common jobs women performed in a siege could be seen as extensions of traditional gender roles: carrying food and drink to those fighting on the walls; carrying water to the artillery batteries, where it was needed to swab down the gun barrel after every round;† caring for the wounded; building fortifications; and repairing the day's damage to the fortifications each night. Women stood

---

* Which were often surrounded by earthwork defenses—it's hard to beat packed dirt when it comes to absorbing artillery rounds.

† As opposed to bringing water to the artillerymen to drink as is commonly assumed.

on the walls and jeered at the besiegers—a dangerous ancestor of trash-talking at modern sporting events. They encouraged the city's defenders. And some of them fought on the walls alongside the city's male defenders. They had every incentive to do so: the metaphorical rape of the besieged city often ended with the literal rape of many of its female inhabitants.*

Many of the free cities of medieval and early modern Germany regulated the role of women in a besieged city. Cities required male citizens to participate in guarding the city and to keep arms in antic-ipation of the need for defense. The same laws required women and children to stay in their homes during civic emergencies, including fires. Some places made an exception in the case of a siege. When the city was besieged, women were allowed to play an active role in its defense by throwing stones, hot water, or pitch from the windows of their homes.

Not all women were willing to wait for the enemy to get that close. Contemporary accounts of sieges from the period describe women using firearms; participating in night raids; joining in the defense of breaches in the walls, where the attack would have been at its most fierce; and fighting hand-to-hand at the improvised bar-ricades that often provided a last line of defense—a far cry from the prescribed gender-appropriate action of throwing hot water out the second story window.

For the most part, these were anonymous heroines, remembered only in the collective. A contemporary chronicler reported that when the young King Louis XIII besieged the Protestant stronghold of Mountauban in 1621, "the women demonstrated their usual courage." When the alarm sounded, townswomen ran to the walls armed with

---

* Historically, noncombatant women have suffered as much violence in the course of war as any soldier on the front lines: taken captive and used as sexual slaves for soldiers, raped, and killed. Many cultures saw suicide as an escape route for women after the fall of a stronghold, an alternative to the horrors often experienced at the hands of enemy soldiers. In medieval India, the Rajputs codified the idea of suicide as a response to the loss of a besieged city in the idea of *jauhar*, the collective ritual self-immolation of women and children performed when the Rajputs saw no hope of victory. The following day, the men would smear the ashes on their foreheads and sally forth in a suicide charge against the enemy. One of the most famous examples of *jauhar* took place at Chittorgarh in 1303, led by the Rajput queen Rani Padmini. Rajput women also committed *jauhar* at Chittorgarh in 1535, when Bahadur Shah of Gujurat besieged the fortress, and in 1567/8 when under siege by the Mughal ruler Akbar.

scythes and prepared to stop the besiegers from climbing the walls by throwing stones down on their enemies; one woman "cut off seven or eight pikes of the enemies with her scythe." Others fought from the "firing steps" or in the ditches that formed part of the city's defenses.[3] During the Thirty Years War (1618–1648), women in the forest of Bregenz, in what is now Austria, defended their communities against Swedish invaders with sickles and pitchforks. In the English Civil War (1642–1651), women in London, Gloucester, Hull, and Lyme drew admiration from their male counterparts for their valor in constructing, repairing, and defending the cities' fortifications. In Lyme, for example, some four hundred women joined their townsmen at the fortifications, where they put out fires caused by incendiary arrows, stood guard duty, fired muskets, and repaired the city's walls with picks and shovels.

Within the larger context of female courage, some women performed acts of bravery that caught the imaginations of their contemporaries. For example, Margaret of Beverly (ca. 1150–1215), aka Margaret of Jerusalem, was a Christian pilgrim to the Holy Lands who was in Jerusalem when the Muslim ruler Saladin besieged the city in 1187 during the Third Crusade.* She is reported to have carried water to the men on the walls and then fought "like a man" in defense of the city, wearing a cooking pot for a helmet,† until she was wounded in action by Saladin's siege engines.

Margaret wasn't the only woman to "fight like a man" under siege. Many are remembered as hometown heroines even if it is difficult

---

* We know more about Margaret than we do about most of her counterparts. Her brother Thomas, a monk at Froidmont in Picardy, wrote a long account of her experiences as a pilgrim. Her adventures did not end with Saladin's capture of the city. In the twelfth-century version of backpacking across Europe, she traveled through the Holy Lands, working as a laundress when she needed cash. She was captured and enslaved twice, and was caught up a second time in the conflicts between Christians and Muslims at Antioch. After leaving the Holy Lands, she toured the pilgrimage sites of Europe before settling down as a Cistercian nun in France.

† The improvised defense of city walls by civilians often required the use of improvised weapons, but the semicomic detail of the cooking pot as helmet carries a whiff of gender condescension. Arab poet and diplomat Usama Ibn-Munqidh, writing at much the same time, reported a similar incident: a Frankish woman who wounded an Egyptian amir by hitting him with a cooking pot. Perhaps this is the (cross-cultural) medieval equivalent of the cartoon routine of hitting someone with a frying pan? A comic shtick with horrifying real-life equivalents and underlying gender anxieties.

to prove they ever existed. A French tavern keeper named Jeanne Maillote, for example, reputedly grabbed an axe and led the people of Lille against the Protestant Hurlus who attacked the city in 1582. The city of Lille erected a statue in her honor in 1935—a time when people might well have wanted to remember the possibility of an everyday hero.

HEROINE OR HARRIDAN?

Kenau Simonsdochter Hasselaer (1526–1588), a fortysomething widow who was a shipbuilder and timber merchant, came to personify the defense of the siege of Haarlem, during the Dutch revolt against Spain (1558–1648).*

In 1572, Frederick of Toledo, son of the new governor of the Spanish Netherlands, led an army of thirty thousand men on a punitive expedition against Dutch towns that supported the Calvinist insurrection. The Spanish army left devastation behind it: cities burned to the ground and their citizens slaughtered. Toledo's army reached Haarlem in December. The city had weak defensive walls and a garrison of some three thousand troops, most of them German mercenaries. Toledo had established a reputation for giving no quarter and was confident the city would surrender. Instead, Haarlem stood its ground. Citizens and soldiers fought together. Kenau organized a division of some three hundred women, who fought alongside the men on the ramparts.

When the starving citizens of Haarlem surrendered in July, the Spanish executed the surviving Dutch members of the garrison, along with a thousand leading citizens of the town. The list of those the Spanish considered "war criminals" did not include Kenau and the women she led. Some historians argue that the absence of women on the list of executed citizens refutes the story of their involvement, but letters and diaries of German mercenaries describe the women of Haarlem fighting beside them, both in the "feminine" style of pouring boiling oil over the walls and in hand-to-hand combat.

---

* Also known as the Eighty Years War and the Dutch War of Independence, the Dutch revolt was a complicated and ugly mess of religion (Protestant versus Catholic), nationalism, and trade rights. The conflict between Protestantism and Catholicism would later fuel the civil wars that tore England and France apart during the seventeenth century.

The first account of Kenau's actions was published before the siege ended: a report of Kenau baiting the enemy from the ramparts, written by a Friesen scholar named Acerius. Acerius's vision of Kenau is the one that stuck. Her name entered the Dutch language. At first the word denoted a spirited woman; it has degenerated over the centuries from its original positive meaning. Today it translates as tartar, battle-axe, or virago.

That's one way to make a woman warrior disappear from history.

JEANNE THE HATCHET

In 1472, Jeanne Laisne* earned the nickname "Jeanne Hachette" for her role in defending the city of Beauvais against the armies of Charles the Bold, the Duke of Burgundy,† who had joined forces with other disaffected noblemen against King Louis XI of France.

The vanguard of the Burgundian army arrived on June 27. Charles had taken—and ravaged—three French towns before he reached Beauvais. The city was well fortified but had no artillery and few soldiers. With only the townspeople and a handful of soldiers to defend the walls, the duke expected the residents would surrender without a fight. Wrong.

When the city refused to surrender, the Burgundian commander ordered a simultaneous attack on two of the city gates. The duke's soldiers rushed into the gap made when their cannon blew a hole in one gate, but the townspeople defended the breach valiantly. Men fought on the walls. Women threw flaming torches down on their enemies, catching the city gate on fire in the process. A few women took part in hand-to-hand combat at the breach.‡ The Burgundian forces were on the verge of overrunning the city's defenses when Jeanne entered the battle, armed with, you guessed it, an axe. As a soldier planted a Burgundian flag on the battlements, she wrested it from him and hurled him off the wall. Her actions rallied the garrison, who held off the besiegers until reinforcements arrived.

---

* Or perhaps Jeanne Fourquet. Both names appear in accounts of the incident.

† So there is no confusion, this is the son of Philip the Good, the Duke of Burgundy, who opposed Joan of Arc.

‡ Some modern accounts claim Hachette organized the city's female defenders. As best as I can tell, this is wishful thinking.

The siege continued for almost a month. In contrast to the usual siege experience, in this case the besiegers grew short of supplies while the besieged had no trouble obtaining provisions. On July 22, Charles the Bold gave up and headed west toward Normandy, burning and pillaging villages and fields for miles around Beauvais. A grateful Louis XI rewarded Hachette for her act of bravery with a lifelong exemption from paying taxes—worth more than a medal. As late as 1907, the town of Beauvais celebrated Hachette's actions with an annual parade led by the city's women, the Procession of the Assault—not unlike the Argive festival honoring the women who fought alongside Telesilla against the Spartans. Today, Hachette is still celebrated with an annual festival and reenactment.

"THE MAID OF SARAGOSSA"

Napoleon Bonaparte's invasion of Spain in February 1808 set revolutions in motion throughout Latin America. It created a different kind of popular movement in Spain itself: resistance. For six years, Spanish patriots, men and women alike, fought against the French occupation in small irregular bands and provided critical support to the British Army in the Peninsular War against France.[*] Twenty-two-year-old Agustina Zaragoza Domenech (1786–1857), who kept a key artillery position from falling into French hands at the first siege of Zaragoza, became the face of that resistance—so much so that British poet Lord Byron and Spanish artist Francisco Goya both created works celebrating her heroism.[†]

Napoleon's invasion of Spain had its official roots in long-simmering tensions between King Carlos IV of Spain and his son Ferdinand. Fearful that his father intended to remove him from the succession, Ferdinand asked Napoleon to help him depose his father.

If Ferdinand had been patient, the throne would have fallen into his hands without the risk of inviting Napoleon to invade. Carlos IV and his wife were not popular with their subjects. In March 1808, a

---

[*] They were termed *guerrillas*—a diminutive of the Spanish word for war, *guerra*. A new word for an old way of conducting war.

[†] Domenech's actions are reported in journals, memoirs, and letters written by both British and French participants in the Peninsular War. They also appear in a heavily embroidered account of the siege by General José Palafox.

Agustina Domenech's exploits in the siege of Zaragoza inspired one of the few heroic etchings in Goya's series "The Disasters of War."

public uprising forced Carlos to abdicate in favor of Ferdinand. The new king arrived in Madrid on March 24, one day after French commander Joachim Murat entered the city at the head of the French army. Dissatisfaction with Carlos IV's corrupt government was so strong that many Spaniards greeted the French as liberators. By the end of April, it was clear the French had come to conquer, not to liberate.

On May 2, rumors spread that the French planned to forcibly remove the remaining members of the royal family to Bayonne, where Carlos and Ferdinand were now held captive, having abdicated in favor of Napoleon's brother. Violent protests erupted in Madrid. A cavalry unit made up of the Muslim slave soldiers known as Mamluks, a souvenir of Napoleon's invasion of Egypt, charged the protesting crowd, which was armed with little more than cudgels and knives. Once the protestors were dispersed, Murat's men rounded up everyone they could find who was armed. Executions lasted through the night and well into the morning.

The brutal repression of the May 2 protest fueled resistance across Spain.

Agustina Zaragoza Domenech was the wife of Juan Roca, a Spanish sergeant stationed at Barcelona. With Ferdinand's abdication, the Spanish army owed its allegiance to Joseph Bonaparte—and indirectly to France. Plenty of Spanish soldiers were unhappy with this arrangement, including Roca. Like many other Spanish soldiers, Roca fled French-occupied Barcelona after the May uprising in Madrid and made his way to Zaragoza, where General José de Palafox had organized resistance against the French. Domenech followed her husband there with their four-year-old son. Soon after reaching Zaragoza, Roca was sent to join a force some hundred miles away, leaving Domenech on her own in Zaragoza when the French army besieged the city on June 13.

Palafox held the French off for two months, from June 13 through August 15, with an improvised force of soldiers and townspeople—similar to those that have defended besieged cities throughout history. Domenech, like other women in the city, took on the tasks women traditionally performed in a besieged city: bringing food and water to the men on the city walls and caring for the wounded.*

On July 2, 1808, the French launched a new attack on the city walls. As Domenech approached an artillery battery near the Portillo gate on the east wall of the city, a French shell destroyed the battery's earthwork defenses and killed or incapacitated most of its gunners before they could fire their last round. The French army stormed the position. Domenech took a linstock—a long pole designed to hold a burning length of wicking, known as a "slow match"—from the hand of one of the fallen soldiers and fired the loaded twenty-four-pound cannon.† Hit by a round of grapeshot at close range, the French retreated. Domenech received a medal, a small pension, and an honorary commission as a lieutenant for her bravery.

---

* Hazardous jobs by any standard. One of the women who carried water to the men fighting on the walls at Zaragoza, Maria Agustin, continued to bring buckets to the walls after she received a serious neck wound that made her left arm useless. She later received a pension from the Spanish government because her war injury left her disabled and unable to work.

† Palafox claimed that he witnessed this event, but he is not a reliable narrator. For instance, he erased Roca from the story. In his version—the one that has made its way into the popular historical imagination in Spain—Domenech was engaged to one of the gunners and snatched up the linstock from his dying hands to fire the cannon, creating a Hallmark movie version of Domenech's heroism. Same military results, more schmaltz.

Domenech was not the only woman to fight at Zaragoza. By all accounts, many women took part in the city's defense. At least two others received official recognition for their services. French horsemen surrounded a peasant woman named Casta Álvarez (1776–1846) as she delivered food and water to a key artillery battery. She grabbed a musket and bayonet and joined the battery's defense. She received a pension and a medal for her role. Manuela Sancho (1783–1863) was wounded defending the convent of San Jose during the second siege. General Palafox, who clearly saw the promotional value of women warriors, mentioned her with honors. She, too, received a pension for her services at war's end.

A WOMAN'S CASTLE IS HER HOME

In periods when sieges dominated warfare, cities were not the only target. Castles mattered.

In *Treasure of the City of Ladies; or the Book of the Three Virtues*, a practical survival guide to life in fifteenth-century France for women of all social classes,* Christine de Pizan (1364–1430) instructed no-blewomen that they must learn military skills in order to defend their own property:† "She ought to have the heart of a man, that is, she ought to know how to use weapons and be familiar with everything that pertains to them, so that she may be ready to command her men if the need arises. She should know how to launch an attack, or de-

---

* Though given the realities of book "publishing" before Gutenberg perfected move-able type in the 1450s, the odds are only members of the privileged classes saw it.

† De Pizan knew what she was talking about when it came to military theory. She was one of the most important European writers of the late Middle Ages and the first woman known to make a living as a writer (with the usual caveat that, with so many women's sto-ries erased from history, we can't really know). She is best known today for her pioneering books about women, but she also wrote two important works on medieval warfare. She released one under her own name—a praise poem about Joan of Arc, who was alive and leading troops at the time. The second, *The Book of Deeds of Arms and Chivalry*, was a textbook for noblemen on how to wage war. It included a discussion of the morality of war as well as practical information on strategy, tactics, and technology, including one of the few medieval accounts of how to use artillery in war. She wrote it anonymously, assuming, no doubt correctly, that no one would take a military manual seriously if they knew a woman wrote it. (Some things don't change.) By the mid-fifteenth century, the book was on the shelves of leading French military commanders. It remained a standard work through the end of the century—important enough that King Henry VII had it translated into English.

fend against one."[4] It was good advice. Noblewomen and queens often found themselves leading the defense of a keep, castle, or manor—even if they didn't have "the heart of a man."[*]

The skills needed to withstand a siege were an extension of housekeeping when the idea that a man's home was his castle was a literal description for members of the aristocracy. In medieval and early modern Europe, noblewomen were often responsible for managing family properties, and consequently for providing the military resources needed for those properties. Provisioning a household that was as much armed fortress as family domicile involved procuring the cannons, small arms, and gunpowder needed for its defense, as well as the day-to-day supplies of food, clothing, and household linens. Noblewomen supervised men-at-arms in the course of daily life and helped mobilize the household's resources for war. Leading its defense was one more step down a familiar road.[†]

We find stories of women leading the defense of a besieged castle/keep/manor in sixth century China, in the dynastic wars of medieval Europe, in the religious wars of seventeenth century England and France,[‡] and in shogunate Japan.[§] Some defended their strongholds for a few days. Lady Blanche Arundell (1583/84–1649), for example, held Wardour Castle with a score of men and her maidservants for six days against an army of more than a thousand parliamentary soldiers. Others hung on for months. Judith of Bavaria (1103–1131), the Duchess of Swabia, defended the city of Speyer for over a year. During the Kenin Rebellion (1201–1203) in Japan, Hangaku Gozen,[¶] sister of the rebel leader, defended the castle of Torisaka against the shogun's army for three months; the castle surrendered only after an enemy arrow wounded her.[**]

---

* Occasionally, not-so-noble women also found themselves under siege. Margaret Paston (1423–1484), the wife of a wealthy landowner and merchant, defended besieged properties three times against noblemen's attempts to seize them by force.

† Women also conducted sieges in the Middle Ages. For instance, Emma of Burgundy (d. 939), queen of France, not only organized the defense of the city of Laon; she also led a siege against Château Thierry in 933.

‡ The English Civil War (1642–1651), in particular, was marked by many sieges of small strongholds. Women on both sides of the conflict led the defense while their husbands were away fighting on other fronts or imprisoned by their enemies.

§ A period that lasted, with a few pauses, from 1185 to 1868.

¶ "Gozen" is a term of address, roughly equivalent to the title "Lady," not a name.

** Japanese "castles" in the twelfth century were wooden stockades—more like a fort in the American West than a medieval European keep.

Some drove the besiegers from their gates. Lady Mongchi, for instance, routed the imperial army that besieged the walled city of Changying in 503 CE. Some forced concessions before they surrendered. Emma of Norfolk (d. 1100) held Norwich Castle against the army of William the Conqueror during the Revolt of the Earls in 1075, the last serious act of Saxon resistance against the Norman Conquest. She was successful enough that she was able to demand safe passage out of England for herself and her men-at-arms before they surrendered.

The unlucky saw their defenses crumble around them. In 1448, Margaret Paston attempted to defend the manor of Gresham with twelve men against a force of a thousand men "arrayed in a manner of war," sent by Lord Molynes to turn the Pastons out. Lord Molynes's men "bore her out at the gates, and cut asunder the posts of the house, and let them fall," then proceeded to rifle the house for valuables.[5]

Some led their men-at-arms, weapons in hand. Hangaku Gozen took a position on the tower of her fortress, from which she commanded her forces and rained down arrows on their attackers in 1201. In 1590, during the French Wars of Religion, Françoise de Cézelly (ca. 1555–1615) organized the defenses of Leucate and led the garrison with a pike in her hands.[*]

Most harangued the enemy and encouraged their men-at-arms. (Sometimes they also harangued their men-at-arms. In 1584, the wife of samurai warrior Okamura Sukie'mon armed herself with a *naginata*,[†] patrolled the besieged castle, and put the fear of the gods in any soldiers she found asleep while on duty.) More than one noblewoman, such as Hungarian nationalist Llona Zringyi (1644–1703),[‡]

---

[*] De Cézelly was so successful in her defense of Leucate that Henry IV, the first Bourbon king of France, made her governor of Leucate in her own right, with the right of passing the position down to her son. Referred to now as the Joan of Arc of Languedoc (what else?), she is the subject of a heroic statue in Leucate. The original statue was erected in 1899. In 1942, the Vichy government, perhaps recognizing the danger of a local hero, ordered the statue taken down, and shipped the bronze to Germany. The town put up a new statue in 1975.

[†] A traditional weapon of samurai women, the *naginata* is a curved blade on a staff, similar to a glaive. Samurai women also carried a long dagger in their sleeves called a *kaiken*, sometimes referred to as a suicide dagger.

[‡] Zrirngyi led the defense of Munkacs Castle, the last stronghold of the Hungarian resistance, against the Hapsburg army over the course of three years of intermittent sieges.

walked her ramparts at twilight in full view of the enemy, giving the besieging army a metaphorical middle finger.

In the case of Nicolaa de la Haye (ca. 1150–1230), the castle she defended was her own. Like Matilda of Tuscany, though on a smaller scale, de la Haye inherited the offices of castellan and sheriff of Lincoln when her father died in 1169 with no male heirs. Also like Matilda, she became involved in the great events of her time— in her case, the conflicts surrounding the absentee King Richard the Lionhearted, his brother John, and England's barons, that resulted in the Magna Carta. (De la Haye was on Team John.) As castellan, she successfully defended Lincoln Castle twice, once in 1191 and once in 1216. Her resistance during the second siege led her enemies to describe her as a "most ingenious and evil-intentioned and vigorous old woman."[6] I suspect she took that as a compliment.

The common feature in these stories is not absence of men, because in most cases these women commanded men-at-arms in the defense of their keep, but the absence of a man in charge.

BLACK AGNES

"Black Agnes" Randolph (c. 1312–1369), who held Dunbar Castle against the army of King Edward III during the second Scottish war of independence, is one of the most colorful examples of a noblewoman who successfully defended a besieged castle.[*]

Edward III's invasion of Scotland in 1338 was the third act in an ongoing struggle between England and Scotland over Scottish independence, Scotland's relationship with France,[†] and the disposition

---

[*] It's hard to tell how much of Agnes's story is fact and how much is poetic license. No contemporary Scottish account of the siege exists, but it is described in both English and French chronicles from the period. The first Scottish source for Agnes's story is a vernacular verse chronicle written by Andrew of Wyntoun, the prior of St. Serf's monastery, around 1420. In the late eighteenth and early nineteenth centuries, when Scottish nationalism and the Romantic movement came to maturity together, Scottish nationalists, most notably Sir Walter Scott, used Agnes's story as a call to pride in the Scottish past—much as Vietnamese nationalists would use the story of the Trung sisters in the twentieth century.

[†] The treaty known as the Auld Alliance, signed in 1293, aligned the Scots and the French against the English. In return for French military and economic support, Scotland committed to invading England if the English invaded France. The alliance would shape relationships between the three countries from the Hundred Years War through the French Revolution.

of the Scottish throne after the death of Robert the Bruce in 1329. When fourteen-year-old Edward succeeded his incompetent and much-despised father to the throne in 1327, he recognized Scotland as an independent kingdom under the rule of Robert the Bruce. He changed his mind two years later when the succession struggles that followed the death of Robert the Bruce offered a chance for England to regain control of its troublesome northern neighbor.* By 1333, the English occupied much of Scotland and the young David II and his court had taken asylum with the French king.

In 1334, Edward's apparent victory took a kick in the shins when Patrick Dunbar, the ninth Earl of Dunbar and second Earl of March, switched his allegiance from Edward III to the Scottish nationalists who supported the claims of Robert the Bruce's son to the throne of Scotland. Dunbar Castle became the center of anti-English resistance in the southeast and an entry point for supplies from France.

Dunbar Castle and the Scots became more than an annoyance in 1337, when Edward declared himself the rightful heir to the French throne through his mother. With what would become the Hundred Years War between England and France on the horizon, the need to split up the Auld Alliance took on new urgency. Dunbar Castle, located on the North Sea coast thirty miles from Edinburgh, was one of the few fortresses remaining in Scottish control and became a primary target.

On January 13, 1338, a troop of four thousand English soldiers and a corps of military engineers under the command of William Montague, First Earl of Salisbury, arrived at the gates of Dunbar Castle. In her husband's absence, Lady Agnes Randolph, Countess of Moray, nicknamed "Black Agnes" for her dark hair and sallow complexion, commanded the castle. Montague was one of the best generals of his day and he expected an easy victory with Dunbar away. He did not take into account the fact that Agnes was a nationalist born and bred: great-niece of Robert the Bruce and daughter of a hero of the first Scottish War of Independence. Not the first time we've seen a besieging army underestimate the defending forces.

---

* Robert the Bruce's heir, King David II, was four years old when his father died. Edward Balliol, who was the son of an earlier Scottish king, and a group of nobles (known as the Disinherited) who had opposed Robert the Bruce thought it was a fine opportunity to regain control of Scotland with the help of a large English army. Like Ferdinand of Spain inviting Napoleon over the border, this didn't work out the way Balliol hoped.

Montague called for the castle to surrender. Despite the fact that her defense force consisted of a few guards and the servants, Agnes is reported to have replied: "Of Scotland's King I haud my house / He pays me meat and fee / And I will keep my gude auld house / While my house will keep me."*

The earl may have expected a cakewalk, but he came prepared with large boulders and catapults capable of hurling them at the castle's defenses. Lady Agnes walked the battlements and yelled insults at the Englishmen below. Between attacks, she walked onto the ramparts with her maids and ladies-in-waiting; they dusted down the damaged walls with white handkerchiefs.

Next Montague brought out a siege engine known as the "sow": an enormous wooden caravan on wheels designed to protect soldiers from attack from above while they undermined the walls of a fortress. Agnes reportedly warned him from the battlements: "Montague, beware, for your sow will farrow." She ordered large boulders dropped onto it from the ramparts—probably the same boulders the English had fired at the castle walls earlier. The boulders crashed through the roof of the sow, destroying the ram and injuring the soldiers inside.

The siege continued into the spring. Supplies grew short in the castle. Before the situation grew so critical that Agnes was forced to surrender, she received unexpected aid. Sir Alexander Ramsay of Dalhousie arrived by boat with forty men and provisions, which he smuggled in through the postern gate on the sea side of the castle, bypassing two Genoese galleys hired by the English to cut off sea access. Agnes presented Montague with a freshly baked loaf of bread and some wine (French no doubt) the following day.

In mid-April, Montague sent for Agnes's brother, John Randolph, Earl of Moray, who was a prisoner of the English. Holding Randolph outside the walls where Agnes could see him, Montague threatened to kill him if she did not surrender. Agnes called his bluff. She told Montague she could only surrender at her husband's command. She reminded him her brother was childless and claimed she would inherit his lands if Montague killed him. Montague effectively said, "Oh, never mind," and sent Randolph back to England for use as a bargaining chip elsewhere.

---

* Agnes is credited with a lot of trash-talking in rhyme. While I'd love to think she was the fourteenth-century equivalent of a rapper, I suspect Andrew of Wyntoun is responsible for the verse.

Finally Montague gave up: his men and resources were needed in France. On June 10, he signed a truce with Agnes, and the English withdrew from Dunbar. Andrew of Wyntoun credits Montague with a ditty that summed up the retreating English commander's frustration: "Came I early, came I late, I found Agnes at the gate."

Four centuries later, Scottish novelist and history buff Sir Walter Scott gave Agnes an accolade that few women warriors can claim: "From the record of Scottish heroes, none can presume to erase her."[7]

When the Second World War began, no one expected siege warfare to play an important role.

Face-to-face battles between large armies had replaced the siege as the dominant act of war.[*] Nobles no longer maintained fortified keeps and the private armies to defend them.[†] The rise of professional armies in Europe in the late eighteenth century, and the subsequent rise of non-European rulers willing to hire European mercenaries to train and command their armies, placed a premium on mobility. The new technology of war—air power, tank corps, mechanized infantry, and mobile artillery—introduced in the First World War and perfected in the second, made the traditional form of the siege, in which citizens fought on the ramparts to defend their homes, seem impossible. For that matter, cities no longer had working ramparts.

And yet, when Germany invaded the Soviet Union on June 22, 1941, Napoleon Bonaparte's often-quoted (but never fully referenced and possibly apocryphal) edict that "the fate of a nation may depend sometimes upon the position of a fortress" proved to still be true.[‡] And women once again played a critical role in the defense at the

---

[*] Though it could be argued that the western front in World War I was one enormous siege.

[†] Armed nobility remained a powerful force into the nineteenth century in Japan, where the samurai class held out until the Meiji Restoration (1868–1912). The last stand of the samurai took place on September 24, 1877, at the Battle of Shiroyama, in which samurai armed with their traditional weapons of swords and bows and their traditional code of honor fought the newly modernized imperial army. It was essentially a battle between the past and the modern world. The modern world won. To put this in context: the samurai fought their last battle twelve years after the end of the American Civil War, which is sometimes described as the first "modern" war—at least when "modern" means the First and Second World Wars.

[‡] Ironic, given Napoleon's performance in Russia.

sieges of Moscow, Sebastopol, Stalingrad, and, most particularly, at the siege of Leningrad.

The siege of Leningrad is generally considered the worst siege in history: 872 days of blockade and bombing that killed between 1.6 and 2 million Soviet citizens.* Women bore the brunt of the siege. At the beginning of 1941, women made up 56 percent of the city's population, thanks to the military draft and Stalin's purges, which claimed more men than women. Over the course of the siege, the shortage of men grew worse, as the call for soldiers continued.

Russia was unprepared for the German attack. Stalin refused to believe it would happen, even after he received a personal warning from the German ambassador in Moscow. Russian media dismissed rumors that German divisions were deploying along the Russian border as propaganda.

When the invasion came, it was swift and ruthless. Germany's Operation Barbarossa was a three-pronged attack of three million troops with 7,000 guns and 3,300 tanks along a two-thousand-mile front. Leningrad (now St. Petersburg) was the primary target for Army Group North, led by Field Marshal Wilhelm Ritter von Leeb. Leeb's instructions were to take the city by July 21, reduce it to rubble, slaughter its inhabitants, and then turn his attention to Moscow. Hitler was so sure of victory that he sent out invitations to celebrate Christmas 1941 in Leningrad.

While the Germans advanced, the people of Leningrad worked to construct concentric defense lines around their otherwise defenseless city. Half a million Leningraders, mostly women,† were drafted to build fortifications first on the Pskov-Ostrov and Luga River defense

---

* The number is horrifying enough as it stands, but it looks even worse if you add two pieces of context:

1. The Soviet Union consistently underreported its losses. (In other words, modern battle statistics are no more reliable than battle statistics from the ancient world.)
2. Estimated Soviet losses at Leningrad exceed the total number of Americans, both military and civilian, who have died in wars from the American Revolution through 2002.

In Cynthia Simmons and Nina Perlina, *Writing the Siege of Leningrad: Women's Diaries, Memoirs, and Documentary Prose* (Pittsburgh: University of Pittsburgh Press, 2002), ix.

† A fact that is often glossed over in standard histories of the siege but is all too clear in photographs of the period.

lines, 180 and 60 miles southwest of Leningrad respectively, and later in Leningrad itself. Between June 22 and August 20, civilian laborers built 620 miles of earthworks. They dug 420 miles of antitank ditches and thousands of miles of defensive trenches. They strung 320 miles of barbed wire across the approaches to the city, constructed the static antitank devices known as "Czech hedgehogs," and built some five thousand earth, timber, and concrete pillboxes—small defensive structures built with peepholes through which a weapon could be fired. It was heavy manual labor performed without the benefit of mechanized construction equipment. Women dug trenches by hand and worked together to carry heavy timber and stones. Driven by reports of the rapid German advance, they worked long days in primitive conditions, with no shelter against the enemy aircraft that strafed their construction sites.

By September the city was under siege. That month alone, the Germans launched two hundred artillery bombardments and twenty-three major air raids against Leningrad, but were unable to break through the city's defenses.

In addition to regular Red Army units, the city was defended by "destruction battalions," which had originally been created to deal with internal security threats, and by nine divisions of the *narodne opolchenie*, a volunteer citizens' militia organized by the Communist Party.* By late August, when the Germans had almost encircled the city, the military command officially encouraged women and teenage boys to enlist: about a quarter of the eligible volunteers were women.

Unlike most home guards in World War II, the *opolchenie* fought. They had little training. Armed with a variety of small arms and hundreds of thousands of bottles of flammable liquid, dubbed "Molotov cocktails" by the Finnish soldiers, their primary task was to stop the advance of German armored divisions by hurling grenades and gasoline bombs at German tanks from slit trenches. A. A. Gusev, a political commissar in the second *opolchenie*, summed up the experience: "Our people are poorly trained and insufficiently armed. We fight more from the soul and heart than from military training."[8]

---

* Translated as "people's army" in accounts of Soviet Russia, *opolchenie* could just as easily be translated as "home guard," "volunteer militia," or "territorial army." The German invasion was not the first time the *opolchenie* had mustered in times of war. The first reference appears in the Russo-Polish War of 1605–1618.

The only real advantage the city's defenders had was that Leningrad was one of Russia's largest centers of manufacturing munitions. Thousands of women replaced their husbands and brothers in Leningrad's factories, the Russian counterparts of Rosie the Riveter. Unlike Rosie, factory workers, male and female, were armed (badly) and received training at the end of their eleven-hour days as members of "worker battalions," intended to defend the city factory-by-factory if need be.

Faced with massive bombardment and starvation—a combination of the newest and oldest techniques of siege warfare—the defenders of Leningrad held out against German troops until January 27, 1944.

Like women before them at Sparta, Haarlem, Zaragoza, or Paris, the women of Leningrad defended their city with courage and grim determination. Because sometimes the distance from the home front to the frontline is only a few short steps.

MOLLY PITCHER(S)?

In 1876, caught up in the patriotic excitement of the first centennial of the American Revolution, the people of Carlisle, Pennsylvania, raised a stone inscribed "Molly Pitcher" over the previously unmarked grave of a local resident, Mary Ludwig Hays McCauley (ca. 1754–1832). In the years before her death, Hays claimed to have served at the Battle of Monmouth, on June 28, 1778, carrying water to the artillerymen, including her husband, William Hays. When Hays was wounded and unable to continue, she stepped in as an impromptu member of the artillery team. A hundred years after the fact, she looked like a shoo-in for the legendary figure of Molly Pitcher.*

One resident of Carlisle, Jeremiah Zeamer, editor of the local newspaper, felt strongly that McCauley should not be so honored. He wrote to Congressman Marlin E. Olmsted that local townswomen remembered McCauley as "a vulgar, very profane, drunken old woman."†

---

* The first known use of the name is a painting titled *Molly Pitcher, the Heroine of Monmouth*, by Nathaniel Currier, of Currier and Ives fame, dated 1848, seventy years after the battle.

† Quoted in Ellen E. Dodge, "Molly Pitcher," *Profiles of Revolutionaries in Atlantic History, 1700–1850*, ed. R. William Weisberger, Dennis P. Hupchick, and David L. Anderson (New York: Columbia University Press, 2007), 11. Not that vulgarity, profanity, and/or drunkenness preclude heroism. Zeamer believed those qualities did, however, preclude being honored with public monuments when so many "Revolutionary heroes who led useful and respected lives" remained obscure. Quoted in Ray Raphael, *Founding Myths That Hide Our Patriotic Past* (New York: New Press, 2004), 40.

Despite Zeamer's objections, there is no reason to think McCauley's account wasn't true. A similar story appears in the memoir of Joseph Plumb Martin, published in the 1830s under the name Private Yankee Doodle. Writing about the Battle of Monmouth, Martin mentions

> one little incident [that] happened during the heat of the cannonade, which I was eyewitness to. . . . A woman whose husband belonged to the artillery and who was then attached to a piece in the engagement, attended with her husband at the piece the whole time. While in the act of reaching a cartridge and having one of her feet as far before the other as she could step, a cannon shot from the enemy passed directly between her legs without doing any other damage then [sic] carrying away all the lower part of her petticoat. Looking at it with apparent unconcern, she observed that it was lucky it did not pass a little higher, for in that case it might have carried away something else, and continued her occupation.[1]

He does not name this irrepressible artillery woman, and there is no direct evidence linking her with McCauley. (On the other hand, there is no evidence that Martin's unknown woman wasn't McCauley, either.) But there is a bawdiness to the story that seems in keeping with Zeamer's later complaints. Moreover, the fact that the Pennsylvania legislature granted her a pension for her services during the war, which may well have included carrying water to the cannon, lends credence to the story.

But McCauley isn't the only serious candidate for the title.

Margaret Corbin (1752–1800) is known to have wo-manned an artillery piece on the field at least once. Corbin followed her husband, John, from one military camp to another during the American Revolution.* They were both on the field at the Battle of Fort Washington in New York City, on November 16, 1776: John as an artilleryman and

---

* Known in the camps as "Dirty Kate," she was no more respectable than McCauley. With the (possible) exception of officers' wives, the women who followed eighteenth-century armies were rough around the edges, if not all the way to the core.

Corbin as a water carrier.* When enemy gunfire killed her husband, Corbin took his place at the cannon. She didn't stop until she was wounded by a blast of grapeshot that mangled her shoulder and left breast. After the battle, the British captured Corbin near her cannon; both the British and the Americans treated her as a combatant prisoner of war. Released on parole, she was assigned to the Continental Army's invalid corps until mustered out of the army in 1783—raising the question of whether she enlisted alongside her husband.† After the war, Congress awarded Corbin a wounded soldier's pension.‡ In 1926, Corbin's remains were transferred from Highland Falls, New York, to the government cemetery at West Point.

That should have been the end of her story. But confusion about identity is a central part of the Molly Pitcher name and legend. In 2016, workmen disturbed the remains. Examination by a forensic anthropologist revealed the bones to be those of an unknown middle-aged man. Corbin's bones are nowhere to be found.

In addition to Hays and Corbin, there are accounts of an unnamed woman who fired a cannon at the Battle of Fort Clinton in the Hudson River Valley in October 1777. There may be at least one more Molly Pitcher whose story remains untold.

---

* The nature of eighteenth-century artillery is important to understanding the Molly Pitcher story. In order to be sure no sparks or hot embers remained in the breech, gunners swabbed out muzzle-loading cannons with wet sponges after each round was fired before they loaded the next powder charge—adding fresh powder before extinguishing embers from the previous round was a short path to "kaboom!" A well-organized artillery battery had casks of water nearby for the purpose of wetting the sponges. But not every team was well organized. Armies were taken by surprise. And casks ran dry over the course of hours of battle. Women in the army's camp often performed the hazardous job of carrying water to the artillery line—in buckets, not pitchers. Firing a cannon was not a one-woman job—it took at least three people. When a gun crew lost a man, it's a fair assumption that the woman who brought the water knew enough to step into the breach as a rammer or a sponger. (Though she probably didn't know enough to perform the mathematical calculations required to place a cannonball on target. A difficult skill to pick up on the fly.)

† It's possible. Some women's names appear on the rosters of local militia.

‡ And a complete set of new clothes! Not a standard benefit for veterans of the time.

CHAPTER SEVEN

IN DISGUISE

In 1876, Cuban-born Loreta Janeta Velazquez (1842—?) published a best-selling account of her adventures as a soldier and spy for the Confederate army of the United States, titled *The Woman in Battle*.*

The daughter of a Spanish father and a French American mother, Velazquez moved from Cuba to New Orleans, where she lived with

---

* Readers have questioned the book's authenticity since its publication, beginning with accusations of fraud from Confederate general Jubal A. Early. Early pointed out factual errors in the text, expressed outrage about Velazquez's morals, and questioned her ability to travel so far and do so much. The book was, he declared, an insult to the Confederacy in general and Southern womanhood in particular. On the other hand, another Confederate general, James Longstreet, claimed to have been aware, in a positive way, that "there was a woman in the ranks with us who . . . was [a] Lieutenant, and called her name Buford"—a variation of the name under which Velazquez reputedly enlisted. Quoted in DeAnne Blanton and Lauren M. Cook, *They Fought Like Demons: Women Soldiers in the Civil War* (New York: Vintage Books, 2002), 197. The sensationalized style of the memoir, and the fact that a Northern man, C. J. Worthington, was listed as the editor (a term that sometimes meant "writer," in the case of memoirs in the nineteenth century), led many historians to conclude the account was fabricated. With more recent research into the role of women soldiers in the American Civil War, historians have verified many of the basic facts about her life through a patchwork quilt of newspaper accounts, government records, and other Civil War memoirs—a task made more difficult by the changing identities she adopted throughout her career. My conclusion is that Velazquez, like Durova, is an unreliable narrator—perhaps not surprising given that her entire career was built on layers of deception—but that her (no doubt) embellished account of her life rests on a core of truth. Ambiguity of evidence makes writing history an art, not a science.

her aunt and attended a Catholic girls' school in the 1850s. As a young teen, she eloped with an American military officer of whom her parents disapproved. (She mentions him only as William.) Together they had three children; all three died in 1860, one soon after his birth and the other two from fever.

Velazquez tells us that as a child she dreamed of emulating the careers of her historical heroes: Catalina de Erauso (1592–1650),* Appolonia Jagiello (1825–1866),† and—surprise—Joan of Arc. (All of whom dressed as men during their military careers.) With the deaths of her children and the growing possibility of Southern secession, Velazquez found her thoughts turning to "reviving my old notions about military glory, and of exciting anew my desires to win fame on the battle-field."[1]

When her husband's home state of Texas seceded from the Union, Velazquez hounded him into resigning his commission and joining the Confederate army. She soon followed him. Having perfected the essential male arts of spitting and swaggering, she disguised herself as a man and entered the Confederate army in June 1861 as Harry T. Bufford, with the self-appointed rank of lieutenant, "ready to start on my campaign with as stout a heart as ever beat in the breast of a soldier."[2]

Since she did not have an official commission, Velazquez attached herself to brigades as the opportunity allowed and moved on when she was threatened with possible discovery as a woman. She claimed to have fought at the battles of Blackburn's Ford, First

---

* A Spanish nun who left the cloister, disguised herself as a man, and fled to the New World, where she enlisted in a small troop of Spanish soldiers under the name of Alonso Díaz Ramírez de Guzman. She fought well but was a problem off the battlefield. She alternated between courting young Spanish women and dueling with young Spanish men. Eventually she killed so many men in duels, including her brother, that she was called before the local bishop, to whom she confessed the truth. She was not punished for either the deaths or the masquerade; instead, she received a generous pension from the king of Spain and an official dispensation from Pope Urban VIII that allowed her to continue dressing as a man.

† A well-born Pole who fought, disguised as a man, in the Krakow Insurrection of 1846 and again in the Hungarian Revolution of 1848–49, in which she rose to the rank of lieutenant. Like many nationalists and socialist reformers who fought in the failed revolutions of 1848, Jagiello emigrated to the United States in 1849. She settled in Washington, DC. Many male "48-ers" enlisted in the Union army when the Civil War began, but there is no sign that Jagiello yearned to pick up a musket and return to battle.

Manassas (or Bull Run, if you prefer), Ball's Bluff, Fort Donelson, and Shiloh, where she was struck in the arm and shoulder by flying shrapnel while helping bury the dead. The doctor who treated her discovered she was a woman, but apparently chose not to reveal her identity.

Thinking it was only a matter of time until her gender was revealed, she decided spying as a woman would do more good for the Confederacy than "plunging into the thick of a fight, as much for the enjoyment of the thing as anything else."[3] As a spy she trafficked in counterfeit currency, posed as a double agent, and may have been involved in a conspiracy to assassinate President Abraham Lincoln. At one point she was hired by a Union agent to find "this woman who is traveling and figuring as a Confederate agent"[4]—when he showed Velazquez a picture of the woman she was to locate, she realized he was hiring her to track herself down.

After the war, Velazquez took part in a Confederate expedition to settle in Venezuela, dabbled unsuccessfully in mining operations in the western United States, and had a son with her third (or perhaps sixth) husband. Finding herself in financial difficulties, she wrote *The Woman in Battle* as a way to earn money to support herself and her son. Then she vanished from the historical record. Perhaps she simply changed her name again and moved on.

Velazquez is a dramatic and controversial example of a type of woman warrior with whom most American readers have at least a passing acquaintance: women who disguised themselves as men in order to fight in the American Civil War.

In 1888, Mary Livermore, a former Union nurse and a leader in the women's suffrage movement, estimated more than four hundred women fought in the Civil War disguised as men—not including women who fought for the Confederacy.[5] Most scholars today agree that between five hundred and a thousand women fought in the war—a small number in the context of the two to three million soldiers who served in the combined Union and Confederate armies.

The women soldiers of the American Civil War may constitute the largest group of women who fought in disguise in a single conflict. Researchers have identified several hundred women who passed as men (sometimes for a very short time) in Europe's armies and navies between 1550 and 1840*—again, a number that is statistically insignificant when we consider the hundreds of thousands of men who fought in European battles during this period. Over time, far more women fought *as women* on the ramparts of besieged cities and towns than ever disguised themselves as men and enlisted.

But if the numbers of women who served at any given time or place are small, the lineage of cross-dressing women soldiers is long. One of the earliest descriptions of such soldiers comes from a twelfth-century work by Byzantine historian Joannes Zonaras, who, writing of Persian soldiers of the third century, reported, "It is said that when the Persian dead were stripped, among them were found women equipped and armed as men."† Accounts of individual women (as opposed to faceless, nameless dead Persians) who fought as men date from as early as Hua Mulan, who was the subject of poetry at least by the sixth century CE, through Milunka Savic, a Serbian woman who fought in the Balkan Wars and World War I.

The idea that some women fought disguised as men was at times a subject of public fascination. In China, variations on the Mulan story have been a fixture of popular culture for 1,500 years. In seventeenth- and eighteenth-century Europe, cross-dressing women who went to sea or to war for love and/or glory—as soldiers, bandits, pirates, or simply adventurers—were the subjects of more than two hundred popular songs and broadsheets—the sixteenth-century equivalent of a supermarket tabloid.‡ Nineteenth-century American

---

* The most important work on this subject has been done by scholars in the field of gender studies rather than by military historians.

† Quoted in Michael R. Evans, "'Unfit to Bear Arms': The Gendering of Arms and Armour in Accounts of Women on Crusade," in *Gendering the Crusades*, ed. Susan B. Edgington and Sarah Lambert (New York: Columbia University Press, 2002), 46. Note the cautious "it is said." Zonaras knows he is looking at the distant past through a telescope. We have a similar account from twelfth-century Muslim historian Imad al-Din Isfahani (1121–1201), a scribe in the court of Saladin and a firsthand observer of the Third Crusade, which he would have called the Frankish wars or the Frankish invasion, from the Muslim side. According to al-Din, Frankish women fought wearing men's clothing and armor and were recognized as women only if they were killed in battle and stripped of their armor.

‡ Broadsheets were the single-sheet predecessors of newspapers and first appeared in the early seventeenth century. Unlike modern newspapers, they were printed on an occasional basis because "news" as a popular commodity was a relatively new product, made possible by the invention of the printing press in the mid-fifteenth century.

newspapers carried on the broadsheet tradition, announcing the occasional discovery of women disguised as men with screaming headlines: "Poses, Undetected, 60 Years as a Man."[6] Memoirs by women warriors—some real, some ghostwritten, some fabricated—became a popular literary genre. A few women soldiers ended their careers on the lecture circuit, where they earned a living by telling their stories while in uniform.

By the end of the eighteenth century, women warriors were such a constant feature in the popular imagination in Britain that Anglo-Irish novelist and playwright Oliver Goldsmith made the satirical suggestion that Britain could solve the manpower shortage in its army by "raising thirty new Amazonian regiments, to be commanded by females."[7] Goldsmith would have been stunned to learn the king of the West African kingdom of Dahomey had done just that. (But that's skipping ahead.)

WHY DID THEY ENLIST?

Despite the (comparatively) large numbers of women who fought as men in the American Civil War, we know little about them as individuals.

Male soldiers wrote an unprecedented number of letters home, astonishing for their quality as well as their quantity. Twenty or thirty years after the end of the war, memoirs by veterans became a popular literary genre. Soldiers of all ranks wrote their stories: some for publication, more as privately printed works distributed to family and friends.

The women who fought are noticeably absent from this flood of written attempts to document/explain/understand the experience of the war. So far, historians have discovered letters from only three of the women known to have fought, and no diaries.* Only two such women are known to have published their memoirs: Loreta Janeta Velazquez

---

* DeAnne Blanton and Lauren M. Cook suggest women soldiers may have suffered from a higher rate of illiteracy than their male counterparts. Having recently spent a chunk of my life reading the letters and memoirs of Civil War nurses, I find that argument difficult to accept. It is probable, however, that women who assumed male identities and joined the army broke off contact with family and friends at home. After all, they left for a reason.

and Emma Edmonds (1841–1898), who served in the Union army for two years as Franklin Thompson. In the absence of personal testimony from these women, historians have traced details of their military careers—the units with which they served, the battles in which they fought, and, in many cases, the way their disguises were uncovered*— through newspaper accounts, pension petitions, muster rolls and other government records, and an occasional remark in the letters and diaries of their fellow soldiers.

We get a more immediate picture of women soldiers from Europe and its colonies in the seventeenth and eighteenth centuries, thanks in part to the popularity of "true stories" and memoirs of women soldiers as a literary genre. Catalina de Erauso's account, which appeared around 1625, is one of the earliest. Flora Sandes's autobiography, published in 1927, is a relative of the genre, though Sandes made no attempt to disguise the fact that she was a woman.

We also get a glimpse into these women's lives from court records of the trials of disguised women soldiers, whether they were arrested for other infractions—petty theft, for instance—that led to the discovery that they were women, or *because* their identities had been discovered. The records of their trials present a less romantic vision of the experience than the popular memoirs, and in some cases give us the direct voices of the women on trial. Since these records were not intended to entertain a popular audience, the temptation to exaggerate or distort was not as strong, though it is important to remember the testimony they report is not necessarily true. As was the case with their American counterparts in the nineteenth century, traces of their stories can also be found, with varying degrees of reliability, in petitions for pensions, broadsheets, newspaper accounts, chapbook biographies, and medical treatises.

One of the most well-documented examples is the trial of Maria van Antwerpen (1719–1781). In 1769, van Antwerpen came before the court of the Dutch city of Gouda, charged with "gross and excessive fraud in changing her name and quality" and "mocking holy and human laws concerning marriage."[8] She had not only disguised herself as a man and enlisted in the army under the name of Machiel van Antwerpen but had courted and married another woman. Worse,

---

* The most common reason for a woman soldier to appear in the historical record.

she had been tried and found guilty for the same offenses in 1751 in the town of Breda.

The trial received a great deal of attention. The story appeared in the popular press (a relatively new phenomenon in the seventeenth century) and was the subject of a news song.* Even before van Antwerpen was sentenced, an "autobiography" titled *De Breasche Hedinne* (*The Heroine of Breda*) hit print stalls in the Netherlands.†

Taken together, these records suggest a variety of reasons why a woman might have chosen to disguise herself and enlist.

One common idea, popular in songs and broadsheets, was that women who enlisted disguised as men did so in order to follow a lover or husband, or in some cases to track down a man who had gone missing. Even in those cases where this was true, the real-life experience was more complicated than that depicted in ballads. In one of the best-known examples, Irish-born Kit Cavanagh (1667–1739), also known as Christian Davies, Christopher Welsh, and "Mother Ross" at various points in her career, claimed she enlisted to search for her first husband after he was forcibly conscripted into the British army in 1692, though later events suggest that wasn't the entire story.‡ She fought as a foot soldier in the Second Dragoons in the Netherlands in the last years of the Nine Years' War. She reenlisted at the start of the War of the Spanish Succession four years later. After *twelve years* as a foot soldier, she located her husband. He was still a soldier and was living with another woman. Cavanagh was clearly in no hurry to leave the military, since she convinced her husband to let her pass as his brother rather than his wife. She continued to serve until 1706, when she was wounded at the of Battle of

---

* News singers were another way current events reached the man in the street and had a broader reach than the printed word in the eighteenth century. Writers took popular tunes and wrote new lyrics to them about current events. Singers were paid to roam the streets and sing the latest tunes. Some songs became so popular that printers compiled collections of greatest hits for sale.

† Written by Franciscus Lievens Kersteman, who served with van Antwerpen's military unit. In the introduction, Kersteman claims he based *The Heroine of Breda* on van Antwerpen's own words—making it an early version of an "as told to" autobiography.

‡ Cavanagh's memoir, *The Life and Adventures of Mrs. Christian Davies, Commonly Called Mother Ross*, was previously attributed to Daniel Defoe and assumed to be fiction. Recent scholarship has established that "Mother Ross" existed and that much of her story can be verified.

Ramillies in the Spanish Netherlands. As often happened, a serious wound meant the jig was up. Although dismissed from service, Cavanagh stayed with the army as a sutler—one of the traditional roles played by camp followers.[*]

The case of Rose Barreau (1773–1843) looks more like a story taken from a ballad than Cavanagh's. Rose had been married only a few days when her husband was called to military service in the army of revolutionary France in March 1793. Unwilling to be separated from her new husband, she disguised herself as a man and enlisted in his regiment as a grenadier under the name Liberté. In July, Rose's husband was wounded during a battle with Spanish troops. Rose continued to fight until she used up her ammunition, then dragged her husband to safety. At that point, she decided it was best to reveal her true sex. (The fact that she was several months pregnant may have contributed to her decision.)

Several women followed their husbands to war, or enlisted with them, in the American Civil War, including Martha Lindley, who left the couple's two children behind with her sister, enlisted in her husband's regiment as Jim Smith, and refused to go home despite her husband's pleas. (There's got to be more to that story.)

Some women, like Emilia Plater[†]and Appolonia Jagiello, described their decisions in terms of patriotism or belief in a cause. That certainly seems to have been true during the French Revolution. Dozens of women enlisted in the army of the Revolution, at first openly and later in disguise after the government made female enlistment illegal. A few appeared before the new Legislative Assembly and demanded

---

[*] From the sixteenth through the mid-nineteenth centuries, women were always a critical part of European armies, though not as soldiers. They cooked, did laundry and mending, nursed the wounded, and scavenged the battlefield for useful gear when the fighting was over. The British army described them as "women on the ration"—such women may have accounted for as much as 10 percent of the British force in the American Revolution. The numbers varied by the type of unit; artillery units, for instance, which as we have seen needed support on the battlefield, tended to have larger numbers of women than other units. Some armies also tolerated women "off the rations"—prostitutes, grog vendors, fences for plundered goods—as long as they did not disturb camp discipline. Like nurses, radio operators, and other noncombatants in modern armies, these women often found themselves in active combat zones. We have no way of knowing how often they picked up weapons and fought back.

[†] Who didn't disguise herself, even though she dressed like a man.

women be allowed to serve. Chocolate-maker and radical organizer Pauline Léon (1768–1838), for example, urged the government to form a female militia and hand out "pikes, pistols, daggers and even muskets for those women who had the strength to serve" and allow them to drill in the Champs de Mars.*

Patriotism wasn't the sole province of revolutionaries. At least one woman, Renée Bordereau, nicknamed L'Angevin, fought on the royalist side. In her memoir, she explained why she chose to go to war:

> I saw forty-two of my relatives perish successively; but the murder of my father, committed before my very eyes, filled me with rage and despair. From this moment on, I resolved to sacrifice my body to the King, to offer my soul to God, and I swore to fight until death or victory.[9]

A clear enough motive by any standard.

Other women claimed they were drawn to the life by the desire for adventure and freedom. Nadezhda Durova appealed to young women who shared her sense of constraint to recognize the role freedom played in her choices:

> Freedom, a precious gift from heaven, had at last become my portion forever! I respire it, revel in it, feel it in my heart and soul. It penetrates and animates my existence. You, young women of my own age, only you can comprehend my rapture, only you can value my happiness! You, who must account for every step, who cannot go fifteen feet without supervision and protection, who from the cradle to the grave are eternally dependent and eternally guarded, God knows from whom and from what—I repeat, only you can comprehend the joyous sensations that fill my heart.[10]

Emma Edmonds reported she was inspired to disguise herself as a man by a moment in the novel *Fanny Campbell, or, the Female Pirate Captain*, when the heroine "cut off her brown curls and donned the

---

* The Legislative Assembly applauded her patriotism, but did not approve the suggestion. Instead the president of the session expressed the hope that their desire to fight would shame men into enlisting. An idea we will see again in the case of the Russian Women's Battalion of Death.

blue jacket and stepped into the freedom and glorious independence of masculinity."* When Babe Bean (1869–1936), who would later fight in the Spanish-American War under the name Jack Grant, was arrested for masquerading as a man in Stockton, California, in 1897, "he" explained his decision in a written deposition: "From a tomboy full of ambitions, I was made into a sad and thoughtful woman. I commenced to be rebellious. . . . How I yearned for that freedom I dreamed of and how often I wished I could enjoy the liberty that the world sees fit to allow a boy."[11]

For many, romance, patriotism, or freedom were less important motivations than a bad family situation, economic need, or the desire for greater opportunity. Women were as likely to join the army to flee a husband as to follow one. Even those who explained their decision in terms of the clarion of freedom typically sought freedom *from* something, whether escaping from a convent, like Catalina de Erauso and Babe Bean, or fleeing an abusive father and a forced marriage with a neighboring farmer, like Emma Edmonds.

The decision was often a financial one: in bad times, the army provided basic necessities. The work was hard, but, unlike Nadezhda Durova and Loreta Velazquez, who came from privileged backgrounds, a majority of the women who disguised themselves to serve as soldiers came from the lower classes of society. It is easy to forget that in earlier centuries, working-class women (i.e., most women) performed hard physical labor. Common domestic tasks, such as laundry, required a heroic effort prior to the application of steam or electricity to women's work.

The story of Mary Anne Arnold, a young Englishwoman who served on board the ship *Robert Small* in 1839, is typical. Arnold was ten when her mother died, leaving Arnold and her eighteen-month-old sister in the care of charitable neighbors, who were no better off than the Arnold family. At first she supported herself by working in the fields and running errands. Then she found permanent employment

---

* *Winfield Courier*, January 24, 1884, quoted in John A. Lynn, *Women, Armies, and Warfare in Early Modern Europe* (New York: Cambridge University Press, 2008), 185. Like Velazquez, Durova, and others, Edmonds is an unreliable narrator. When asked by a reporter if her book could be considered "authentic," Edmonds answered, "Not strictly so." Quoted in Laura Leedy Gansler, *The Mysterious Private Thompson: The Double Life of Sarah Emma Edmonds, Civil War Soldier* (New York: Free Press, 2005), 198. Scholars generally agree that she served as a soldier. Her adventures as a spy are probably fictional.

in a rope factory in the town of Sheerness in north Kent. With two older brothers in the navy, she spent time on the docks, where she soon realized boys her age who went to sea earned more money, were better fed, and were "in every way in a superior condition to her." It wasn't a difficult decision to make. She "determined to renounce the petticoats and become a sailor."*

Such choices were not limited to Europe and its colonies. In 1804, pirates captured an Englishman named Penmal off the coast of Algeria. He noticed several pirates who "were appreciably smaller both in waist and breadth of shoulder, with their voices and cheeks completely devoid of hair." At first he assumed they were adolescent boys, common in naval crews on British ships at the time. He was stunned to learn it was not unusual for a childless widow to take a place on board a pirate ship—it was a more secure living than that of a widow with no family support.[12]

Looking at their stories as a whole, one thing is clear: women who joined the military disguised as men were part of a larger phenomenon of women who chose to pass as men. After revealing her true sex, Catalina de Erauso spent the last years of her life working as a muleteer under the name Antonio de Erauso. Emma Edmonds† traveled as a Bible salesman named Franklin Thompson for several years before she enlisted in the Union army. Babe Bean spent five or six years disguised as a man prior to enlisting to fight in the Spanish-American War.

Passing as a man gave these women access to more than a better wage. As men, they could travel more easily, get a better education, own property, enjoy more political rights (i.e., vote), and, in some cases, marry other women.

Perhaps the most extraordinary example of a woman who seized opportunities otherwise denied her by disguising herself as a man is the case of Dr. James Barry (ca. 1789–1865), née Margaret Buckley,

---

* Our information about Mary Anne Arnold comes from a letter written by an officer on the *Robert Small* after her shipmates discovered Arnold's true gender during the tarring and shaving ceremony practiced on many British ships when they crossed the equator. In the course of telling Arnold's story, the officer praised her as having done "her work as a strong active boy." Dated October 20, 1839, the letter appeared in the *Sydney Morning Herald* on July 10, 1840.

† Christened Sarah Emma Evelyn Edmondson. Changing her name from Edmondson to Edmonds was simply the first in a series of reinventions that began when she ran away from home at the age of fifteen.

the daughter of an Irish shopkeeper. At the age of eighteen, Buckley changed her skirts for breeches, lied about "his" age,* and enrolled as a medical student in Edinburgh—more than fifty years before the first woman officially obtained her medical degree in Great Britain.† After passing "his" Royal College of Surgeons examination, Barry enlisted in the British Army as a hospital assistant in 1809. He served in the Army for forty-seven years, from the Napoleonic Wars to Crimea, rising to become a senior inspector general of army hospitals. He fought for medical reforms. He provided medical care to the neglected and oppressed. He performed one of the first successful caesarean sections. And he fought at least one duel over a woman's honor. His contemporaries considered him bad-tempered, eccentric, effeminate, and an excellent doctor.

At Barry's death in 1865, the woman who laid out "his" body reported to a scandalized press not only that Dr. James Barry was a woman but that the doctor had given birth. When asked by the General Register Office whether it was true, the doctor who signed Barry's death certificate, Major D. R. McKinnon, answered that Barry's gender was none of his [McKinnon's] business.[13]

CATHY WILLIAMS, AKA WILLIAM CATHAY

Cathy Williams (more or less 1844–1892)‡ was the first African American woman known to have served in the United States Army—a two-year stint in which she passed as a man.

---

* Like many women who disguised themselves as men, Barry reduced her age so she could pass as a boy too young to shave. This caused problems when "he" wanted to take the examination for his degree, because the university administrators suspected he had lied about his age in the other direction and declared him too young to get the degree.

† Elizabeth Garrett passed the Society of Apothecaries' examinations that allowed her to practice medicine as a doctor in 1865. The society immediately changed its rules so other women could not get certified through this path. Not the only case illustrating the value of loopholes in allowing women to take strides forward.

‡ It's often difficult to get biographical information about women—as late as the nineteenth and twentieth centuries, social conventions conspired to disguise women in the historical record. Multiply that difficulty many times over in the case of a freed slave. The two data points we have for Williams's birthday are her army enrollment in 1866, when she claimed to be twenty-two, and her pension application in 1891, when she claimed to be forty-one. If you do the math, you find one of those claims must be wrong. Possibly neither is accurate. It is likely Williams did not know her exact age.

Born a slave near Independence, Missouri, she was a "house girl" on the Johnson plantation in Cole County, near the Missouri capital of Jefferson City, when the Civil War began. After General Nathaniel Lyons's troops captured Jefferson City, which had become a rebel stronghold, the Eighth Indiana Volunteer Infantry claimed Williams and other escaped or displaced slaves as "contrabands."* She traveled with the regiment for the rest of the war, working as a laundress.

When the war was over, she was free for the first time, but without family, home, or job. We can only speculate as to why she chose to enlist. It is probable that, like many women who walked a similar path before her, her motivation was as basic as economic security. She could earn more as a soldier than as a laundress, or even as a cook, which was the highest paid, most prestigious job available to black women in the United States in 1866.

In November 1866, she enlisted for a three-year term of service as "William Cathay" at Jefferson Barracks in St. Louis.† After what must have been a cursory medical examination, she was assigned to the newly formed Thirty-Eighth United States Infantry Regiment—one of six all-black regiments of "Buffalo Soldiers" created by Congress in August 1866 with a view toward filling the need for soldiers created by westward expansion.

It does not appear that her company ever engaged in combat. Even if her fellow soldiers experienced battle, the odds are good Williams would not have been with them. She spent most of her military career on sick call: she was hospitalized five times in four different hospitals over the two years that she served. Apparently no one discovered she was a woman during any of these hospital visits—which raises questions about the quality of the medical care black soldiers received at the time. Or, perhaps, doctors repeatedly discovered the truth about her gender and didn't bother to report it.

On October 14, 1868, Private William Cathay was discharged from the army for medical reasons. In June 1891, she filed an application for an invalid pension based on her military service. In February

---

* The term used by the Union army to describe escaped slaves who sought Union protection prior to the Emancipation Proclamation. Derived from the concept of "contraband of war," the term used the concept that slaves were property as the reason why they could not be returned to their owners.

† Many women chose a male version of their own name. Maria van Antwerpen, for example, enlisted once as Jan van Ant and another time as Machiel van Antwerpen.

1892, the Pension Bureau rejected her claim on the grounds that no disability existed, not on the grounds that she was a woman and therefore her enlistment in the army was illegal.*

Cathy Williams vanishes from the historical records after the Pension Bureau rejected her claim. She was not a military hero. She did not earn medals or commendations. She probably never faced an enemy in the field. But she earned a place in history.

DISGUISE AND DISCOVERY

One thing these women shared was the constant threat of discovery.

For the most part, their disguises involved no more than cutting off their hair, donning men's clothing,† and adopting a few "mannish" habits. As one newspaper described a woman who enlisted in the 107th Pennsylvania Infantry in the American Civil War, "He [she] could smoke a cigar, swagger and take an occasional 'horn' [drink] with the most perfect sangfroid."[14] A few bound their breasts. (Catalina de Erauso claimed to use a poultice that made her breasts disappear!) Velazquez wore a false mustache and a wire cage under her clothing to disguise her shape: an anti-corset as it were. Court reports of the trials of cross-dressing women occasionally reveal nitty-gritty details of how women maintained their deception, including descriptions of devices such as silver tubes and leather-covered horns that were intended to help women urinate standing up. (Without noticeable success, if the trial records are to be believed.)

Because they lacked facial hair and had higher-pitched voices, women often posed as adolescents when they enlisted.‡ It was a short-term strategy. Pretending to be a boy placed an upper limit on how long women could serve without detection, because at some point a woman could no longer pass as a boy too young to shave, no matter how boyish her figure or bulky her clothes.

---

* By 1891, the Pension Bureau had dealt with a number of women who applied for military pensions. In fact, Pension Bureau records are a prime source for verifying the military details of women who served in the Civil War disguised as men.

† Often with a coat a size or more too large for obvious reasons.

‡ Ironically, they aimed for the same age range as actual boys who claimed to be older than they were so they could enlist.

But their primary disguise seems to have been in the eyes of their beholders. Until the mid-twentieth century, trousers in general and military uniforms in particular were such a strong male symbol in Europe and the Americas that it was difficult for observers to recognize the wearer was a woman as long as she made some effort to "walk like a man," even in cases where the woman involved did not fit any standard ideas of masculinity.* Loreta Velazquez summed up the effect better than anyone: "Clothing, and particular cuts of clothing, have a great deal to do towards making us all, men or women, appear what we would like the world to take us for."[15]

The most common causes of discovery were wounds, illnesses, and, to a lesser extent, pregnancy.† Kit Cavanagh, for example, maintained her disguise for fourteen years before a serious wound blew her cover. Deborah Sampson (1760–1827), who enlisted as a soldier in the American Revolution under the name of Robert Shurtleff, was wounded in an engagement near Tarrytown, New York. Like other

---

* There may have been an element of "don't ask, don't tell" in the apparent inability of fellow soldiers to recognize a woman in their midst. Durova speculated that her fellow soldiers might have suspicions about her gender: "There were times when the conspicuous courtesy of their behavior toward me and the decorum of their words serve notice that, although they are not quite convinced that I shall never have mustaches, they at least strongly suspect the possibility. My fellow officers, however, are very amicably disposed toward me and think quite well of me. There is no way I can lose their good opinion: they have been the witnesses and comrades of my life under arms." (*The Cavalry Maiden*, 169) The general consensus about such cases was summed up by Lt. Col. Arthur Fremantle, who wrote in his memoir of a woman who fought as a private in the Confederate army: "Her sex was notorious to all the regiment, but no notice had been taken of it so long as she conducted herself properly" (quoted in Blanton and Cook, *They Fought Like Demons*, 128).

† At least six of the women known to have disguised themselves as men and enlisted as soldiers in the American Civil War went into battle while pregnant—and blew their covers with their astonished comrades-in-arms when they gave birth. The most dramatic of these is the case of an unnamed New Jersey woman who fought through her first and second trimesters at the Seven Days' Battles and at Antietam, where she was wounded. Apparently her gender (and her pregnancy) went undetected because she returned to her regiment. She was promoted to corporal before the Battle of Fredericksburg; a soldier who knew her described her at the time as "a real soldierly thoroughly military fellow." In her third trimester, she fought at Fredericksburg and was promoted to sergeant for gallant conduct. She gave birth soon after. Many shocked soldiers wrote home about the incident. Unfortunately, none of them bothered to give either her real name or the name under which she enlisted (Blanton and Cook, *They Fought Like Demons*, 15).

women in the same situation, she treated the injury herself in order to prevent discovery, digging a musket ball out of her own thigh. According to the same source, she lost her cover when she was hospitalized with a fever.* During the American Civil War, women soldiers from both sides of the conflict were wounded and their disguises pierced: one Union soldier was seriously wounded in the leg and shoulder at the Battle of Shiloh; Confederate soldier Mary Ann Clark was "wounded in the thigh a considerable place above the knee" at the Battle of Richmond, Kentucky;[16] another female soldier was found on the battlefield the morning after the Battle of Perryville, Kentucky, wounded in the left side.

As a general rule, whether or not a wound led to discovery depended on its location and its severity. Women who were wounded in the face, hand, calf, or foot had a chance of escaping detection; women who were shot in the upper body, thigh, or groin did not. If at all possible, women soldiers tended to their own wounds to avoid the intrusive eyes of others.

As we have seen before in the twelfth-century accounts of Joannes Zonaras and Imad al-din, some soldiers were discovered to be women after their dead bodies were found on the battlefield. For example, after the battle of Leucate in 1637, the French bishop of Albi discovered bodies of women among the Spanish dead as he administered last rites to dying soldiers on the battlefield. (He gave the fallen women what he undoubtedly felt was the highest praise available: "They were the real men, since those who had fled, including certain officers, had conducted themselves like women.")† In the American Civil War, burial parties discovered women soldiers after the battles of Bull Run, Shiloh, Gettysburg, Resaca, Petersburg, and Appomattox. As late as

---

* Much of what we know about Sampson comes from a romanticized biography titled *The Female Review, or Memoirs of an American Young Lady,* by publisher and newspaper editor Herman Mann in 1797. Historians have not been able to corroborate all the incidents in Mann's account from other sources, including the story that she treated her own wound. At least, not yet. Even if the story is not true, it is in keeping with the experiences of other women in her situation.

† Quoted in Lynn, *Women, Armies, and Warfare in Early Modern Europe,* 96. We've seen this before: the highest praise to give a woman is that she is as brave/smart/competent as a man. The worst thing you can say about a man is that he acted like a woman. Or as Xerxes put it in the fifth century BCE: "My men have turned into women, my women into men." After a few millennia it gets a little tiresome.

the First World War, the London *Graphic* reported fifty Russian soldiers who were found to be women after their deaths.[17]

A number of women were identified by children, who apparently were less easily confused by a pair of pants than were the adults around them. A handful were recognized by acquaintances or family members, who did a double take and realized that the soldier who looked a lot like Maria from down the street in fact *was* Maria from down the street. Some were discovered because they failed to master stereotypically male gestures or leave behind female habits. Two women in the Union army were discovered when they automatically reached for an apron to catch an apple tossed to them by fellow soldiers. Others were unveiled when taken prisoner.

Some were found out almost at once. Others managed to maintain a male identity for months, or even years. A number of women deserted when they feared discovery was imminent. A few, like Catalina Erauso and Rose Barreau, chose to reveal themselves rather than suffer the possible costs of exposure, or because they decided they wanted to leave the military. Others served their terms without discovery and only revealed themselves to the larger world after their service was over.

Perhaps the most amazing thing is how often their disguises succeeded.

THINLY DISGUISED

Milunka Savic (1892–1973) joined the Serbian army when her brother was sent to fight in the First Balkan War. According to some versions, she followed him; in other versions she took his place. (Shades of Hua Mulan!) She earned her first medal for bravery and a promotion to corporal in 1913 at the Battle of Bregalnica in the Second Balkan War.

Like many of her counterparts, her secret was uncovered when she was wounded—hit by a Bulgarian grenade in her tenth combat charge in the Second Balkan War. Savic was called before her commanding officer. He was unwilling to punish her, given her stellar performance as a soldier, but he also didn't want to keep a woman in a combat unit. He suggested she transfer to the Serbian nursing corps. Savic told him she wouldn't take a position that did not involve carrying a gun and fighting for her country. He said he needed to think about it and would give her an answer the next day. Savic told him she would wait right there. She meant it literally. After an hour of watching Savic stand at attention, unmoving, the officer promoted her to sergeant and sent her back to the infantry.

Savic remained in the Serbian army through World War I.* She was awarded two Karadorde Stars with Swords—the highest Serbian military honor—one for single-handedly capturing twenty German soldiers and the other for capturing twenty-three Bulgarians.

As the war went on, France was given command of the under-armed and undermanned Serbian army. After overcoming the usual official uncertainties about allowing a woman to remain in the army, Savic performed as heroically for the French as she had for Serbia. She received the Légion d'Honneur twice, as well as the Croix de Guerre from France, the Cross of St. George from Russia, the Most Distinguished Order of St. Michael from Great Britain, and the Milos Oblic Medal from Serbia.

At the war's end, after seven years of continuous service in three wars, she refused a military pension in France and went back to Serbia, where she settled into civilian life.

In World War II, Savic, then in her forties, found a new way to serve her country: she opened a small hospital to care for the wounded. When the Germans reached Serbia, they arrested her and put her in a concentration camp. Sources disagree as to why. Some claim it was because she nursed wounded members of the resistance—which seems plausible. Others say she was arrested because she refused to attend a dinner given by a high-ranking German officer—which seems unlikely. She survived thanks to a German officer who recognized her as a war hero and arranged for her release.

When Savic died, on October 5, 1973, she was buried with military honors. A street in Belgrade is named after her—one of the standard honors given to half-forgotten women warriors in the modern world.

---

* Savic wasn't the only woman to serve in the Serbian army in World War I. Flora Sandes (1876–1956), the daughter of an English rector, arrived in Serbia as part of a Red Cross nursing unit. She enlisted in the Serbian army as a private in 1915. She was wounded twice in combat, participated in the final offensive against Austria and Bulgaria, and was demobilized in 1921. Unlike Savic, Sandes never tried to hide the fact that she was a woman, though she happily donned a male uniform.

AFTER HER WAR WAS OVER

Military authorities responded with different degrees of severity to revelations that a woman had invaded their ranks, depending on the circumstances under which the woman was discovered and the reactions of the officers in charge. Those who were discovered in the course of committing another crime, or who were clearly involved in a lesbian relationship, received the harshest treatment. Maria van Antwerpen was twice sentenced to exile, not because she enlisted as a soldier but because she married other women. Some were arrested under suspicion of being prostitutes or spies.*

As with other women warriors, we often do not have the full story for women who fought in disguise. They enter the historical record for a single moment, often the point at which they are discovered, and vanish almost immediately. One Confederate officer clearly contributed to the historian's problem: when a woman was discovered under his command, he ordered her removed from the camp and "never asked her name, or the name under which her sex was concealed."[18]

For the most part they were required to leave the military, though not always, as we saw in the case of Milunka Savic. (Private Frank Deming was discharged from the Seventeenth Ohio Infantry on grounds of a congenital disability, described on the muster roll as "being a woman.")[19] Some left the military, but not the camp. Kit Cavanagh was not the only woman who accepted a traditional female occupation at the edges of the military—sutler, laundress, nurse, and, occasionally, spy†—after being discovered. Others reenlisted with another regiment as soon as the opportunity arose.

A lucky few received military pensions, generally with help from friends in high places. Kit Cavanagh was admitted in old age to the Royal Hospital at Chelsea, a home for military pensioners that was founded by Charles II in 1682, and buried with military honors. In the Netherlands, William of Orange, later William II of England, gave Elizabeth Sommeruell an annuity for her valor in the Franco-Dutch War (1672–1678). Louis XIV rewarded Géneviève Prémoy (1660–1706) with a pension and a knighthood in the order

---

* The negative counterparts of enlisting for love or patriotism.

† The rationale appears to have been that a woman who had successfully disguised herself once could do so again.

of St. Louis after her cover was blown.* At least four women received pensions for their service in the American Revolution: Deborah Sampson and Anna Maria Lane (d. 1810),† who fought disguised as men, and the possible "Molly Pitchers," Margaret Corbin and Mary Ludwig Hays McCauley. The United States government was less generous to women veterans of the Civil War. It took eight years, the support of many of her comrades from the Second Michigan Infantry, and an act of Congress for Emma Edmonds to receive a pension in 1884.‡ Without similar support, Cathy Williams's pension application was denied.

Others exploited public fascination with the phenomenon of women soldiers to their benefit. The most common way of doing this was to write a memoir, with or without a ghostwriter, but a few women took things further. Hannah Snell (1723–1792)§ and Deborah Sampson both took their stories to the stage, where they appeared in uniform and demonstrated the weapons drill known as the manual of arms—a relatively new feature in European armies at the time, designed to allow soldiers to load and fire weapons in formation. Both later applied for and received pensions for their war service, and both were the subjects of popular romanticized biographies written during their lifetimes. Snell used the money she received for her biography

---

* Prémoy ran away from home and enlisted in the regiment of the Prince of Condé in 1676 as Chevalier Balthazar at the age of sixteen. "He" rose through the ranks disguised as a man. When "he" was wounded in the breast at the Siege of Mons in 1691, "his" deception was discovered. After granting Prémoy a pension, Louis decreed that she wear a skirt thereafter but allowed her to wear the clothing and accoutrements of a male soldier on her upper body. She published a popular autobiography titled *History of a Dragoon* in 1704. (See how sticky the pronouns can get?)

† Lane enlisted in the same unit as her husband and fought in several battles, including one at Germantown, where she was wounded. She received her pension in 1808 because "in the revolutionary war, in the garb, and with the courage of a soldier, [she] performed extraordinary military services and received a severe wound at the battle of Germantown." In Sandra Gioia Treadway, "Anna Maria Lane: An Uncommon Common Soldier of the American Revolution," *Virginia Cavalcade* 37, no. 3 (Winter 1988): 134.

‡ She seems to have been popular with her fellow soldiers. In 1897, she became the only woman admitted into the Grand Army of the Republic.

§ Snell enlisted as James Gray in 1745, after her husband abandoned her. She initially joined the Sixth Regiment of Foot and then deserted and reenlisted in the British Royal Marines. As a marine, she fought the French in India, where she was shot in the groin at the battle of Pondicherry in 1748. She hired a local woman to tend the wound rather than allow the ship's male surgeon to treat her and expose her secret. Back in England, she revealed her true identity to her fellow marines.

to open a public house in Wapping, England, that she named The Widow in Masquerade, or the Female Warrior. In case anyone missed the reference, Snell dressed like a man even though everyone knew she was a woman.

Snell, Durova, and a handful of others continued to wear men's clothing after their service was over, presumably unwilling to lose the freedom they had experienced as trouser-wearing soldiers. A handful of cross-dressing women soldiers did not simply *dress* as men when their war was over, but *lived* as men until their deaths. Catalina de Erauso, for example, spent the rest of "his" life in Mexico, working as a muleteer under the name Antonio de Erauso. At the other end of the golden age of women soldiers, Babe Bean settled in San Francisco as Jack Grant at the end of the Spanish-American War. For the next thirty years, Grant helped the city's hungry and the homeless. After his death, "Uncle Jack" Grant was revealed to be a woman, who had found a way to "enjoy the liberty that the world sees fit to allow a boy."[20]

World War I marked the last ripple of women who fought as men.

More extensive medical examinations made it difficult for women to avoid disclosure before they enlisted. In at least one case, the combination of the draft and the Medical Examination Board uncovered the disguise of a woman who was living as a man in London as effectively as any battlefield surgeon unveiled a woman soldier in earlier wars. Albert F. Albert (a fake name by any standard) worked as a printer. When "he" was called up, his employer asked for a deferment since he was a skilled and valued craftsman. The deferment was refused and Albert was ordered to report to the Medical Examination Board in August 1916. He arrived at the examination board with a National Health Service form documenting a cardiac condition. It was not enough. Albert—later described as slightly built, smooth-skinned, and soft-voiced—was subjected to a medical examination and found to be a woman. When the recruiting sergeant was asked why he had not suspected Albert was a woman, he said he had no reason to do so. Many of the young men who were called up "have effeminate voices and when a great many men are being dealt with . . . individual characteristics are passed without comment."[21]

At the same time that it became more difficult to enlist, increasing manpower demands on the part of all the combatant powers made it easier for women to make official contributions to their nations' war efforts, though few of them would fight. More women signed up as ambulance drivers, land girls, telephone operators, munitionettes, members of various service auxiliaries, and soldiers in the all-female units of Bolshevik Russia than had ever disguised themselves as men and enlisted as soldiers in all-male units. No false mustache, urination aid, or spitting required.

CHAPTER EIGHT

NO DISGUISE
NEEDED

On March 17, 1917, US Secretary of the Navy Josephus Daniels took what was then the bold—and controversial—step of admitting women into the navy as yeomen.* Hundreds of women between the ages of eighteen and thirty-five headed to recruiting stations to enlist. By the time the United States entered World War I, on April 6, 1917, two thousand women had enlisted as "Yeoman (F)." By 1918, the number of female yeomen had increased to eleven thousand.

Daniels had no intention of creating women warriors. The navy recruited women to "free a man to fight" by taking over clerical duties.

---

* In what many Americans found to be a shocking oversight, regulations in the Naval Act of 1916 did not specify that US citizens had to be male to join the navy. A similar loophole was pointed out in the French Assembly in 1792, when women attempted to join the Revolutionary Army. Unlike the United States Congress, which let the loophole stand, the assembly passed a law on April 30, 1793, that explicitly barred "unnecessary women" from the army. (In other words, laundresses and other women plying the traditional trades of camp followers were allowed to stay.) Women who previously joined the army as soldiers were dismissed. (Though not all of them left.)

Most "Yeomenettes"* were indeed assigned to clerical jobs, but the list of jobs the navy considered suitable for women grew as the war went on. Women also worked as radio operators, supervisors for naval shipments, telegraph operators, commissary stewards, fingerprint experts, and camouflage designers. Florence Whetsel, for instance, who was a telephone operator experienced at switchboard repair before the war, enlisted with an electrician's rating and spent much of the war at the navy yard in Bremerton, Washington, drawing charts of submarine activities.

Once the navy realized that young women in uniform were good publicity, female yeomen were trained to march and perform basic military drills so they could parade in support of war bond drives, troop send-offs, and other official events where goodwill was valuable. Although they were not allowed to serve at sea, female yeomen received the same pay as sailors and marines at the same rank, a uniform allowance, medical care, and war risk insurance.†

Daniels is sometimes given credit for being the first to allow women to join the modern military, but both Britain and Russia beat the United States to the punch. Britain recruited women to become "the girl behind the man behind the gun" as part of Queen Mary's Women's Auxiliary Army Corps (WAAC) in 1916. Under the supervision of their own noncommissioned female officers, "female Tommies" traveled to the front, drove ambulances, ran printing presses, and dug graves. Bolshevik Russia took things one giant step further: in the short period between the Russian Revolution in February 1917

---

* Adding a feminine or diminutive suffix to a noun does more than make the noun feminine in a grammatical sense. It also trivializes female accomplishment by presuming that the base noun is masculine: a poet is a more serious creature than a poetess, for example. Daniels, who objected to the nickname, summed up the issue: "I never did like the 'ette' business. If a woman does a job, she ought to have the name of the job." The official designation, "Yeoman (F)," made it clear women were the institutional equivalent of men who held the same rank. A revolutionary concept that we still haven't come to terms with as a society. Quoted in Lettie Gavin, *American Women in World War I: They Also Served* (Niwot: University Press of Colorado, 1997), 4.

† The US Army didn't do as well by the young women it "enlisted" to serve as telephone operators in France. General John Pershing placed a request with the Department of War for a hundred uniformed female telephone operators who spoke fluent French. Called Hello Girls by the soldiers, they made army communications possible. Most worked behind the lines; a few traveled with Pershing. Like the soldiers with whom they worked, they risked their lives. Unlike those soldiers, they were not considered part of the army and did not receive any of the benefits extended to soldiers during or after the war.

and the Bolshevik coup d'état in October 1917, roughly four thousand Russian women served in combat.*

In fact, allowing women to openly join the military wasn't as new as it seemed at the beginning of the twentieth century.

Seven hundred years before young Scythian women died in battle and were buried with weapons as grave goods, General Fu Hao (ca. 1200 BCE) flourished and fought to defend the Shang dynasty in Bronze Age China (ca. 1600–046 BCE)[†]—the earliest woman warrior I know of for whom we have a name and a story. She was one of three major wives of the emperor Wu Ding and a successful military commander in her own right. Traditional Chinese histories, written centuries after the fact, tell us that Wu Ding, the twenty-third ruler of the Shang dynasty, was a powerful emperor who ruled for fifty-nine years, but they don't mention Fu Hao at all. We know her history from a true primary source: inscriptions on some 250 oracle bones, the earliest Chinese written records.[‡]

Various oracle bone inscriptions from the Shang period refer to Fu Hao as a royal consort, a general, and a landholder in her own right. She led military campaigns and presided over sacrificial ceremonies in the emperor's name. Some oracle bones, inscribed during her lifetime, ask questions regarding her health or the tactics to pursue in a specific military campaign. Others, inscribed on behalf of the emperor, ask whether he should send Fu Hao or another general on a specific campaign, or if he should assume command himself. The inscription on one oracle bone suggests she led a force of thirteen thousand men on a campaign—an interpretation some scholars contest, since most Shang forces ranged from three thousand to five thousand troops. Other oracle bones document sacrifices made on her behalf after her death.

---

* That number would multiply a hundredfold in World War II.

† The second dynasty to rule China. Women warriors have played a role in China for a long, long time.

‡ Used in the art of "scapulimancy," or bone divination, oracle bones were a way for Shang aristocrats to consult their ancestors on matters of concern: Would the weather be good? (Some human fascinations are consistent across the millennia.) Would the hunting trip or military campaign succeed? Would she survive childbirth? Was this a good time to perform a certain religious ceremony? What did my dream mean? Now those questions give us a glimpse into the lives and concerns of the Shang ruling class.

Chinese archaeologists established Fu Hao's place in history without doubt in 1976, when a team under the direction of Zheng Zhenxiang* discovered an undisturbed Shang tomb near Anyang, the site of the Shang capital in modern Henan province—the same region where most of the oracle bones were found. Because it had never been looted, the tomb included a larger quantity of grave goods than any previously excavated Shang tomb. At first, the richness of the grave goods and the large number of weapons led archaeologists to assume it was the tomb of a male ruler. Inscriptions on some of the seventy bronze vessels found in the tomb identified the site as the tomb of Fu Hao. Her grave goods included more than a hundred weapons, as well as thousands of ornamental objects in bronze, jade, bone, opal, and ivory, and the remains of sixteen slaves, buried with her to serve her in the afterlife. The bronze goods alone totaled 1.6 metric tons.

Scholars have pieced together a picture of Fu Hao's career from sources that were never intended to provide a narrative.† It appears she not only directed her own troops but also served as the ancient Chinese version of a task force commander in campaigns that included forces led by other generals. She participated in virtually every important military campaign at the height of Wu Ding's reign.‡ She led an army against the Tu Fang, a tribe of invaders from the north who had been a problem since the beginning of Wu Ding's reign. For a year and a half, Fu Hao and other Shang generals, including Wu Ding himself, led repeated assaults against the Tu Fang. With the Tu Fang defeated, Fu Hao then led Shang forces against three more attacking forces: the armed horsemen§ of the Qiang Fang in the northwest, the Yi Fang in the southeast and southwest, and, sharing the command with her husband, the Ba Fung in the southeast. Soon

---

* By coincidence, the first female archaeologist in China.

† There is disagreement about which inscriptions are relevant and how they should be arranged. As a result, the chronology of military campaigns against the "barbarian" forces that attacked the Shang during Wu Ding's reign varies substantially from one scholarly work to another. Regardless of how individual scholars arrange the chronology, one thing is clear: Fu Hao played a critical role in all of the military campaigns.

‡ Some historians claim that her role was merely symbolic and question whether she actually wielded any of the weapons found in her tomb, leaving me (and at least one military historian who specializes in ancient China) to ask whether they make the same claims about the male Shang commanders who are also known only through inscriptions on oracle bones, written in much the same terms as those used to describe Fu Hao. I think not.

§ And possibly horsewomen, if they came from one of the Eurasian steppe peoples.

after she returned, victorious, to Anyang, Fu Hao fell ill.* She died shortly thereafter.

Fu Hao was not the only woman warrior during the Shang dynasty. The oracle bones give us the names of at least a hundred women who were active in Shang military campaigns. Most were the wives of Shang kings or powerful local lords or officials.† Unless (until?) we find one of their tombs, we are unlikely to know more. It is not impossible. In 2001, Chinese archaeologists reported the discovery of a tomb of an unnamed woman who was buried with a large cache of weapons, dating from the Western Zhou dynasty (1046–1071 BCE).

After her death, Fu Hao vanished from Chinese history until Chinese scholars discovered that oracle bones were historical documents in the late nineteenth century,‡ but the idea of the woman warrior never entirely vanished as a possibility. From the Warring States period (246–221 BCE) to the Ming dynasty (1368–1644), Chinese women§ led armies in unsettled times, with the expectation that once the crisis was past they would return to their traditional roles as daughter, wife, or mother. Some were teenage girls; some were tough old broads. They defended the border against invasion by barbarians and, like their counterparts in other times and places, organized the defense of besieged cities. They led peasant uprisings and helped put them down. (One woman who led a peasant revolt declared herself empress.)¶ They helped defend existing dynasties and establish new ones. They raised armies and inherited them. Sometimes they held official ranks in the Chinese military or government.** Qin Liangyu (1574–1684), for instance, began her military career by following

---

* From exhaustion, what else? (This is an *old* idea.)

† A relationship with a powerful man was always the easiest road to power, military and otherwise, for a woman in the ancient world. (Or the not-so-ancient world for that matter—the widow's walk to power remains well trodden in the modern world.)

‡ The language used on the oracle bones was rediscovered in 1899 by a Chinese scholar named Wang, who was stunned to realize that the piece of "dragon bone" he had purchased to be pounded into medication was inscribed with what looked like a primitive form of Chinese writing.

§ Loosely defined. A number of China's women warriors were not of Han ethnicity.

¶ Chen Shuozhen (d. 653) led a rebellion of fourteen thousand peasants against Tang Emperor Gaozong. Her self-proclaimed reign as empress lasted two months.

** I've said it before, but it's worth repeating: China is shorthand for a geographic region with shifting borders and a cultural continuum. For any given woman, it is more accurate to refer to her role in a specific Chinese state or dynasty. For our purposes that would be confusing.

her husband as the "pacification commissioner" of Shizhu, an area in modern Sichuan province, and eventually attained the rank of regional commander, the highest military rank under the Ming dynasty. More often, their heroism was recognized after the fact with a commemorative title—at least if they were on the winning side.

The stories we know are shaped by the sources in which they appear. Many of these examples were included in collections of biographies of "exemplary women" rather than in the official Chinese histories. One such collection includes short biographies of fifty-five "remarkable women," most of them women warriors. These accounts are closer to parables with morals than biographies as we know them today: the women who are highlighted fit a number of standard categories, such as filial daughter or chaste widow. As a result, we get incidents, or a series of incidents, in which a seeming transgression of the social norm is shown as being rooted in Confucian ethics of filial piety and loyalty. Most of the examples we know begin their military careers as the mothers, wives, or daughters of Chinese officials, and they either fight beside their kinsmen or in place of male relatives who are unable to carry out the tasks.

China also produced women warriors who were less malleable. Lady Qi Wang (c. 1530–1588), for instance, who led the defense of a coastal fort against Japanese pirates in 1561, was described by her contemporaries as "rude, unreasonable and aggressive"—not an exemplar of Confucian ideals of womanhood.[1] The stories of rude and aggressive women don't make the collections of exemplary tales; instead they are hidden in plain sight in the biographies of others.

SAMURAI WOMEN:
WARRIORS AND OTHERWISE

In medieval Japan, samurai was a class distinction, not a job description. Women who were born into the samurai class were samurai, whether or not they were warriors. Most learned to use the *naginata* for self-defense and carried double-edged daggers on their belts, primarily for self-defense in a confined space but sharp enough to allow the owner to commit suicide by severing her jugular vein should the need for such an action arise. In fact, during the Tokugawa regime, women from the warrior class were legally required to learn at least the basic martial skills needed to defend themselves and their family honor. As members of the warrior class, even those women who

In this nineteenth-century woodblock print, female samurai Tomoe Gozen brandishes a naginata.

did not fight were governed by the martial code of loyalty and honor known as *bushido*. They shared the disgrace when their male relations failed on the battlefield, following them into exile and even death.

If the written evidence is to be believed, few samurai women became samurai warriors who fought alongside men on the battlefield. The most famous was the twelfth-century warrior Tomoe Gozen.* Gozen reportedly fought alongside the hero Minamoto Kiso Yoshinaka in the Gempei War (1180–1185).† She was one of the last soldiers to stand beside him in his final battle at Awazu in 1184. Many scholars consider Tomoe Gozen a fictional character, though they accept Minamoto Kiso Yoshinaka as a historical figure.‡

---

* The primary source for Tomoe Gozen's story is *The Tale of the Heike*. Japan's answer to *The Iliad*, *The Tale of the Heike* was compiled from unwritten traditional sources into a single text in the mid-thirteenth century. It is an epic account of the struggle between the Taira and Minamoto clans for control of Japan at the end of the twelfth century.

† In which two samurai clans—the Taira and the Minamoto—duked it out for control of Japan. The Gempei War ended with the Minamotos' victorious establishment of the first shogunate—a form of government by military dictatorship in the name of a puppet emperor that would last in various forms from 1192 to 1867. Yoshinaka was a cousin and rival of the future first shogun. The two Minamotos were involved on the side in a winner-take-all struggle for dominance within the Minamoto clan. Yoshinaka lost. Tomoe Gozen lost with him.

‡ Tomoe Gozen is not the only woman warrior to suffer from this historical double standard. For example, some scholars believe Telesilla did not organize the defense of Argos against Sparta, though they are perfectly willing to accept the historicity of the Spartan attack.

Most of the samurai women who left a trace in the written accounts of Japan's interminable internal wars appear in the context of sieges rather than on the battlefield. For the most part, such women performed the traditional roles expected of samurai women in the defense of a stronghold: cooking, nursing the wounded, loading guns, filling cartridges, putting out fires caused by enemy cannon, dropping rocks on the enemy army, and preparing trophy heads for viewing. (Yes, you read that correctly.) Some, like western noblewomen in the same position, picked up weapons and led the defense. Fujinoye, for example, kept besieging warriors from taking Takadachi Castle in 1189 by holding the stairs with her *naginata* and sword. She defeated two of her attackers in hand-to-hand combat.*

A few took a quintessentially samurai approach and led a "forlorn hope" sortie against their besiegers. In 1577, Ueno Tsuruhime led thirty-three other women in a suicidal charge against the army of a rival warlord—preferring to die in battle instead of committing the ritual suicide prescribed by her husband. The tactic failed. The besieging samurai proved reluctant to kill women who fought back. Thwarted in their effort to earn an honorable death on the battlefield, the women of Ueno Tsuruhime's squadron retreated to the castle, where they committed mass suicide. Similarly, near the end of the Amakusa rebellion in 1589–90, three hundred women from the largely Christian stronghold at Hondo cut off their hair, tied up the hems of their kimonos so they could move freely, armed themselves with weapons and rosaries, and made a final desperate attack against the enemy. In this case, their opponents did not hesitate to fight back: only two of the women survived. The men who fought against them honored them with a variation of an idea we've seen before: "The warriors of Hondo were not men. They were women and children, yet the men who were fighting were surpassed by the dauntless courage of these warriors."[2]

In the nineteenth century, when the world of the samurai was coming to an end, some women from samurai families joined their fathers, husbands, and brothers in the fight against the forces of the Meiji emperor in the Boshin War. For example, Yamamoto Yaeko

---

* After the battle was over, she reportedly wrote a poem about her feelings on the subject—hard to imagine Black Agnes Randolph or that "most ingenious and evil-intentioned and vigorous old woman" Nicolaa de la Haye doing the same.

(1845–1932), the third daughter of a gunnery instructor, cropped her hair and participated in night sorties during the siege of Aizu in 1868, armed with two swords and her personal Spencer repeating rifle.* After her father died in the siege, she took over his command of the male soldiers who manned an elderly four-pound cannon at the entrance of Crane Castle and held the position through the month-long siege.

The most notable examples of samurai women who fought against the Meiji were the Joshigun, a group of thirty women who also fought at Aizu. The women of Aizu had received serious combat training, particularly in the use of the *naginata*. That training was tested when imperial forces attacked the well-fortified Crane Castle. Many samurai women committed suicide or were killed by their relatives in order to avoid capture by the imperial army: they had no reason to expect leniency if they were captured. The Joshigun chose to fight.

The Joshigun were an ad hoc group of volunteers, formed the day after the imperial army attacked. On October 10, 1868, led by Nakano Takeko (1847–1868),† the women charged the imperial army, armed with the traditional samurai weapons of *naginata* and swords. At first the imperial army thought it was being attacked by a group of adolescent boys, because many of the younger women had cut off their hair and tied it back in the style typically worn by young men, and they wore loose trousers. When the soldiers realized they were fighting against women, the cry went up to take them alive‡—their brief hesitation gave the Joshigun the chance to kill many of the soldiers before they were themselves gunned down. According to one report, Takeko, "with her tied-back hair, trousers, and steely eyes, radiated an intense *male* spirit and engaged the enemy troops, killing five or six with her *naginata*."§ She took a bullet to her chest at the

---

* Not all members of the samurai class rejected modern weapons.

† The daughter of an Aizu official, Takeko was also the adopted daughter of a martial arts master who ran a school in Aizu for training girls in martial arts. Takeko may have worked alongside him as an instructor.

‡ Probably not for chivalrous reasons.

§ By now I don't have to point out the fact that the highest compliment the chronicler could give her was to compare her to a man—right? Quoted in Diana E. Wright, "Female Combatants and Japan's Meiji Restoration: The Case of Aizu," *War in History* 8, no. 4 (November 2001): 409.

height of the battle. Dying, she asked her sister to cut off her head and bury it so no imperial soldier could take it as a trophy.

Now that's a samurai warrior!

THE KING'S WIVES

In the seventeenth through the nineteenth centuries, the kingdom of Dahomey in West Africa, in what is now the Republic of Benin, employed troops of trained full-time women soldiers who fought alongside their male counterparts.* The Europeans who encountered them in the eighteenth century dubbed the Dahomean soldiers "black Amazons." The Dahomeans called them *abosi* (the king's wives)† or *minos* (our mothers).

Members of the female regiments lived in the palace, which was off limits to all men except the king. Unlike other palace women, such as concubines, they were required to remain celibate. In compensation, they enjoyed more autonomy than most women in Dahomey. In their time off they swaggered like any other band of elite soldiers with a three-day pass: drinking, dancing, and singing rowdy songs, many of them to the effect that the men could stay behind and plant crops, a job Dahomeans considered women's work, while the minos headed out to eviscerate their enemies. They not only disdained "women's work" but claimed that by proving themselves equal to, or better than, their male counterparts on the battlefield, they had become men.‡

For much of their existence, the minos' weapon of choice was the smooth-bore, muzzle-loading flintlock, the same weapon carried in North American and European wars from the eighteenth through the mid-nineteenth centuries. Most early references to Dahomey's women warriors describe them carrying muskets and comment on

---

* The primary historical sources for the women warriors of Dahomey are accounts written by European soldiers, explorers, missionaries, colonial officials, slave traders, and merchants. We also have oral traditions recorded in Benin in the 1970s by anthropologist Amélie Degbelo.

† Not queens in the Western sense.

‡ It was not unusual for women warriors to use language that elevated women by comparing them to men and denigrated men by comparing them to women. Women warriors are the product of the same culture as the men around them.

their prowess with the weapon. British traveler John Duncan, invited to a display of marksmanship by Dahomey's women warriors, was impressed: "I was certainly surprised to see the certainty of their deadly aim.... Very few missed their object; and I did not observe one who fired wide of a man's body."[3] Serious praise for marksmanship with a notoriously inaccurate weapon.

Most European travelers echoed his opinion.

As in the American Revolution, the slow reloading time and inaccuracy of the flintlock meant battles were often decided by hand-to-hand combat. Dahomean soldiers, male and female alike, carried machetes, a weapon that French trader Edmond Chardoin reported they "wield with much skill and with which they lop off a limb or a head with a single blow as if it were an ordinary cane of bamboo."[4] Others carried a uniquely Dahomean weapon: a blade eighteen inches to three feet long that folded into a wooden handle. Effectively a giant straightedge razor, it took two hands to use. Fascinated Europeans reported the minos were rumored to use the razor to collect body parts as trophies.

The minos fought not in units alongside men but in separate units commanded by women. The units were not easily distinguished from each other in the field because their uniforms were similar: sleeveless, kilt-length tunics and shorts. According to an Egba oral tradition, when Dahomey attacked the capital of the Yoruba kingdom of Egba in 1851, the city's defenders were unaware they had been retreating before women soldiers until one of the minos fell into Yoruba hands. The Yoruba traditionally castrated the first prisoner taken during a battle. When they stripped their prisoner and discovered she was a woman, the Yoruba soldiers were so outraged at the idea they had been fighting against women that the tide of battle turned.* The Egba do not say what retribution they took on the woman, but I suspect it was ugly.

Oral history traces the origin of the minos to a group of women who hunted elephants for King Wegabja (ca. 1645–1680). Known as the *gheto*, they were presumably responsible for supplying him with ivory and meat.† While the jump from women hunting elephants to

---

* Since the Yoruba had been fighting Dahomey on-and-off for more than forty years at that point, it's hard to believe word wouldn't have gotten around.

† Dahomey still had female elephant hunters in the late nineteenth century.

This drawing of a Dahomean warrior, by a European observer, emphasizes her musket and her "trophy."

women fighting the enemy seems logical enough, there is no direct link to prove it is true. The closest tie we have is a probably apocryphal story that when King Gezo (r. 1818–1858) praised his female elephant hunters for their courage, they answered "a nice manhunt would suit them even better."[5]

The first eyewitness account of women deployed as soldiers in Dahomey dates from 1734. In 1727, Dahomey conquered the neighboring kingdom of Whydah (now Ouidah), a wealthy coastal trading state. In 1729, encouraged by the director of the local English entrepôt,* the ruler of Whydah regained control of the country with a large army while King Agaja (r. 1718–1740) of Dahomey fought off an attempted invasion of his country by the Yoruba kingdom of Oyo, in what is now central Nigeria. The Dahomean army suffered heavy losses in the battle against the Yorubans, but Agaja was determined to recapture Whydah, manpower shortage or not. According to British slave trader William Snelgrave (fl. 1719–1743), Agaja "ordered a great number of Women to be armed like Soldiers, and appointed Officers to each Company, with Colours, Drums, and Umbrellas [symbols of rank], according to the *Negroe* Fashion. Then ordering the Army to march, the women soldiers were placed in the Rear, to prevent Discovery."[6] Snelgrave doesn't tell us whether or not these women fought, but a similar ploy used in the Battle of Tenochtitlan in 1521† suggests they would have. The chronicles of Tlatelolco tell us that at the end of the battle, when his troops and those of his allies had been decimated by disease and Spanish gunfire, the Aztec leader Cuauhtémoc ordered the women of the city to cut off their hair, disguise themselves as men, and fight the Spanish. Would an experienced elephant hunter do less?

European observers agree the minos numbered between eight hundred and nine hundred women during the eighteenth century. The size of the corps grew in the two years after King Gezo seized power from his brother in 1818. By the 1840s, European visitors

---

* Europeans in Africa in the eighteenth century always had a straight-edged razor to grind.

† The last battle between the Aztecs and the Spaniards.

estimated the number of female soldiers at between three thousand and eight thousand.[*]

The women warriors of Dahomey came to an end with the arrival of the French in the late nineteenth century.

The first Franco-Dahomean war began in 1890. The war lasted two months and included two major engagements; Dahomey's women warriors fought in both of them. The Battle of Cotonou began before dawn on March 4. The French fielded a small force of 359 men, most of them Senegalese and Gabonese *tirailleurs* trained and led by French officers. They were armed with eight-shot repeating rifles and equipped with four field pieces that shot grapeshot. A Dahomean army of several thousand soldiers, armed for the most part with muskets and led by its women warriors, attacked the log stockade of the trading post around five o'clock in the morning. The battle lasted for four hours, but despite the Dahomeans' manpower advantage, they could not hold out against the superior French firepower, particularly after dawn, when a gunboat stationed offshore supported the troops in the trading post with cannon fire. The second major conflict of the war, the Battle of Atchoupa on April 20, was a repeat of the first: rifle and artillery fire demolished the charging Dahomean forces before they could get within musket range. Even so, a few women managed to get close enough to engage French soldiers in hand-to-hand combat before they fell to bayonet thrusts.[†]

---

[*] Richard Burton—the nineteenth-century explorer and proto-anthropologist, not the twentieth-century actor—was the British consul in Dahomey in 1863. He claimed his British predecessors in Dahomey had been hoodwinked as to the numbers of female warriors by "the heroines [being] marched out of one gate and in through another," so they could be counted more than once. See Richard F. Burton's 1864 *A Mission to Gelele, King of Dahome* (New York: Praeger, 1966), 263. Unlike other European observers, including members of the French army who would fight opposite the minos twenty years later, Burton was as dismissive of the women warriors' military skills as he was of his predecessors' observation skills. Writing to his friend Richard Moncton Milnes, Lord Houghton, Burton said, "They manoeuvre with the precision of a flock of sheep, and they are too light to stand a charge of the poorest troops in Europe . . . an equal number of British charwomen, armed with the British broomstick, would . . . clear them off in a very few hours." Quoted in Edward Rice, *Captain Sir Richard Francis Burton: The Secret Agent Who Made the Pilgrimage to Mecca, Discovered the Kama Sutra and Brought the Arabian Nights to the West* (New York: Charles Scribner's Sons, 1990), 378. Unfortunately, with Burton, it is hard to separate truth from quip.

[†] French accounts of the battle suggest the Dahomean soldiers had never faced bayonets before and consequently were impaled in large numbers—which seems odd, since they were familiar with other types of long, sharp metal weapons.

Peace negotiations after the Battle of Atchoupa resulted in a treaty in which Dahomey recognized the French protectorate over Porto-Novo and occupation of Cotonou. Both sides knew the peace was just a pause before war would resume.

The last Dahomean king, Béhanzin (r. 1890–1894), realized his army didn't stand a chance without modern weapons. He used the period of peace to stock up on rapid-firing, breech-loading rifles purchased from European merchants in the port cities of West Africa. By the time of the second Franco-Dahomey War in 1892, the Dahomean army had between four thousand to six thousand modern rifles in a variety of makes from different countries, including American Winchesters, Austrian Mannlichers, and French weapons that had been captured by Germans in the Franco-Prussian war of 1870 and shipped to Africa for resale. European observers were as complimentary of the minos' handling of the newer, more powerful weapons as they had been about their ability with a musket: "I don't know who taught them military tactics, the handling of arms, and shooting," one French lieutenant said after encountering the minos in a firefight, "but that one certainly didn't steal his money."[7]

The French, too, realized they had come to the first war inadequately prepared; it would take more than a few hundred troops to conquer Dahomey. They beefed up their forces to 2,200 troops, adding members of the French Foreign Legion, French marines, engineers, artillery, and cavalry, and additional Senegalese *tirailleurs*. Almost half the French fighting force was African.

With both sides primed for war, a minor incident between Dahomean troops and a French gunboat became the excuse for the Second Franco-Dahomean War. On the morning of September 19, an estimated four thousand to five thousand Dahomean troops attacked the French camp at Dogba—the first battle in a war that would last seven weeks and destroy the Dahomean army. French eyewitnesses reported that the women warriors were first-class troops, and conspicuous in every battle.

The turning point of the war came on October 6 at the battle of Adégon. Of the 434 women who fought in the battle, 17 survived. At that point, it became clear to King Béhanzin that Dahomey would not simply be defeated but crushed.

On November 3, the king directed a last ditch battle against the French: a mass assault against the French camp that lasted for four hours. At day's end, Béhanzin retreated. Some of the minos attempted to recruit girls to join their ranks. But the war was over. By the time Dahomey sued for peace, only fifty or sixty of its women warriors were still able to bear arms.

Veterans of Dahomey's all-female regiments survived into the twentieth century. Several travelers reported encounters with elderly women who claimed to be former minos. The most touching of these comes from a friend of historian Hélène d'Almedia-Topor, who tells the story of an ancient woman he and his friends used to see on the street of Cotonou when they were boys, around 1930. On one occasion, they startled her with a sharp noise. As they watched, she straightened to attention, fired an imaginary rifle, pounced on an imaginary enemy, and stabbed him with an imaginary dagger. She performed a victory dance, holding up an imaginary trophy of severed genitals, then shrank, confused, into old age again. An adult explained to the shaken boys: "She is a former warrior. . . . In the time of our former kings, there were women soldiers. Their battles ended long ago, but she continues the war in her head."[8] As what soldier does not?

THE FIRST WOMEN'S
BATTALION OF DEATH

When World War I began, Russian law prohibited women from joining the army. Nonetheless, women found ways to fight with the Russian army. Some women took the "traditional" route and disguised themselves as men, taking advantage of the general confusion to bypass medical inspections and other formalities. Others applied directly to unit commanders for the chance to enlist. As the war went on and manpower shortages became dire, individual commanders chose not to enforce the law. When women couldn't convince a commander to let them enlist, they often appealed to a higher authority. (At least one invoked the memory of Nadezhda Durova to strengthen her case.) The number of petitions became burdensome enough that in June 1915—ten months after Russia entered the war—the army established a policy for dealing with them. Thereafter, all requests were referred to the tsar for his personal approval.

In 1917, the February Revolution brought with it the possibility of change. The Provisional Government proclaimed all subjects of the empire free and equal citizens, with the rights and duties that went with citizenship. Many women assumed their new status included their right as citizens to bear arms in their country's defense.[*] By the spring of 1917, the idea of an all-female military unit was in the air.[†] Individual women proclaimed their desire to serve. Women's groups sent petitions to the government asking for permission to form all-female military units.

At the same time that women were eager to join the army, men on the front were desperate for the war to stop. For two and a half years, the army had suffered shortages of food and materiel, heavy casualties, and brutal defeats at the hands of the Germans. From the perspective of the front line, the February Revolution had done nothing to improve their lot. The Provisional Government was no more effective at running the war than the imperial government it replaced. The introduction of democracy to the military decision-making process in the form of soldiers' committees resulted in endless wrangling about every action and made it difficult for officers to enforce orders. In fact, many units voted to remove their officers, and then followed up the vote with force. Morale was low and the desertion rate was high. In May, units at the front experienced mass mutinies. It was not clear that Russia could continue to fight.

Many people thought an all-female battalion was the solution, believing the presence of women in the trenches would raise morale, or at least shame male soldiers into fighting.

In late May 1917, despite having serious reservations about the value of such units, Minister of War Alexander Kerensky approved the creation of a single all-female battalion under the leadership of

---

[*] The relationship between citizenship, the right to bear arms, and the right to vote has been a tangled one ever since the concept of universal male suffrage arose in the eighteenth century. In several countries, including the United States, legislators argued against giving women the vote because they could not fight to defend their country.

[†] The story of Russian women who fought in the First World War can be pieced together from several different types of sources. Soviet archives hold dozens of petitions from women who sought to become soldiers in the years from 1914 to 1917. In addition, some women who fought in the war, both as individuals and as part of the later official units, left accounts of their experiences. Alongside these accounts in their own words, we have contemporary news coverage of the Soviet women soldiers. Russia's women soldiers caught the public imagination at home and abroad. Books, magazines, and newspapers carried stories about the women. The most extensive account outside of Russia appeared in *The Red Heart of Russia* by American journalist Bessie Beatty.

Maria Bochkareva (1889–1920), a semiliterate peasant from Siberia who had already fought for two years alongside male soldiers.[*]

Bochkareva's story is similar to that of women who joined the army disguised as men in earlier centuries. She was born into a desperately poor peasant family and went to work at the age of eight. When she was fifteen, she married a local peasant, Afanasi Bochkarev, in an attempt to escape her father, who was an abusive alcoholic. Afanasi proved to be as brutal as her father. She fled again, this time with a petty criminal named Yakov Buk. They lived together for three years. When Buk was arrested for fencing stolen goods in May 1912, Maria followed him into exile in Siberia, where he began to drink heavily and became physically abusive.

When the war began in 1914, Bochkareva saw it as an opportunity to escape. She traveled to her childhood home of Tomsk and attempted to enlist in the Twenty-Fifth Tomsk Reserve Battalion. The commander explained it was illegal for women to serve in the imperial army. Bochkareva pushed. The commander sarcastically suggested she ask the tsar for permission to enlist—not that far-fetched a suggestion as it turned out. Bochkareva convinced (or perhaps bullied) the commander to help her write a telegram to Tsar Nicholas II. To the amazement of everyone, and the possible chagrin of the commander, she received a thumbs-up from the tsar.

With the tsar's permission, she enlisted in the Fourth Company of the Twenty-Fifth Reserve. Her unit was sent to the western front in February 1915. For two years she served with distinction. She was wounded three times—the third time a shell fragment pierced her spine, leaving her paralyzed. She learned to walk again and returned to the front. She earned several military honors for valor, including the St. George Cross.

Bochkareva was an avid proponent of an all-female brigade. She began to recruit for the First Women's Battalion of Death as soon as she received approval to form the unit,[†] helped by the Petrograd

---

[*] Much of what we know about Bochkareva comes from her memoir, an as-told-to account written with the help of Russian émigré journalist, Isaac Don Levine. Published in New York in 1919, Bochkareva's memoir, like those of Durova, Edmonds, and Velazquez, must be used with care due to fabrications, omissions, and embellishments.

[†] The women's battalion was not the only unit to receive the designation "battalion of death." The designation indicated that all members of the unit had sworn they were willing to fight to the death. Members of such units had a special skull-and-crossbones insignia for their caps and red-and-black chevrons for their sleeves.

Women's Military Organization. Some two thousand women enlisted initially, far exceeding expectations. The realities of war and
Bochkareva's rigid leadership style whittled the battalion down to
three hundred by the time they were sent to the front.*

The social backgrounds of the women who enlisted varied. Bochkareva was barely literate, but roughly half the women who served
under her had a secondary education, and 25 to 30 percent had completed some degree of higher education. Professionals and women
from wealthy families trained alongside clerks, dressmakers, factory
workers, and peasants. Some had already served in the war in medical
or auxiliary positions and were eager to do more; as one woman said,
"Women have something more to do for Russia than binding men's
wounds."[9] At least ten had fought previously in all-male units. Thirty
of them had been decorated for valor in the field.

Bessie Beatty, an American journalist who reported on the Russian Revolutions and the subsequent civil war for the *San Francisco
Bulletin*, spent ten days living with the battalion in its barracks. When
she asked the women why they had enlisted, many told her it was "because they believed that the honor and even the existence of Russia
were at stake and nothing but great human sacrifice could save her."[10]
Others joined because "anything was better than the dreary drudgery
and the drearier waiting of life as they lived it."[11] A fifteen-year-old
Cossack girl from the Urals, who managed to enlist despite the re-
quirement that all volunteers be at least eighteen, joined because her
father, mother, and two brothers had all died in battle. "What else is
left for me?" she asked Beatty.

On June 21, after less than a month of rigorous training, their hair
cut in a style any modern recruit would recognize, and wearing uniforms that didn't fit,† the First Women's Battalion of Death marched
in procession to St. Isaac's Cathedral for the consecration of their battalion standards. Enthusiastic crowds cheered and a group of soldiers
and sailors boosted Bochkareva onto their shoulders. Bessie Beatty
trumpeted the significance of the unit and the event to her readers.
This was "not the isolated individual woman who has buckled on a

---

* She lost eight hundred women because she refused to allow them to establish a
soldiers' committee.

† The Russian army did not have the resources to produce women's uniforms. The
women received standard uniforms designed for male soldiers. Boots were a particular
problem.

sword and shouldered a gun throughout the pages of history, but the woman soldier banded and fighting en masse—machine gun companies of her, battalions of her, scouting parties of her, whole regiments of her."[12]

Two days later, Bochkareva and her soldiers left for the Russian western front. Kerensky sent the unit to an area that suffered from dangerously low morale. A few days before the women arrived, a regiment had been forced to disband due to massive desertions. Their posting was deliberate—a test as to whether the presence of women would affect the morale of male soldiers.

The First Women's Battalion of Death experienced its first taste of battle on July 9 as part of an offensive against a German position. When the order came to attack, nothing happened. Three regiments of the infantry division to which they were attached convened their soldiers' committees and debated whether or not to fight. After several hours, the women, anxious to prove their worth, decided they would advance without the support of the other regiments. Joined by a few hundred male soldiers, they advanced with few casualties. Eventually, more than half the soldiers in the division joined them in the advance. Together they took the first and second lines of the German trenches.

The Women's Battalion of Death in the field.

The women and a few male soldiers held off six German counter-attacks on their position. They retreated only when they ran out of ammunition. Before retreating, they captured two machine guns and a number of Germans, including two officers, who were not happy about being taken prisoner by women. One officer was so distraught with the shame of being captured by women that the Russian women tied him down for fear he would commit suicide—a variation of the Yoruba rage at finding they had retreated before an army of women.

The First Women's Battalion of Death inspired the creation of similar units throughout Russia. Between five thousand and six thousand women volunteered for combat. The Provisional Government established fifteen more official units; grassroots women's groups organized at least ten others. Several of these units saw active duty.

Despite the success of the First Women's Battalion of Death at the front, military authorities believed the units were more trouble than they were worth. The units were formed as a means of improving morale among male troops. Instead, male soldiers became increasingly hostile to the presence of women soldiers over the course of the summer. By September, the military had stopped enlisting women and was discussing proposals to disband existing women's combat units.

In October, the Bolsheviks seized power from the Provisional Government in a relatively bloodless coup.* On March 3, 1918, the Bolshevik government signed a separate peace treaty with Germany and began demobilizing the army, including the all-female units. Because the great experiment of women soldiers was publicly linked with the Provisional Government, many women soldiers were branded as counterrevolutionaries during the first chaotic months of Bolshevik rule and suffered violence at the hands of their countrymen.† Some joined anti-Bolshevik forces in the civil war that followed the October Revolution. Others enlisted in the Red Army, which welcomed women during the civil war—though most of them were placed in noncombat positions.

Maria Bochkareva fled to the United States, where she met with President Woodrow Wilson to plea for the United States to intervene in Russia. (And took the time to "write" her memoir.) She returned to Siberia in 1919 and organized a women's paramedic unit on

---

* The blood came later.

† It was easy enough for a woman who wanted to blend back into the civilian population to discard her uniform, but a shaved-head was difficult to disguise.

behalf of the White Russians. She was captured by the Bolsheviks on Christmas Day 1919, tried as an enemy of the state, and shot on May 16, 1920. She was thirty years old.

Russia's women soldiers were celebrated during the First World War, but they were conspicuously absent from Soviet histories of the war and the revolution that followed it because of their connection to the failed Provisional Government. Nonetheless, they would serve as a precedent when Soviet Russia once again faced an external enemy in the form of Nazi Germany.

The Second World War offered opportunities for unprecedented numbers of women to openly enlist, no disguise needed. The numbers of women involved, the terms under which they enlisted, and how close they came to combat varied depending on how desperately the nation involved suffered from a manpower shortage. For the most part, they filled support positions. At first, they were assigned jobs as drivers, cooks, or typists. As the war went on, the jobs classified as suitable for women expanded to include hundreds of jobs away from the front line, including radio and telephone operators, mechanics, and engineers.

The United States was the most conservative in its implementation of women's military units, not surprising since it was the last of the combatant nations to enter the war, and the one in which women civilians were at the least risk of finding themselves threatened by an enemy army. The initial bill that established the Women's Army Auxiliary Corps (WAAC)—to serve "with" the army, not "in" the army— limited enlistment to twenty-five thousand women. (A year later, the WAAC was converted from auxiliary to active duty status with the creation of the Women's Army Corps, or WAC.) The US Navy, Coast Guard, and Marines followed the Army's lead a few months later, though WAVES, SPARS, and female marines were not allowed to serve outside the United States (unlike army and navy nurses and women in the WAAC).* Several months later, Congress raised the ceiling on female enlistment—the first of several legislative changes required to fill the military's needs. By war's end, some 350,000 American women had enlisted in the various branches of the armed services.

---

* Oddities and twisty thinking abound when you look closely at the history of women in the modern military.

In Great Britain, the women's auxiliary units of all three military services, which had been disbanded at the end of the First World War, were reactivated before the Second World War began. Originally organized as women's auxiliaries, the Women's Royal Naval Service (WRNS), the Auxiliary Territorial Service (ATS), and the Women's Auxiliary Air Force (WAAF) were given military status in 1941 as part of the National Services Act.* The act also allowed for women to be conscripted into war work or the armed forces—a historical fact often forgotten in arguments about whether or not women should be included in the draft.†

Britain stretched the definition of noncombatant to accommodate public opinion with little reference to logic. Members of the WAAF were not allowed to fly military aircraft, but they operated more than a thousand barrage balloon sites, designed to deter enemy bombers.‡ Some "Wrens" took part in planning naval operations, including the D-Day landings. They operated small harbor launches and tugs throughout the war. Anecdotal evidence suggests WRNS led groups of smaller landing craft south of the English coast and towed disabled vehicles back through the Solent strait for repairs.§ Back on land, as the need for able-bodied men in the field army became desperate, members of the ATS were assigned to integrated male-female anti-aircraft (AA) units, where they did everything except fire the guns—a concession to public opinion that allowed the government to claim the women in AA jobs were not in combat, unlike the men standing next to them.

The Soviet Union made the most dramatic use of women soldiers: 8 percent of all Soviet combatants were women. Eight hundred thousand women served in the Red Army in World War II. Most, like

---

* Military status brought with it two-thirds the pay of men of equal rank.

† At first the law provided for the conscription of single women and widows without children between the ages of nineteen and thirty. As the war went on, the upper age limit was pushed to forty-three. Women who had served in World War I were eligible for conscription up to the age of fifty. Britain drafted 125,000 women over a period of three years. An additional 430,000 volunteered during the same period.

‡ When it became necessary to free up male pilots for combat, Britain formed the Air Transport Auxiliary (ATA), which had no military status and consequently could allow women to fly military aircraft (speaking of oddities and twisty thinking).

§ As is so often the case when talking about women warriors, it is almost impossible to trace the extent of WRNS involvement in the complex maneuvers of D-Day. Smaller vessels, including those of the types "manned" by WRNS, did not maintain ships logs.

enlisted women in Britain or the United States, worked in support positions, but several hundred thousand fought at the front as snipers, machine gunners, tank crews, antiaircraft personnel,* and three regiments of female bombers, fighter pilots, navigators, and airplane mechanics. Between 100,000 and 150,000 Soviet women were decorated for bravery during the war. Ninety-one women received the Gold Star Hero of the Soviet Union, including more than thirty female fighter pilots and air crewmen. More than half of them received the honor posthumously.

Even in Germany, where Nazi orthodoxy stated women could best serve the Third Reich by bearing children, some 450,000 women joined female auxiliary units. They filled 85 percent of the German army's support posts. Thousands of German women served in AA units; like their British counterparts, they were not allowed to fire the guns. Although members of the female auxiliary units wore uniforms and were under military discipline, they were never officially described as soldiers. (Unofficially, they were known as *Blitzmädchen*—the man on the street knows a woman warrior when he sees one.)

After the First World War, combatant nations discharged female recruits and disbanded all-female units. When World War II was over, tired nations attempted to forget a world in which women had been mobilized to build airplanes and to fly them. Soviet Russia made the most explicit attempt to erase all memory of women's role in the war; the government told members of the all-female pilot regiments: "Do not speak of the services you rendered."[13]

In the United States, attempts to pass a bill that would allow women to serve as permanent regular members of the armed services met with serious opposition in 1947, despite the support of General Dwight D. Eisenhower and Admiral Chester W. Nimitz. During the war, opponents of women in the military argued women should not be exposed to the stress of the army in war. Now they argued that without the pressure of a military emergency, when women could free

---

* Unlike in Britain and Germany, women in Russian antiaircraft units were allowed to fire the guns. If you have ace female snipers in your army, no one is likely to be queasy about women shooting down planes, except enemy pilots. One German pilot testified to their effectiveness: "I would rather fly ten times over the skies of Tobruk [over all-male British ack-ack] than to pass once through [Russia where] the fire of Russian flak [was] sent up by female gunners." Quoted in D'Ann Campbell, "Women in Combat: The World War II Experience in the United States, Great Britain, Germany, and the Soviet Union," *Journal of Military History* 57, no. 2 (April 1993): 319.

Lyudmilla Pavlichenko was one of the most successful snipers in World War II, with 309 confirmed kills (almost 50 percent more than the acclaimed Audie Murphy).

up men for combat assignments, women could play no useful role in the military. The bill's opponents were not able to stop it entirely, but they were able to impose serious restrictions on women's ability to participate in the military. President Harry S. Truman signed the Women's Armed Services Integration Act into law on June 12, 1948. The final bill included a cap on female enlistment of 2 percent of the total armed force of the United States and a ban on women having command authority over men.

In the seventy years since, women have been further integrated into the American military one painful step at a time, always accompanied by political opposition and the perception by some branches of the public that women cannot and should not fight.

WAS SHE
OR WASN'T SHE?

Female samurai aren't the only women warriors who are finding their way back onto the historical battlefield, undisguised, thanks to forensic archaeology in general, and DNA testing in particular.

The existence of female warriors in Viking Age Scandinavia is a hot-button topic, with passionate defenders on both sides of the argument.

Medieval texts dealing with the Viking period, written a few centuries after the fact, include stories of Scandinavian women fighting alongside men, told with varying degrees of realism. A tenth-century Irish source reports a female warrior, Inghen Ruaidh ("Red Girl"), who led a Viking fleet to Ireland. Saxo Grammaticus, author of the twelfth-century *Gesta Danorum* (*Deeds of the Danes*), tells us "there were once women among the Danes who dressed themselves to look like men, and devoted almost every instant of their lives to the pursuit of war'"*—the examples he gives include the warrior Lagertha, who later provided the model for a character in the television series *Vikings*. Many scholars dismiss these references to women warriors as

---

* Like some observers today, Saxo wasn't sure women warriors were a good thing. He went on to say "they devoted those hands to the lance which they should rather have applied to the loom. They assailed men with their spears whom they could have melted with their looks, they thought of death and not of dalliance." See Saxo Grammaticus, *Gesta Danorum: The History of the Danes*, vol. 1, trans. Peter Fisher (Oxford, UK: Clarendon Press, 2015), 477.

purely fictional, sometimes describing them as male sexual fantasies.* A smaller number of scholars argue that we shouldn't automatically dismiss these accounts as having no historical roots, pointing out that scholars have discovered a historical basis for many of the semilegendary male characters in the sagas. Similarly, physical artifacts such as fragments of tapestry and brooches depicting female figures holding weapons or riding on horseback are assumed to be representations of Valkyries, without considering the possibility they could represent real-life armed female warriors riding into battle.

Even though we know of a number of cases of Viking women buried with weapons, scholars have been reluctant to acknowledge they might have used those weapons to fight. When a male burial includes weapons, the argument goes like this: "Warriors were men. Therefore it is likely, if not 100 percent certain, that a man buried with a weapon was a warrior." When a female burial includes weapons, scholars speculate on why she might have been buried with "male" grave goods, or reinterpret the weapons as everyday tools, rather than concluding that she was a warrior, even with the caveat that a woman warrior was an exception rather than the norm.

The spectacular ship burial from 834 CE found at Oseberg, Norway, in 1903 presents an extreme example of how far scholars will bend and stretch to avoid this conclusion. Unlike most Viking ship burials, the Oseberg ship held the remains of two women who were buried with two axes and other objects traditionally associated with men, including the ship itself. The burial included none of the grave goods traditionally associated with women—i.e., jewelry.† Many interpretations of the Oseberg burial remove the women from the center of the picture, and the power associated with their burial, by positing that one of them was the wife of a powerful man, or that their burial was a religious offering. Scholars have questioned whether the "male-related" objects actually belonged to the women and suggested the axes might be kitchen implements rather than weapons. One scholar went beyond these typical responses to finding a woman buried with weapons or other emblems of power and suggested a male

---

* The medieval equivalent of the scantily clad women warriors that graced the covers of pulp fiction novels in the mid-twentieth century, or their controversial counterparts in modern pop culture, perhaps? (Though Saxo didn't seem to find the idea titillating.)

† Their absence could be explained by the fact that the grave had been looted long before the archaeologists arrived.

skeleton had been buried with the women, but his bones had been ritually removed from the grave with the purpose of using them for magical or religious practices, leaving no trace behind.*

Polite scholarly bickering over whether or not Scandinavian women went a-viking became somewhat less polite when DNA evidence regarding a Viking burial made a public splash in 2017.

In 1871, Swedish archaeologist Hjalmar Stolpe excavated an unusually well-furnished grave at Birka, a town in central Sweden that was a key Viking trading center in the eighth through the late tenth centuries and is the site of the largest, most well-known Viking burial ground. The grave goods in grave Bj581 included the complete equipment of a Viking warrior: sword, spear, armor-piercing arrows, a battle knife, two shields, and two horses. Archaeologists saw the evidence of a warrior and assumed the individual buried with the goods was male. For 130 years, the "Birka man" was considered a defining example of a high-status Viking warrior.

In 2014, assumptions about the "Birka man" were overturned when Stockholm University bioarchaeologist Anna Kjellström examined the warrior's pelvic bones and mandible and determined they were those of a woman. The image of the male warrior in a patriarchal society is so deeply embedded in our culture that some archaeologists blamed Kjellström's finding on errors made by the archaeologists who excavated the site in 1871. Perhaps the bones were mislabeled. Maybe more than one skeleton had been jumbled together.

DNA testing on the warrior buried in Bj581 was the only way to settle the controversy. A team led by Uppsala University archaeologist Charlotte Hedenstierna-Jonson tested two types of DNA from the skeleton. One, mitochondrial DNA, would show whether the bones belonged to one person. The other, nuclear DNA, would identify whether the body was male or female—the simplest of all DNA tests. No one could argue about the test results. The bones belonged to one person, with a genetic affiliation to modern Swedes, and she was a woman.

Presented with irrefutable evidence that the "Birka man" was a woman, some scholars questioned the relationship between the grave goods and the person with whom they were buried.† Some suggested

---

* You have to give the man points for imagination.

† Ironically, some of the scholars whose work has expanded our understanding of women as prominent players in the Viking world over the last thirty years are among the most determined opponents of the new status of the "Birka woman."

that perhaps the weapons reflected the status and role of the family rather than the individual.* Others posited the existence of a second (male) body, now missing, to whom the weapons belonged—a theory not supported by the relationship between the grave goods and the nontheoretical human remains in the grave. Because the skeleton shows no signs of weapons-related wounds, some argued that even if the grave goods belonged to her she was not a warrior.† In short, people believed the remains in grave Bj581 were those of a warrior as long as those remains were assumed to be male. Once the gender identification changed, so did the archaeological interpretation, which was based on our ideas of gender roles rather than on objective facts drawn from the remains. Apparently double standards apply to those long dead as well as to the living.

There is no reason to believe women warriors were a normal part of Viking culture based solely on the revelation that the "Birka man" was a woman. At the same time, there is no reason to believe female burials with weapons are as rare as previously thought. Thousands of Viking graves have been excavated over the last 150 years. It is possible archaeologists have misidentified other Viking graves as those of men based on the inclusion of weaponry in their grave goods. In his careful analysis of known examples of possible women warriors, published in 2013, before Anna Kjellström upset the status quo in Birka, Polish archaeologist Leszek Gardela noted:

> Although many Viking Age cemeteries were excavated in the twentieth century, some of the sites have not been documented in a satisfactory manner. Very often, what we have at hand are just very vague descriptions of particular graves with no plans, drawings or photographs. Moreover, in a lot of cases the sex of the deceased was not determined with the application of anthropological (osteological) methods, but only on the basis of the finds that accompanied the deceased. . . . In such "traditional" approaches weapons were usually regarded as clear indicators of men, while jewelry and tools for textile production were seen as characteristic for females. It is possible,

---

* No one asks this kind of question when a male burial site includes similar grave goods. In fact, no one asked this kind of question about grave Bj581 when they believed these items had been buried with a man.

† An objection no one raised when everyone thought she was a he, perhaps because only two out of forty-nine similar male burials at Birka show signs of sharp-force trauma.

therefore, that some of the graves excavated in the early 20th century that were described as belonging to men (on the basis of male objects that accompanied the deceased) may have actually belonged to biological females. In order to determine this with more certainty, however, one would have to conduct a new analysis of the skeletal material—and unfortunately this is not always possible.[1]

In the same study, Gardela describes another grave at Birka that contained weapons alongside the remains of both a man and a woman. He points out that it has always been assumed the weapons belonged with the man, even though everything else about the grave suggested the woman was the more important of the two. Perhaps, he hints, the grave tells a different story to someone willing to look with fresh eyes.

The "Birka man" is not the only instance of archaeologists reconsidering the gender identification of remains. In 1997, archaeologist Jeannine Davis-Kimball published a paper in the September/October issue of *Archaeology* titled "Chieftain or Warrior-Princess?" in which she challenged the traditional interpretation of the gender of a richly accoutered Issyk skeleton, dubbed the Issyk Gold Man by the Russian archaeologists who excavated it in 1969. Based on the resemblance of the striking headdress to those buried with high-status women in early nomad cultures, the presence of earrings and other artifacts that typically were not included in male burials of the period,[*] and the skeleton's slight stature,[†] Davis-Kimball argued that the Gold Man was likely a high-status Gold Woman, weapons and all. Davis-Kimball's suggestions did not raise the same furor as Anna Kjellström's outing of the Birka "man," in either scientific circles or the popular press.[‡] While a few colleagues pushed back, others admitted she could be right. Even the physical anthropologist who examined the bones in the lab after the excavation agreed: "The bones were very

---

[*] As noted before, this is the flip side of assuming the presence of weapons means the remains are male.

[†] Russian archaeologists drew on the same assumptions that helped adult women pass themselves off as adolescent boys and enlist in the army, and described the "Gold Man" as a young chieftain based on his build.

[‡] With no equivalent to Lagertha to catch the imagination, ancient nomadic warriors of the Russian steppes don't have the same emotional resonance for the American public as female Vikings.

small and could have belonged to a female. It was probably the prestigious artifacts, particularly the sword and dagger, that made [Kemal] Akishev [the Kazakh archaeologist who discovered the Gold Man in 1969] think the skeleton had been a male chieftain."[2]

Unfortunately, no bone samples from the Issyk skeleton are available for DNA testing—a casualty of Soviet archaeological practices. Whether the Gold Man was actually a Gold Woman will remain an open question.

INSIGNIFICANT
EXCEPTIONS?

In the sixteenth century, Gaspard de Tavannes, a military commander in the French Wars of Religion, argued, "Women should be
women, not captains; if the illness of their husbands or the minority
of their children constrains them to enter combat, it is tolerable for
one or two times when necessary"[1]

In 1976, speaking about the first class of women to enter the United
States military academies, General William Westmoreland, former
army chief of staff and former superintendent of West Point, made a
similar point in less polite terms: "Maybe you could find one woman
in 10,000 who could lead in combat, but she would be a freak, and
the Military Academy is not being run for freaks."[2] (General Westmoreland apparently found it more difficult to accept the possibility of
women combat commanders than his sixteenth-century counterpart,
who would have seen women fighting in sieges. So much for progress.)
Many of the senior male cadets shared his viewpoint and did their best
to drive their new female classmates out of the academies.*

---

*A nurse in the American Civil War wrote about a similar experience a hundred
years earlier when she described the reception of another group of women in another un-
welcoming military institution. Army surgeons, like the West Point cadets, "determined
to make [the women's] lives so unbearable that they should be forced in self-defense to
leave." Did I say, so much for progress? In Georgeanna Woolsey Bacon and Eliza Woolsey, Letters of a Family During the War for the Union 1861–1865 (London: Forgotten
Books, 2015), 142.

Forty plus years later, every attempt to allow female soldiers the same opportunities as their male comrades in arms is met with some variation of "maybe a few exceptions can [fill in the blank], but the average woman can't."

The belief that women warriors are "insignificant exceptions" has deep historical roots. (And apparently isn't going anywhere.) When we describe women warriors of the past as Joan of Arc look-a-likes or as Amazons, we reinforce that belief. By making them larger-than-life we set their actions outside the reach of ordinary women.[*]

You can argue that many of the women discussed in this book were exceptions in their time and place, whether they were queens, inspired revolutionaries, saints, viragos, patriots, or simply ordinary women doing extraordinary things in times of crisis.[†] The fact that sources so often describe them as having "fought like a man" makes it clear their contemporaries and/or their chroniclers saw them as exceptions—and perhaps as one of Westmoreland's freaks.

As long as you focus on one historical figure, or one cluster of women, or on one historical period, it is easy to believe any individual woman warrior was indeed an exception who stood outside the norm of her time—created by a national crisis or an anomaly of inheritance—and who consequently stands outside the norm of history as a whole. One of John Keegan's "insignificant exceptions." There is, after all, only one Joan of Arc. The number of women who enlisted disguised as men in any given war is statistically insignificant. The circumstances that led women to fight at the siege of Sparta or Tenochtitlan or Leningrad were desperate. And so on.

Looking at women warriors in isolation, it is also easy to accept the way in which the accomplishments (or even existence) of a specific woman warrior are dismissed. That Telesilla or Kenau Simonsdochter Hasselaer or Artemisia II didn't do what the sources claim she did. That an unknown man stood behind Matilda of Tuscany pulling the military strings.[‡] That Fu Hao played no more than a symbolic role on the battlefield. That Mawiyya or Kit Cavanagh didn't exist. That any ancient remains buried with a sword are male.

---

[*] A fact that doesn't seem to stop young girls from identifying with Joan of Arc. Or with "Molly Pitcher," for that matter. Dream big!

[†] The essence of the citizen soldier.

[‡] Unlikely as it seems, a number of historians have worked very hard over the years to identify him, without suggesting any viable candidates.

That the women who stood on the ramparts and fought back don't count as warriors because if they were soldiers (and therefore men) the fact that they stepped forward to fire a cannon or picked up a rifle wouldn't be worth remarking on.* Looking at women warriors in isolation, it doesn't matter that Katherine of Aragon successfully defended England against invasion because everyone knows the important part of her story is Henry Tudor's inability to father a son. You can overlook the fact that Alexander the Great or Edward the Elder of England had a sister who led troops into battle.

When you step back and look at women warriors across the boundaries of geography and historical period, larger patterns appear—parallels not only between the stories of the women themselves but in the ways their stories are told and not told. Some times, places, and social structures are more accepting of women warriors than others. (As a general rule, horse-based cultures, honor cultures, and tribal societies do a better job with the concept than large empires or regular armies—with the extraordinary exception of China.) The accomplishments of women are questioned, undercut, and ignored by scholars in consistent ways across periods. There are unexpected linkages between women, particularly between mothers and daughters— looked at in the context of Cynane, Matilda of Tuscany, Katherine of Aragon, and Amina of Zazzau, the legend that the Trung sisters learned the arts of war from their mother seems a lot more possible.

But the main thing that struck me when I looked at women warriors across cultures rather than in isolation is how many examples there are and how lightly they sit on our collective awareness. I began with hundreds of examples. I ended with thousands. In the last weeks of writing this book I continued to discover new examples almost daily, sometimes as many as a dozen at a time.† The most well-documented women—Matilda of Tuscany, Njinga, Begum Samru—are increasingly the subjects of academic monographs and occasionally break into the zeitgeist/popular media. As I write this, the Dahomey "Amazons" are enjoying a flurry of popular interest thanks to their (thin) parallels with the all-female army in the Marvel Studios film *Black Panther* (2018). At the other end of the spectrum, I found stories that

---

* An actual example from the "have your cake and eat it too" school of writing about women in war.

† I reached the point where all I could do was make a note and keep going. A good problem to have.

were no more than a trace in a footnote, an aside in a paragraph about something else entirely, or a reference to a statue commemorating an obscure local heroine. In many cases, a single sentence sums up everything we know about an individual woman warrior.

In the end, I left out many more examples than I included:

Gesche Meiburg, the Maid of Braunschweig, who stood on the fortifications when the city was under siege in 1615, armed with a sword and a musket. A contemporary illustrated broadsheet reported (in verse) that she "behaved valiantly / wounded a number of warriors / and put out their lights."[3]

Lozen, the younger sister of the Apache war leader Victorio, who was a regular member of Apache war and raiding parties in the late nineteenth century. Her brother described her as "a shield to her people."[4]

Mika Etchebéhère, who commanded a column on the republican side in the Spanish Civil War, described with pride by the men she led as "a female captain with more balls than all the male captains in the world."*

Captain Linda Bray, the commanding officer of a military police company in the United States force that invaded Panama in 1989, who led her men in an unexpected firefight with Panamanian forces who had occupied a K-9 Corps compound.

Exceptions within the context of their time and place? Yes. Exceptions over the scope of human history? Not so much. Insignificant? Hell, no!

---

* Sometimes you just have to accept the compliment in the spirit in which it was intended.

SUGGESTED READING
AND RESOURCES

MAPS AND GENERAL REFERENCES

Ancient History Encyclopedia (Ancient.eu) includes maps, interactive timelines, useful bibliographies, and a wide range of illustrated articles about the ancient world.

The TimeMap of World History (TimeMaps.com) is designed as an educational tool. It includes maps and brief essays for the same scope of time and place as *Women Warriors*.

I have mixed feelings about *Encyclopaedia Britannica Online* (Britannica.com), which is the reference equivalent of the little girl with the curl right in the middle of her forehead. But when it's useful, it's very useful indeed.

The various editions of the *Oxford Atlas of World History*, edited by Patrick O'Brien, are a good source of historical overviews with detailed maps that show changes over time. If you want to go in deeper, I strongly recommend the various *Palgrave Concise Historical Atlases*, which focus on particular regions and include extensive bibliographies.

Alas, I can't point you to a one-size-fits-all general history of the world or historical dictionary.

A HANDFUL OF BOOKS THAT STRUGGLE WITH THE BIG QUESTIONS

Davis-Kimball, Jeannine. *Warrior Women: An Archaeologist's Search for History's Hidden Heroines*. New York: Warner Books, 2002.

Fraser, Antonia. *The Warrior Queens: The Legends and the Lives of the Women Who Have Led Their Nations in War*. New York: Vintage Books, 1994.

Hay, David J. *The Military Leadership of Matilda of Canossa, 1046–1115*. Manchester, UK: Manchester University Press, 2008.

Jansen, Sharon L. *The Monstrous Regiment of Women: Female Rulers in Early Modern Europe*. New York: Palgrave Macmillan, 2002.

Lynn, John A. *Women, Armies, and Warfare in Early Modern Europe*. New York: Cambridge University Press, 2008.

Mayor, Adrienne. *The Amazons: Lives and Legends of Warrior Women Across the Ancient World*. Princeton, NJ: Princeton University Press, 2014.

A FEW GOOD BIOGRAPHIES OF INDIVIDUAL WOMEN WARRIORS

Alpern, Stanley B. *Amazons of Black Sparta: The Women Warriors of Dahomey*. New York: New York University Press, 2011.

Castor, Helen. *Joan of Arc: A History*. New York: HarperCollins, 2015.

Heywood, Linda M. *Njinga of Angola: Africa's Warrior Queen*. Cambridge, MA: Harvard University Press, 2017.

Keay, Julia. *Farzana: The Woman Who Saved an Empire*. London: Tauris, 2014.

Tucker, Phillip Thomas. *Cathy Williams: From Slave to Buffalo Soldier*. Mechanicsburg, PA: Stackpole Books, 2002.

ACKNOWLEDGMENTS

Depending on how you count, I've spent the last eighteen months, or four years, or three decades thinking about the women warriors who appear in these pages. I had a lot of help along the way, but there are a handful of people to whom I owe special thanks:

Leila Campoli, agent extraordinaire, who pushed me to think harder about the context and the audience for *Women Warriors* and found us a good home at Beacon Press.

Amy Caldwell, my editor at Beacon Press, who gave me room to explore ideas and be opinionated, but never let me fall into the abyss of weirdness. Her questions and suggestions made *Women Warriors* a better book.

Teri Embree and her staff of reference librarians at the Pritzker Military Library, who not only helped me find answers and sources but also helped me frame the questions.

Longtime blog reader Paul Hancq, who volunteered to be my Pentagon research assistant, got me copies of elusive articles and regularly reminds me that I am not the only person who finds this stuff interesting.

My accountability buddies Amy Sue Nathan and Evelyn Herwitz and the ever-changing members of a top secret, permanent, floating Facebook writing challenge group who cheered me on, listened to me grumble, and kicked my behind as appropriate.

And last but never least, my husband, Sandy Wilson, who is the reader in my head and in my heart. He read drafts, asked hard questions, talked through problems, and got me out of the house in spite of myself. Without him, this book wouldn't have happened.

NOTES

EPIGRAPH

Quoted in Ingrid Strobl, *Partisanas: Women in the Armed Resistance to Fascism and German Occupation (1936–1945)* (Edinburgh: AK Press, 2008), 17.

INTRODUCTION: "WOMEN DO NOT FIGHT"

1. David Hay, *The Military Leadership of Matilda of Canossa, 1046–1115* (Manchester, UK: Manchester University Press, 2008), 3.

2. Rachel Swaby, *Headstrong: 52 Women Who Changed Science—and the World* (New York: Broadway Books, 2015), xiii.

3. Plato, *The Republic*, trans. G. M. A. Grube (Indianapolis: Hackett Publishing, 1974), 114–15.

4. Grace Paley, "Of Poetry and Women and the World," *The Grace Paley Reader* (New York: Farrar, Straus & Giroux, 2017), 235.

5. From an email interview between Linda Grant De Pauw and Rosemarie Skaine, March 3, 1996. Quoted in Skaine, *Women at War: Gender Issues of Americans in Combat* (Jefferson, NC: McFarland, 1999), 139.

6. Hay, *The Military Leadership of Matilda of Canossa*, 11.

CHAPTER ONE: DON'T MESS WITH MAMA

1. Plutarch, "Life of Lycurgus," *Plutarch on Sparta*, trans. Richard J. A. Talbert (London: Penguin, 1988), 39.

2. Herodotus, *The Histories*, Book 1, trans. Aubrey de Selincourt (Baltimore: Penguin, 1965), 96–101.

3. Ibid.

4. Ammianus Marcellinus, *Roman History*, vol. 1. 15.12.1, trans. John C. Rolfe (Cambridge, MA: Harvard University Press/William Heinemann, 1956), 195.

5. Quoted in Lorraine Bayard de Volo, "Drafting Motherhood: Maternal Imagery and Organization in the United States and Nicaragua," in *The Women and War Reader*, ed. Lois Ann Lorentzen and Jennifer Turpin (New York: New York University Press, 1998), 246.

CHAPTER TWO: HER FATHER'S DAUGHTER

1. Quotations from "Poem of Mulan" are from *Mulan: Five Versions of a Classic Chinese Legend, with Related Texts*, ed. and trans. Shiamin Kwa and Wilt L. Idema (Indianapolis: Hackett Publishing, 2010), 1–3.

2. Liu Xu et al., "The Old History of the Tang Dynasty," quoted in *Amazons to Fighter Pilots: A Biographical Dictionary of Military Women, vol. 1: A–M*, ed. Reina Pennington (Westport, CT: Greenwood Press, 2003), 343.

3. Nadezhda Durova, *The Cavalry Maiden: Journals of a Russian Officer in the Napoleonic Wars*, trans. Mary Fleming Zirin (Bloomington: Indiana University Press, 1988), 3.

4. Ibid., 8.

5. Ibid., 15.

6. Ibid., 38.

7. Ibid.

8. Ibid., 51.

9. Ibid., 62.

10. Ibid., 126.

11. Ani Pachen and Adelaide Donnelley, *Sorrow Mountain: The Journey of a Tibetan Warrior Nun* (New York: Kodansha International, 2000), 55.

12. Ibid., 111.

13. Ibid., 139.

14. Quoted in the *New York Times* obituary by Douglas Martin, "Ani Pachen, Warrior Nun in Tibet Jail 21 Years, Dies," February 18, 2002.

15. Pachen and Donnelley, *Sorrow Mountain*, 282.

16. Gayle Tzemach Lemmon, "How Dads Can Raise Strong Women," Time.com, June 19, 2015, http://time.com/3928792/fathers-day-dads-and-daughters.

CHAPTER THREE: THE WIDOW'S RAMPAGE

1. Vitruvius, *On Architecture*, trans. Richard Schofield (New York: Penguin, 2009), 54.

2. Sozomen, *The Ecclesiastical History of Sozomen, Comprising a History of the Church, from A.D. 324 to A.D. 440*, trans. Edward Walford (London: Henry G. Bohn, 1855), 308.

3. Ibid., 307–8.

4. James Baillie Fraser, *Military Memoir of Lieut.-Col. James Skinner* (London: Smith Elder, 1851), quoted in Julia Keay, *Farzana: The Woman Who Saved an Empire* (London: Tauris, 2014), 69.

5. Quoted in Nicholas Shreeve, *Dark Legacy: The Fortunes of Begum Samru* (Calcutta: Rupa & Co., 1998), 51.

6. John Wilson Croker, *The Croker Papers, 1808–1857*, ed. Bernard Pool (New York: Barnes & Noble, 1967), 100.

7. Quoted in Dian H. Murray, "Cheng I Sao in Fact and Fiction," in *Bold in Her Breeches: Women Pirates Across the Ages*, ed. Jo Stanley (London: Pandora Books, 1995), 212.

CHAPTER FOUR: THE MOST POWERFUL PIECE ON THE CHESSBOARD

1. Quoted in Marilyn Yalom, *Birth of the Chess Queen: A History* (New York: HarperCollins, 2004), 214.

2. Quoted in Giles Tremlett, *Isabella of Castile: Europe's First Great Queen* (New York: Bloomsbury, 2017), 153.

3. A. M. Hocart, *Kings and Councilors: An Essay in the Comparative Anatomy of Human Society* (orig., 1936; Chicago: University of Chicago Press, 1970), 98.

4. John Keegan, *A History of Warfare* (New York: Vintage Books, 1993), 76.

5. Edward Gibbon, *The History of the Decline and Fall of the Roman Empire*, vol. 1 (New York: A. L. Burt, 1900), 204.

6. Quotations from Herodotus throughout this section are from Herodotus, *The Histories*, Books 7 and 8 (Baltimore: Penguin, 1965), 446–47 and 520–33.

7. *William of Malmesbury's Chronicle of the Kings of England from the Earliest Period to the Reign of King Stephen*, ed. J. A. Giles (New York: AMS Press, 1968), 123–24.

8. Quoted in Giles Tremlett, *Catherine of Aragon: The Spanish Queen of Henry VIII* (New York: Walker & Company, 2010), 169.

9. Quoted in David Starkey, *Six Wives: The Queens of Henry VIII* (New York: HarperCollins, 2003), 142.

10. Tremlett, *Catherine of Aragon*, 172.

11. John Sadler, *Flodden 1513: Scotland's Greatest Defeat* (Oxford, UK: Osprey, 2006), 86.

12. Quoted in Linda M. Heywood, *Njinga of Angola: Africa's Warrior Queen* (Cambridge, MA: Harvard University Press, 2017), 45.

13. Wilhelmina, Queen of the Netherlands, *Lonely But Not Alone* (London: Hutchinson of London, 1960), 147–48.

14. Ibid., 154.

15. Ibid., 151.

16. Quoted in Lynne Olson, *Last Hope Island: Britain, Occupied Europe, and the Brotherhood That Helped Turn the Tide of War* (New York: Random House, 2017), 25.

CHECKPOINT: A QUEEN IN ALL BUT NAME

1. Hay, *The Military Leadership of Matilda of Canossa*, 1–12.

2. Quoted in ibid., 89.

CHAPTER FIVE: JOAN OF ARC OF [FILL IN THE BLANK]

1. Henry Miller, *The Colossus of Maroussi* (1941), quoted in April Kalogeropoulos Householder, "The Life and Legacy of Laskarina Bouboulina: Feminist Alternatives to Documentary Filmmaking Practices," PhD diss., University of Maryland, 2006, 29.

2. Halina Filipowicz, "The Daughters of Emilia Plater," in *Engendering Slavic Literatures*, ed. Pamela Chester and Sibelan Forrester (Bloomington: Indiana University Press, 1996), 43.

3. Svetlana Alexievich, *The Unwomanly Face of War: An Oral History of Women in World War II*, trans. Richard Pevear and Larissa Volokhonsky (New York: Random House, 2017), 27.

4. Quoted in Philip Demertzis-Bouboulis, *Laskarina Bouboulina* (Spetses, Greece: Bouboulina's Museum, 1997), 20.

5. Filipowicz, "The Daughters of Emilia Plater," 43.

6. Thomas B. Marquis, *Cheyenne and Sioux: The Reminiscences of Four Indians and a White Soldier*, ed. Ronald H. Limbaugh (Stockton, CA: Pacific Center for Western Historical Studies, University of the Pacific, 1973), 16.

7. Mari Sandoz, *Cheyenne Autumn* (New York: McGraw-Hill, 1953), 79.

8. Householder, "The Life and Legacy of Laskarina Bouboulina," 8.

CHAPTER SIX: WO-MANNING THE RAMPARTS

1. Pausanias, *Pausanias's Description of Greece*, Book 2, 20.8, vol. 1, trans. J. G. Frazer (New York: Bilbo and Tannen, 1965), 102.

2. *Plutarch's Lives, Vol. 9, Pyrrhus* 29.6 (London: William Heinemann, 1914), 447.

3. Quoted in Brian Sandberg, "'Generous Amazons Came to the Breach': Besieged Women, Agency and Subjectivity During the French Wars of Religion," *Gender & History* 16, no. 3 (November 2004): 675–76.

4. Christine de Pizan, *Treasure of the City of Ladies; or the Book of the Three Virtues*, trans. Sarah Lawson (New York: Penguin, 1985), 129.

5. Quoted in H. S. Bennett, *The Pastons and Their England* (Cambridge, UK: Cambridge University Press, 1951), 63.

6. Quoted in Kate Norgate, *The Minority of Henry III* (London: Macmillan, 1912), 37.

7. Sir Walter Scott, "Provincial Antiquities of Scotland," *The Miscellaneous Prose of Walter Scott*, vol. 7 (Edinburgh: Robert Cadell, Adam and Charles Black, 1834), 415.

8. Quoted in Richard Bidlack and Nikita Lomagin, *The Leningrad Blockade, 1941–1944: A New Documentary History from the Soviet Archives* (New Haven, CT: Yale University Press, 2012), 40.

CHECKPOINT: MOLLY PITCHER(S)?

1. Quoted in John Todd White, "The Truth About Molly Pitcher," in *The American Revolution: Whose Revolution?* ed. James Kirby Martin and Karen R. Stubaus (Huntington, NY: Robert E. Krieger, 1977), 105.

CHAPTER SEVEN: IN DISGUISE

1. Loreta Janeta Velazquez, *The Woman in Battle: The Civil War Narrative of Loreta Velazquez, Cuban Woman and Confederate Soldier* (Madison: University of Wisconsin Press, 2003), 50.

2. Ibid., 69.

3. Ibid., 220.

4. Ibid., 516.

5. Mary Livermore, *My Story of the War: A Woman's Narrative of Four Years Personal Experience as a Nurse in the Union Army* (Hartford, CT: A. D. Worthington, 1888), 116, 119–20.

6. San Francisco Lesbian and Gay History Project, "'She Even Chewed Tobacco': A Pictorial Narrative of Passing Women in America," in *Hidden from History: Reclaiming the Gay and Lesbian Past*, ed. Martin Bauml Duberman, Martha Vicinus, and George Chauncey Jr. (New York: New American Library, 1989), 184.

7. "Female Warriors: Containing a Humble Proposal for Augmenting the Forces of Great Britain," in *The Works of Oliver Goldsmith*, vol. 1., ed. J. W. M. Gibbs (London: George Bell and Sons, 1885), 315–20.

8. Quoted in Rudolf M. Dekker and Lotte C. Van de Pol, *The Tradition of Female Transvestism in Early Modern Europe* (New York: St. Martin's Press, 1989), 1.

9. Quoted in Marilyn Yalom, *Blood Sisters: The French Revolution in Women's Memory* (New York: Basic Books, 1993), 199.

10. Durova, *The Cavalry Maiden*, 32.

11. Quoted in San Francisco Lesbian and Gay History Project, "'She Even Chewed Tobacco,'" 189.

12. Quoted in Jo Stanley, "In the Right Place at the Right Time," in Stanley, *Bold in Her Breeches*, 131.

13. Rachel Holmes, *Scanty Particulars: The Scandalous Life and Astonishing Secret of Dr. James Barry, Queen Victoria's Preeminent Military Doctor* (New York: Random House, 2002), 51.

14. Quoted in Richard H. Hall, *Women on the Civil War Battlefront* (Lawrence: University of Kansas Press, 2006), 131.

15. Velazquez, *The Woman in Battle*, 185.

16. Quoted in DeAnne Blanton and Lauren M. Cook, *They Fought Like Demons: Women Soldiers in the Civil War* (New York: Vintage Books, 2002), 11.

17. Vern L. Bullough and Bonnie Bullough, *Cross Dressing, Sex, and Gender* (Philadelphia: University of Pennsylvania Press, 1993), 160.

18. Blanton and Cook, *They Fought Like Demons*, 113.

19. Ibid., 107.

20. Quoted in San Francisco Lesbian and Gay History Project, "'She Even Chewed Tobacco,'" 189.

21. Bullough and Bullough, *Cross Dressing, Sex, and Gender*, 162.

CHAPTER EIGHT: NO DISGUISE NEEDED

1. Quoted in *Biographical Dictionary of Chinese Women: Tang Through Ming, 618–1644*, ed. Lily Xiao Hong Lee and Sue Wiles (Armonk, NY: M. E. Sharpe, 2014), 413.

2. Quoted in Stephen Turnbull, *Samurai Women, 1184–1877* (New York: Osprey, 2010), 45.

3. Quoted in Stanley B. Alpern, *Amazons of Black Sparta: The Women Warriors of Dahomey* (New York: New York University Press, 2011), 96.

4. Quoted in ibid., 65.

5. Quoted in ibid., 21.

6. Quoted in ibid., 29–30.

7. Quoted in ibid., 97.

8. Quoted in ibid., 210.

9. Quoted in Laurie S. Stoff, *They Fought for the Motherland: Russia's Women Soldiers in World War I and the Revolution* (Lawrence: University of Kansas Press, 2006), 34.

10. Bessie Beatty, *The Red Heart of Russia* (New York: Century Co., 1918), 101.

11. Ibid.

12. Ibid., 91.

13. Quoted in Amy Goodpaster Strebe, *Flying for Her Country: The American and Soviet Women Military Pilots of World War II* (Dulles, VA: Potomac Books, 2009), 71.

CHECKPOINT: WAS SHE OR WASN'T SHE?

1. Leszek Gardeła, "'Warrior Women' in Viking Age Scandinavia? A Preliminary Archaeological Study," *Analecta Archaeologica Ressoviensa* 8 (2013): 276.

2. Quoted in Jeannine Davis-Kimball, *Warrior Women: An Archaeologist's Search for History's Hidden Heroines* (New York: Warner Books, 2002), 106.

CONCLUSION: INSIGNIFICANT EXCEPTIONS?

1. Quoted in Sandberg, "'Generous Amazons Came to the Breach,'" 677.

2. Quoted in Donna McAleer, *Porcelain on Steel: Women of West Point's Long Gray Line* (Jacksonville, FL: Fortis Publishing, 2010), 31.

3. Quoted in Ulinka Rublack, "Wench and Maiden: Women, War and the Pictorial Function of the Feminine in German Cities in the Early Modern Period," *History Workshop Journal* 44 (Autumn 1997): 7.

4. Quoted in Kimberly Moore Buchanan, *Apache Women Warriors* (El Paso: Texas Western Press, 1986), 27.

INDEX

IMAGE CREDITS

Page 2: "Rani of Jhansi," © Victoria and Albert Museum, London.

Page 45: "Nadezhda Durova," HIP/Art Resource, New York.

Page 108: "Joan of Arc," De Agostini Picture Library/Bridgeman Images.

Page 113: "Trung Sisters," History/Bridgeman Images.

Page 124: "Buffalo Calf Road Woman," National Anthropological Archives, Smithsonian Institution, Washington, DC.

Page 138: "Agustina Zaragoza Domenech," © The Metropolitan Museum of Art; image source: Art Resource, New York.

Page 181: "Tomoe Gozen," History/Bridgeman Images.

Page 186: "Dahomey," History/Bridgeman Images.

Page 194: "Women's Battalion of Death," Harris and Ewing Collection, Prints and Photographs Division, LC-USZ62-68359, Library of Congress, Washington, DC.

Page 199: "Lyudmilla Pavlichenko," FSA/OWI Collection, Prints and Photographs Division, LC-USW3-007334-D, Library of Congress, Washington, DC.